D0894224

RATLINE

ALL THIS WAS INSPIRED BY THE PRINCIPLE—which is quite true within itself—that in the big lie there is always a certain force of credibility; because the broad masses of a nation are always more easily corrupted in the deeper strata of their emotional nature than consciously or voluntarily; and thus in the primitive simplicity of their minds they more readily fall victims to the big lie than the small lie, since they themselves often tell small lies in little matters but would be ashamed to resort to large-scale falsehoods. It would never come into their heads to fabricate colossal untruths, and they would not believe that others could have the impudence to distort the truth so infamously. Even though the facts which prove this to be so may be brought clearly to their minds, they will still doubt and waver and will continue to think that there may be some other explanation. For the grossly impudent lie always leaves traces behind it, even after it has been nailed down, a fact which is known to all expert liars in this world and to all who conspire together in the art of lying.

—Adolf Hitler , *Mein Kampf,* vol. I, ch. X

HIS PRIMARY RULES WERE: never allow the public to cool off; never admit a fault or wrong; never concede that there may be some good in your enemy; never leave room for alternatives; never accept blame; concentrate on one enemy at a time and blame him for everything that goes wrong; people will believe a big lie sooner than a little one; and if you repeat it frequently enough people will sooner or later believe it.

—OSS *Psychological Report on Adolf Hitler*

◊ ◊ ◊ ◊ ◊

AN EXHIBITION HAS OPENED IN RUSSIA showing visitors part of a skull which officials claim was Adolf Hitler's. The fragment, with a bullet hole through it, has been kept in a secret vault for decades . . .

The authenticity of the claim has been questioned since Moscow first announced it had the fragment in 1993.

Hitler biographer, Werner Maser, said the fragment was fake. However, director of the exhibition Aliya Borkovets insisted that "no doubts remain" about its origin.

—BBC News 26 April 2000

◊ ◊ ◊ ◊ ◊

DEEP IN THE LUBYANKA, HEADQUARTERS of Russia's secret police, a fragment of Hitler's jaw is preserved as a trophy of the Red Army's victory over Nazi Germany. A fragment of skull with a bullet hole lies in the State Archive.

So when American academics claimed that DNA tests showed the skull to be that of a woman, they challenged a long-cherished tale of the hunt for Hitler's remains.

—*The Times*, 9 December 2009

RATLINE

Soviet Spies
Nazi Priests, and
the Disappearance of
Adolf Hitler

PETER LEVENDA

IBIS PRESS
Lake Worth, FL

Published in 2012 by Ibis Press
A division of Nicolas-Hays, Inc.
P. O. Box 540206
Lake Worth, FL 33454-0206
www.ibispress.net

Distributed to the trade by
Red Wheel/Weiser, LLC
65 Parker St. • Ste. 7
Newburyport, MA 01950
www.redwheelweiser.com

Copyright © 2012 by Peter Levenda

All rights reserved. No part of this publication may be
reproduced or transmitted in any form or by any means, electronic
or mechanical, including photocopying, recording, or by any information
storage and retrieval system, without permission in writing from
Nicolas-Hays, Inc. Reviewers may quote brief passages.

Please note that every attempt has been made to determine the proper
copyright holder of the images presented here. We apologize for any
inadvertent errors and request you contact us with corrections.

ISBN 978-0-89254-170-6

Library of Congress Cataloging-in-Publication Data

Levenda, Peter.
  Ratline : Soviet spies, Nazi priests, and the disappearance of Adolf Hitler /
Peter Levenda.
    p. cm.
  Includes bibliographical references.
  ISBN 978-0-89254-170-6 (alk. paper)
  1. Hitler, Adolf, 1889-1945—Exile. 2. War criminals—Germany—History—
20th century. 3. Fugitives from justice—Germany—History—20th century.
4. Nazis—Middle East—History. 5. Nazis—South America—History. I. Title.
  DD247.H5L395 2012
  940.53'145--dc23   2012005055

Book design and production by Studio 31
www.studio31.com

Printed in the United States of America

CONTENTS

INTRODUCTION

For when the truth is with us in one place, it is buried in another.
—Norman Mailer[1]

September, 2011

THE SUN WAS GOING DOWN OVER THE FIELD OF TOMBS. I picked my way gingerly over the stone slabs that were set down in an almost haphazard fashion, threatening to twist an ankle with every step. Leading the way was a plainclothes security guard. Around me a small crowd was gathering: young, dangerous-looking men with curious expressions. I was the only foreigner in the cemetery, probably the only foreigner for miles.

But I was not the only foreigner they had ever seen. Recently, visitors had been coming from Europe and the Middle East to pay their respects in this nondescript plot in an obscure graveyard on the far side of the world.

Thirty-two years ago, I had been on a similar expedition and had nearly disappeared in the torture cells of a Nazi estate in the Andes mountains. I had been alone that time, trusting to luck and my instincts to survive what was certainly a foolish mission to uncover one of the links of the Ratline in Pinochet's Chile. This time, after a bone-rattling eight hour drive through small towns, tea plantations, and remote forests, I achieved my objective just as the muezzin began calling the faithful to prayer.

I hoped that was a good sign.

I was there with a professor of anthropology from Indonesia's largest university. She served as interpreter and camera operator, a task far beneath her but one that she shouldered without complaint. She would provide my cover story to the guards, that I was a relative from abroad seeking the grave of his uncle. But the guards knew

---

1 Norman Mailer, *The Gospel According to the Son*, New York: Random House, 1997, p. 4

exactly whom I was seeking. The name on the tombstone had become famous, but the "real" identity of the corpse was more famous still.

As I finally reached the tomb, a stone box surrounded by a neat wrought-iron fence and gate, one of the guards leaned down over it and reverently whispered the name of the cemetery's most notorious inhabitant:

"Hitler."

How I came to be there, and why I began to take this outrageous story seriously, is the theme of this book. I'd been researching Nazism for decades, with a particular emphasis on Nazi mystical ideas as well as on the escape routes used by Nazi war criminals to escape justice, the "rat lines." I have appeared numerous times on television documentaries concerning the strange beliefs that fueled the Nazi Party. I've been asked to speak on this subject to groups in Asia, Europe and North America, and have been interviewed for radio and podcast more times than I can remember. But in all of those years of describing and trying to explain the motives of Nazi war criminals I had never seriously entertained the theory that Hitler had escaped Berlin at the end of the war. While I like to think I have an open mind, the idea of "Hitler in Argentina" was just too paranoid—and just too wrong—to be believed. After all, there was ample evidence to prove that Hitler committed suicide in the Berlin bunker on April 30, 1945. I had written about it. I knew the facts of the case. There was nothing to question.

Nothing, that is, until the year 2008, fully sixty-three years after the end of World War II.

I had been threatened by Nazis and neo-Nazis in Latin America, as well as by Klansmen and neo-Nazis in the United States. In most cases, the threats were empty, but in Chile in 1979 the threat was very real and immediate. They were torturing and killing people at Colonia Dignidad, and I could very easily have been one of them. I had lived with the constant presence of Nazism in its various forms for decades. So how could I have missed what was possibly the biggest story concerning the Third Reich for the last sixty-plus years?

The answer lies in the psychological force that history has over us all. When a historian writes something down, it becomes the truth.

We do not realize that this "truth" is only one of several—perhaps many—possible narratives. A selection process takes place when one writes history. One leaves out certain, awkward or unpalatable facts in favor of others that advance one's thesis and thereby a kind of consensus reality is created. It's a fictional world like any other but—like the so-called "reality" shows on television—it *seems* genuine and unscripted. We rarely get the opportunity to go behind the scenes, talk to the producers and directors of our shared reality system, in order to satisfy ourselves that what we see and hear is "real".

We have to take "real" on faith.

July, 2008

Faith.

The cry of the muezzin floated over the hot and humid tropical air, carrying with it a memory of ancient Arabia and old conquests by fire and sword. Mecca. Baghdad. Granada. Palm trees bent calmly under the weight of time and torpor, providing a shade that was more suggestion than reality. Men in sarongs and flip-flops were walking slowly in the direction of the mosque, smiling gently and murmuring comments or prayers. In the distance, as always, the volcano with its ever-present plume commanded the landscape like a giant waving a flag.

Along the side streets, food vendors were setting up in anticipation of the end of the day of fasting. Charcoal grills were lit, and colorful bunches of exotic fruit—hairy rambutans and foul-smelling durians, weird-looking snakefruit with its coarse and scaly purple shell and green starfruit with their almost translucent skin—were piled on rickety wooden tables next to packages of instant noodles and pink and yellow shrimp-flavored chips. The sun was setting, and the talk among the students sitting on the mats of the *lesehan*—a kind of impromptu restaurant set out on the sidewalk, without chairs, where people sat on the ground and waited for their food to arrive—turned to the topic of the day. In this case, Adolf Hitler.

The year was 2008. I had been visiting the Universitas Gadjah Mada—the ubiquitous UGM—in the city of Yogyakarta for the second time in two years. My friends there were mostly anthropology students and teachers, and they knew of my interest in the Nazi Party largely through my book on the subject, *Unholy Alliance* and through a talk I gave at UGM the previous year. As we feasted on *tempe, ayam kampung,* and *kancong belacan,* they told me of a news story making the rounds of a man who was buried in Surabaya. A white man. A foreigner.

The story had originally come out in the 1980s, in a local magazine article written by an Indonesian doctor. The doctor claimed to have met this foreigner—Georg Anton Pöch—in the 1960s when Pöch was running a clinic on the faraway island of Sumbawa. He lived there with his wife—another white foreigner—and the doctor was suspicious of them. They did not seem to have any real medical knowledge, yet they were running a clinic on this remote island, far to the east of Bali, on the other side of Lombok.

The night grew around us, the comfortable darkness adding to the sense of conviviality as the smell of grilled satay became overwhelming. The most ancient dish in the world, it is simply meat—lamb, beef or chicken—grilled on wooden sticks over an open flame, but it commands respect everywhere in Southeast Asia. As we ordered a few dozen sticks of satay and the necessary accompaniment—a spicy peanut sauce for dipping—the story became more complex and I listened politely, prepared to dismiss the speculation as fantastic.

For the whole point of this story was that the mysterious foreigner was none other than the icon of twentieth century evil: Adolf Hitler, the Führer himself!

THE WHOLE IDEA WAS PREPOSTEROUS, of course. Everyone knew that Hitler had committed suicide in the Berlin bunker on April 30, 1945. I wrote about it myself in *Unholy Alliance,* and noted the significance of the date for April 30 is the German pagan holiday of Walpurgisnacht, made famous in Bram Stoker's novel, *Dracula.* Stories about Hitler having escaped were legion, but they were largely the stuff of half-baked conspiracy theories and the pulp novels that cater to them. No responsible historian would take such an allegation seriously.

But Hitler had become big business lately, in Indonesia as in the rest of the world. His autobiography and political manifesto—*Mein Kampf*—was available in Indonesian translation as were *The Protocols of the Learned Elders of Zion* and Henry Ford's *The International Jew.* The founder of Jemaah Islamiyyah (or JI, the terrorist group linked with Al-Qaeda and responsible for the Bali Bombings of October 12, 2002) told me to my face that there was an international conspiracy of Jews and Freemasons to rule the world. It was 2007, and I was sitting in his *pesantren* in the nearby city of Solo where I was part of a group called Psychologists for Peace. Our local contact had finagled an interview with one of the most dangerous men in Indonesia as part of our itinerary, and it was an opportunity I could not pass up. I sat and listened to this ageing terrorist in the white turban in 2007 use the same words, phrases and slogans of 1930s Germany and wondered if I had somehow wandered into a time warp. How could there be anti-semitism in a country that had virtually no Jews? How could they fear Freemasonry in a country that had no Masonic lodges?

So Hitler was on the minds of many people. I understood that. As I slid a chunk of grilled lamb off its flimsy wooden stick I listened with half my attention to the story of an old European man named Pöch and how they had confused him with the dead Nazi of sixty years ago.

And then, they dropped the bombshell, and this book is the result.

A little background:

IN 1979, I WENT ON A HAZARDOUS TRIP to Pinochet's Chile to investigate a mysterious German colony in the Andes mountains. It was a country under martial law and military dictatorship. Six years previously the democratically-elected president of Chile—Salvador Allende Gossens—was overthrown in a military coup with assistance from the Nixon administration. As a Socialist, Salvador Allende was not an "acceptable"[2] government leader where Richard Nixon and Henry Kissinger were concerned, and they lent covert support to the generals comprising the coup leadership in the days and months leading up to the event. In the ensuing battle for Chile, Salvador Allende was

---

2 That Nixon and Kissinger were determined to do all they could to remove Allende from power—including covert action—is now no longer debatable. See, for instance, the CIA-issued report "CIA Activities in Chile", September 19, 2000 in response to the Hinchey Amendment to the 2000 Intelligence Authorization Act. This report can be found on the George Washington University site http://www.gwu.edu/~nsarchiv/news/20000919/index.html last accessed May 19, 2011.

slain and his supporters were rounded up throughout the country, imprisoned, tortured and killed. Among them was an American citizen, Charles Horman, who was murdered by security forces at the National Stadium in Santiago shortly thereafter. His case became the basis for the Costa-Gavras film, *Missing*.

The coup took place on September 11, 1973.

WHAT WAS NOT GENERALLY KNOWN or understood at the time was the extent to which Nazi and neo-Nazi organizations were involved in the military coup and in the events preceding it as well as the torture of political prisoners that took place in succeeding months and days. In fact, the assassination of former Chilean ambassador to the United States—Orlando Letelier—and his American colleague Ronni Moffitt in Washington, DC in 1976 by agents of the Chilean secret police was organized and directed by an American neo-Nazi, Michael Vernon Townley. Some of this was covered in my book, *Unholy Alliance*, which first was published in 1994 and which uses my visit to Chile as the introduction to a study of Nazi ideology.

Attempts to publish my account of the visit to Chile met with stiff resistance in 1979 and the years that followed. There was a general disbelief among Americans that Nazis were living openly in Chile. When I spoke of the mysterious Colonia Dignidad—a Nazi enclave high in the Andes to the south of Santiago where I was briefly detained on that trip—the response was "They are probably unpleasant people, maybe even Germans, but they are not Nazis." This was even the reaction from the Simon Wiesenthal Center, whose founder expressed doubt that the Colony had anything to do with Nazis or the escape routes war criminals had been using for years.[3] Although I had seen the Colony with my own eyes and been interrogated by the Colony's founder—Paul Schäfer, replete with military uniform, fatigue cap and Sam Browne belt—my story was ignored or treated with lofty disin-

---

3 See Guy Walters, *Hunting Evil: The Nazi War Criminals Who Escaped & The Quest to Bring Them to Justice*, New York: Broadway Books, 2009, p. 371. For awhile Wiesenthal believed that Josef Mengele—the "Angel of Death" of Auschwitz—had used the Colony as a safe haven some months before my arrival; the report turned out to be false (if we accept that Mengele died in Brazil in February of 1979).

terest. Even though the Colony had clearly arranged for the military roadblocks that stopped my bus on the return from the Colony to Santiago, to ensure that I was still aboard, and thus proved the close cooperation that existed between the Colony and the government of Chile, my story was considered fictional. The mainstream media—which included respected historians and even organizations that were supposed to specialize in this information (such as the Simon Wiesenthal Center)—had decided that they would not take seriously the story of a Nazi estate in the Andes, with electronic gates, bodyguards, and a sinister clinic that "disappeared" men, women and children. A month after I returned to the States, in fact, the columnist Jack Anderson published an article about the Colony where it was revealed that it had operated as a torture and interrogation center for the Pinochet regime and that it had been investigated by the CIA and Amnesty International. Anderson's column appeared in the mainstream media, but Jack Anderson himself had been on Nixon's famous "enemies list" and even had been targeted for assassination by White House "Plumbers"—E. Howard Hunt and G. Gordon Liddy—a plot that fell through when the Watergate scandal took center stage.[4]

Yet, there was still no interest in the only existing eye-witness account of the Colony by an American citizen who lived to tell the tale.

A FEW YEARS LATER, another American citizen—Boris Weisfeiler—went hiking in the Andes mountains. He was discovered by Chilean security forces, arrested and taken miles away to the lethal embrace of the Colony. No one knows why.

He was never seen again.

And still, no one wanted to pursue this story.

I BRING THESE STORIES UP to provide a context and to establish a baseline for the information that follows. My personal experience in investigating the escape route taken by Nazi war criminals—the Ratline—is representative of many others who have dared to pursue this story. Serious investigators have been ridiculed or sidelined. We have been

---

4 See G. Gordon Liddy, *Will*, New York: St Martin's Press, 1980, p. 208–211

told that we misinterpreted what we saw, or that we didn't see what we saw. We were told that we were dupes, victims of disinformation and were being paranoid, hysterical, or just simply nuts. The fact that there was political pressure brought to bear on this story—with regard to Colonia Dignidad—and in the post-Watergate era no less—should have been enough to encourage an editor somewhere to run with it.

But none did.

None, that is, until 1994 when John Douglas at Avon decided to publish *Unholy Alliance.* The book went in and out of print quickly. It became something of a cult classic, with second-hand copies of the rack-sized $6.99 paperback going for more than sixty dollars on auction sites until it was re-released by Continuum in 2002, this time with a foreword by Norman Mailer.

By then, Pinochet was gone from power in Chile and in 1996 there was a raid on the Colony by Chilean security forces who came to arrest Paul Schäfer on child abuse charges. That raid—and further raids that took place over a period of several years—revealed a cache of buried weapons and secret documents. Schäfer was not to be found, however, for he had fled across the border to Argentina where he was eventually located (in 2005), arrested and brought back to Chile to face imprisonment for 27 counts of child abuse. He would die in prison on April 24, 2010.

REVELATIONS CONCERNING THE human rights abuses, torture, kidnapping, and child abuse that came out of the government raids—as well as eyewitness testimony over several decades—proved the basic elements of the story I had tried to tell back in 1979. Interviews with Colony residents further revealed that Colonia Dignidad had been used as a safe house for Nazi war criminals on the run. Its location near the Chilean-Argentine border in the Andes made it an ideal location to run to, or run from (as Schäfer proved in his own escape). While my research was considered inconvenient by the mass media at the time—and is still ignored in South Florida, where the anti-Castro (and pro-Pinochet) Cuban element is strong, politically and culturally—the facts as I stated them in *Unholy Alliance* were nevertheless demonstrably true.

Other researchers were not so lucky.

Paul Manning's masterful work on the complex Nazi program for expatriating their ill-gotten gains—*Martin Bormann: Nazi in Exile*—was picked up by renegade publisher Lyle Stuart after every other publisher turned it down. Manning was a colleague of iconic newsman Edward R. Murrow at CBS Radio and served during World War Two in both the European and Asian theaters of operation, and reported live on the surrenders of both the Nazis and the Japanese. As a newsman and journalist, his credentials were above reproach and his methods impeccable, and in fact he became a speechwriter for Nelson Rockefeller after the War. For his research on the Bormann material, he even had the written support of former CIA Chief Allen Dulles ... at least, until he got too close.

Whether or not Bormann survived the war to live in Latin America is immaterial to the documents and evidence Manning gathered for his book on the number-two man in Hitler's Germany showing financial arrangements and wire transfers between German and Argentine banks to fund the underground Nazi network of safe houses and ratlines after the War. His thesis—that Bormann survived the war—was roundly criticized by the very people who were his colleagues and they used that to discredit his entire investigation, an investigation with explosive material and solid evidence to back it up. Lyle Stuart paid for his participation in the project by having his legs broke—it is said—during the very week he published Manning's work.[5] Manning's son, Gerald, was subsequently murdered in what Manning's family believed was an act of retribution by Nazi agents.

Ladislas Farago, the widely respected historian of the Second World War and author of such books as *Patton* and *The Game of the Foxes*, risked his credibility towards the end of his life by publishing *Aftermath: Martin Bormann and the Fourth Reich*. Detailing a lengthy investigation in South America on the hunt for Bormann, including dangerous meetings with unpleasant men, *Aftermath* is full of documentation not only on the search for the Nazi Reichsleiter but also on the culpability of the Roman Catholic Church in providing escape

---

5 See, for instance, journalist David Emory's biographical sketch of Manning on his website, Spitfire List, http://spitfirelist.com/about-paul-manning/ accessed January 12,2012.

routes for Nazi war criminals, of whom Bormann was only one among very many. It was, in fact, *Aftermath* that alerted me to the existence of Colonia Dignidad and inspired me to take the trip to Chile to see it with my own eyes.

Farago, however, was savagely attacked and continues to be attacked even now, thirty years after his death, because of *Aftermath*. Academics and professional historians—siding with the view that Bormann died in Berlin in May of 1945—ridicule his research, his interviews, and his documentation insisting that he was the dupe of unscrupulous individuals who created a kind of "cottage industry" in Bormann's sightings. In fact, there was no irrefutable evidence of Bormann's demise until DNA testing on a skull fragment in 1998, a full eighteen years after Farago's death, and even then, that evidence has been questioned due to the presence of red clay in the skull: a substance that does not exist in the Berlin soil where the skull was found (thus suggesting that Bormann had died elsewhere and was buried in Berlin, only to be "discovered" a little while later).

Again, the bulk of Farago's work on the Nazi escape routes was ignored and especially his revelations concerning Catholic Church complicity in those escapes. Like Manning, he lost his credibility and his prestige for suggesting that Martin Bormann had escaped to Argentina after the War. Like Manning, Farago had based his conclusions on government documents and personal interviews—sometimes in perilous circumstances.

I knew all of this that sultry tropical night as I sat and listened to my friends talk about the rumor that Hitler had escaped to Indonesia. One of them had a copy of one of the news articles and she pointed me to a description of the old foreigner's documents, left behind in the care of a local woman he married after his first wife left him . . . or mysteriously disappeared.

I am always interested in documents, and put down my satay, wiped my fingers on a thin paper napkin, and picked up the article. I started to scan it when one word jumped out at me and dropped the proverbial bomb in the middle of my dinner.

That one word was *Draganovic*.

THE MAN ALLEGED TO HAVE BEEN HITLER died in January, 1970. Thus the diaries and other documents he left behind had to have been written some time before. In 1970 Draganovic was not a household name. He was known to very few people in the world, basically only Nazi hunters and intelligence agents. To come across that name in those documents could only mean that whoever it was who had died in 1970 was someone whose escape from Europe had been orchestrated by the same man who helped so many others flee justice: Krunoslav Draganovic.

Monsignor Krunoslav Draganovic.

Draganovic was a Croatian priest of the Catholic Church, and a devoted Nazi. His segment of the Ratline was known as the "monastery route" because it used Vatican credentials, Red Cross passports, and monasteries and churches as safe houses along the escape routes. It was a Ratline used by many of the most infamous Nazi war criminals including members of the dreaded SS.

That meant that whoever it was who died in Indonesia in 1970 was a Nazi and a war criminal. No one else would have been able to use the monastery route. No one else would have needed it. And among the papers left behind by this mysterious European was a passport number as well as an itinerary of the route he used to escape Europe and wind up in Indonesia.

As I sat and studied what little information there was available to me on this man, I began to feel that strange sensation that accompanies the beginning of a new quest. It is part excitement at the prospect of a chase, mixed with anxiety over the knowledge that one could be wasting years of one's life in a fruitless search for data over forty years old.

One thing was for certain, though. A Nazi had escaped justice and wound up in Indonesia, of all the places on earth. Most Nazis were perfectly happy with South America or the Middle East. There was virtually no evidence at all that any Nazis made it as far as Southeast Asia, on the other side of the world. (At least, that is what I thought at the time.) Yet, here it was. Definitive proof that *someone* did.

Why did this man travel so far from his fellow Nazis? Why did he pick as remote an island as he could find in Indonesia, rather than stay more comfortably in one of the larger cities on one of the larger islands? Jakarta, say, or even Bali? Why settle in a country that was in the midst of political turmoil?

I resisted, of course, the idea that this was Hitler. Like everyone else of my generation, I grew up with the firm conviction that Hitler had died like everyone had said he had died: in the bunker, on April 30, 1945.

Then, in December of 2009, a real shock came in the form of a report that Nick Bellantoni—the State Archaeologist of Connecticut—had managed to examine a piece of what the Russians claimed was Hitler's skull. And the conclusion of that examination?

The skull was that of a woman. And it was not Eva Braun. The Russians did not have Hitler's skull.

In fact, suddenly there was no forensic evidence that Hitler died in the bunker.

Indeed, *there was no evidence that Hitler had died at all.*

THOSE OF US WHO ARE FAMILIAR with police procedurals and television crime dramas like *Law and Order* and *CSI* know the importance of DNA evidence. When there is no DNA evidence—or, as in this case, no body at all—a crime is very hard to prove. When your only eyewitnesses are Nazis and Soviet spies, then you had better look for another case . . . or another line of work. And when the case is more than sixty-five years old and most of your witnesses are dead . . . well, you don't have a case anymore.

If everything we had been told about Hitler's death, cremation and burial was a lie from the beginning then it was starting to look like the Indonesians might have a point.

Then, in 2010, the Justice Department released a report by the Office of Special Investigations (OSI) which detailed how Nazi war criminals were protected from prosecution by the US Government since the earliest post-war days; protected by American intelligence, the military, and even industrial corporations.

THERE WAS NOTHING FOR IT. I had to find out who was buried in that Indonesian cemetery. Hitler or not, this was a key to some larger mystery. Questions had to be asked. Consensus reality had to be challenged. The truth, however improbable or counter-intuitive, had to be revealed. My trip to Chile in 1979 had been hazardous, and I was lucky to have left the country alive. What would be the case with Indonesia? If I pursued this story, would I wind up in a Javanese jail . . . or worse? Certainly no one was covering up this story anymore. It was forty years old; more than sixty-five years old if you count from the end of World War Two. Would anyone still care if I went poking around in the cemeteries, rain forests, and archives of this ancient land? I had already seen Abu Bakr Basyir, the infamous "Bali Bomber," and lived to tell the tale. I had crawled around Tantric temples and half-buried ruins in the punishing heat. Not too far away or long ago, in China, I had visited military installations and prison factories and survived none the worse for wear. I had met with neo-Nazis and Klansmen and lived to write about it. So, how hard could this be?

But . . . was there something else to find, something I did not as yet suspect?

Everything you know is wrong.
   —The Firesign Theater

The first casualty of war is the truth.
   —Arthur Ponsonby

War is the continuation of politics by other means.
   —Carl von Clausewitz

I HAD REASON TO BE SUSPICIOUS.

After all, I was told again and again in the 1970s and 1980s that Colonia Dignidad had nothing to do with Nazis, with torture or interrogation, or with the military regime of General Augusto Pinochet. I was told this by editors of mainstream media outlets as well as by the Simon Wiesenthal people, military historians, and others. They were all seriously mistaken—if not actually lying for a variety of reasons that had nothing to do with me or with the facts of the case but which had more to do with political agendas.

The very fact of the Colony itself is proof of the existence of an extensive network of escape routes and safe houses used by those who supported (and still support) the Nazi regime and its ideology.

It was when I was being told repeatedly that I did not see what I saw, that I did not experience what I experienced, that I began to realize that truth truly is the first casualty of war, as well as of politics since "war is a continuation of politics by other means".

It reminded me of the old Groucho Marx saying, "Who are you going to believe? Me, or your lying eyes?"

The implication was that the interested parties—from the government to the media to the "official" Nazi hunters themselves—all knew about the Colony (otherwise, how could they have made these assessments?) and chose to deny what they already knew to be true. And to steadfastedly deny it for decades.

And that leads us to the present story.

There are many uncomfortable revelations in this book. The passage of time since the end of World War Two has not made any of them more palatable or excusable. We will learn about the complicity of our most cherished institutions—sacred and secular in the escape of some of the world's most notorious war criminals. We will see men obsessed with a new enemy—Communism eagerly enlist the support of persons who had performed medical experiments on living human beings or who slaughtered them in the death camps or as slave labor. *We will even see a sinister connection from that remote tropical island to an American serial killer who was executed in 2011.*

Even more, we will see how history was "managed" by the intelligence agencies of the United States, Great Britain and the Soviet Union—among many others—to present the world with the biggest lie of all. Had I not experienced politically-motivated censorship first hand, I may not have been able to write this story.

Quite simply, I would not have believed it myself.

CHAPTER ONE

THE OFFICIAL STORY

Anyone who undertakes an inquiry of such a kind is soon made aware of one important fact: the worthlessness of mere human testimony.

—Hugh Trevor-Roper[6]

THE AUTHORITATIVE AND DEFINITIVE NARRATIVE since 1947 on the death of Adolf Hitler has always been *The Last Days of Hitler*, by Hugh Trevor-Roper. It is a well-written and compelling account of the final moments of the Third Reich, with all the pettiness, office politics, meanness, sniping, and gossiping that characterized the end of the Nazi regime. One reads this book with the same breathless intensity that one passes the scene of a traffic accident on the highway: too fascinated and appalled at this demonstration of human mortality to turn away and look somewhere else. The figures of Hitler, Bormann, Goering, Goebbels and others are all sharply and theatrically drawn. Their weaknesses and pathos come across strongly and there is no space in Trevor-Roper's account for any other point of view, any other perspective, any other characterization. It reads like an abridged version of Gibbons' *Decline and Fall of the Roman Empire*. With tanks.

And this is its problem. In it's strident tone and impatience with critics it has presented posterity with certain difficulties, not the least of which is the fact that the lack of forensic evidence *of any kind* seemed to have been no impediment to the conclusion of the author that Hitler committed suicide with a pistol, alongside his wife Eva Braun who died of cyanide poisoning, and both around three o'clock in the afternoon of April 30, 1945.

What we have in the case of the deaths of Hitler and Braun is a purely circumstantial case: one with no *corpus delicti*, no foren-

---

6 Hugh Trevor-Roper, *The Last Days of Hitler*, Chicago: The University of Chicago Press, 1987 edition, p. 12

sic evidence (or forensic evidence whose provenance is uncertain or unproven), and conflicting eyewitness testimony. Add to that the almost unbearably arrogant and self-assured tone of Trevor-Roper's report—based on research that was conducted over the space of only six weeks and included testimony from prisoners of war with every motivation imaginable to deceive, embellish, and create out of whole cloth—and you are left with exactly the report that was intended: a piece of psychological warfare, an artfully-created and stylistically-elegant propaganda device.

Trevor-Roper glides over the various inconsistent testimonies of Nazi officers with the blithe air of someone too busy with weightier concerns to concentrate on the minutiae. He ridicules those who disagree with him, even as he admits that eyewitness testimony is the least reliable of all sources of evidence. He reveals that the motive behind his report was an intelligence agenda, set by MI6[7]: to counteract the effects of the Soviet insistence that Hitler was still alive and being protected by . . . British intelligence.

With all of that in hand, and admitted as such in writing by its author, how is it possible to come to any other conclusion than the report was a work of fiction—a cover story—camouflaged as fact?

YET, THERE THE REPORT WOULD STAND, a Maginot Line erected against all other interpretations of the events of April 30, 1945. One criticized or objected at one's peril, for certainly the insidious might of British Intelligence was its foundation and its champion. Dick White, the MI6 officer who had commissioned Trevor-Roper in September of 1945 to write the report, later became head of MI6 itself and was knighted in the process. As far as the British (and, to a large extent, the Americans) were concerned, Trevor-Roper had put paid to any speculation about the survival of the twentieth century's most notorious political leader. Trevor-Roper himself admits that British Intelligence not only approved his writing of *The Last Days of Hitler*, but that they supported it as well.[8] It is a revealing admission, for it proves beyond

---

7   MI6 is also known as the Secret Intelligence Service or SIS, England's equivalent to America's CIA. MI6 should not be confused with MI5, which is Great Britain's internal security apparatus, equivalent to the American FBI.

8   Trevor-Roper, p. 25

any reasonable doubt that the Trevor-Roper narrative is a work of art—the "craft of intelligence"—and not history. There is certainly no science in his text, no pretense towards establishing the facts of the case by anything other than comparing testimonies of various Nazis and coming up with the distillation of these interrogations that best serves the cause. It was, after all, this same approach to intelligence that presented the world with the "weapons of mass destruction" in Iraq.

IN ORDER FOR US TO GAZE, calmly and without prejudice, on the data that suggests Hitler may have escaped Berlin before its capture by the Russians and may have survived in another country, on another continent, we should examine certain elements of Trevor-Roper's work of imagination in order to address—and dispense with—the "facts" that he insists are the critical issues. We begin with the intelligence agenda itself, the one that MI6 called (appropriately enough) "Operation Nursery."

Operation Nursery

> For my book was written, in the first place, for exactly the same reason which made the Russians frown upon it: to prevent (as far as such means can prevent) the rebirth of the Hitler myth.
> —Hugh Trevor-Roper[9]

A British intelligence officer, Hugh Trevor-Roper (1914–2003) crafted the narrative concerning Hitler's ultimate fate, beginning in September 1945 on a mission—called Operation Nursery—from the Secret Intelligence Service, or MI6. This intelligence operation is the source of the story we have all been told since then. It is the authoritative version. It is based on a handful of interviews with former members of Hitler's personal staff, only some of whom served in the bunker up until the fall of Berlin in May, 1945. This eventually became Trevor-Roper's best-selling book entitled *The Last Days of Hitler*. It

---

9 Trevor-Roper, p. 49

stands today as the definitive account of Hitler's alleged suicide, even though there are barely thirty-five pages in the original edition that deal directly with the death itself. The reason for this is simple: there was no forensic evidence to work from. There were only statements of eyewitnesses, all of whom were Nazis and most of whom were in the SS. And, according to Trevor-Roper himself, eyewitness testimony is ultimately unreliable.

> Such is the value of unchecked human testimony, on which, however, much of written history is based.
> —Hugh Trevor-Roper[10]

IF ONE WERE TO TAKE ALL THE TESTIMONY of all of the witnesses who have since written books or who have left behind transcripts of their interrogations by British, American and Russian intelligence officers, and compared them to each other we would soon begin to realize that there is virtually no consensus on critical points of the story. Some of this we can put down to the chaos and trauma of the last days of the war and the fact that the witnesses were not members of the victorious Allied forces but were the losers in that conflict, running in fear for their lives when they were captured and imprisoned. Germany had been completely overrun. Entire cities had been reduced to rubble, including Berlin. There was widespread hunger, disease, and reportedly terrible abuse at the hands of the Soviet forces who raped and killed, seemingly without restraint.

Thus, that there would be discrepancies in these stories is understandable. But that leaves us with a problem. Whom to believe? Which version is really authoritative?

That depends on the agenda you wish to promote. History was being written by the victors to satisfy intelligence objectives and not to illuminate this dark matter of defeat and violent death. This was war, and the Allied forces were themselves about to discover that their respective agendas did not match. The Soviets had one set of goals in mind at the end of the conflict, and the Americans another.

---

10 Trevor-Roper, p. 226, footnote 1

And the British, another still. Hugh Trevor-Roper admitted he did not speak or read German. His experience in the war up to that point was limited to signals intelligence and the code-breaking teams that were intent on decoding Abwehr radio communications. Prior to the war, Trevor-Roper had been an Oxford-educated historian and had published a study of the life of William Laud, Archbishop of Canterbury at the time of Charles I and the English Civil War of the seventeenth century. Trevor-Roper was an accomplished stylist with an acerbic wit who wrote history with an eye towards communicating the sweep of events and the stature (and idiosyncracies) of history's personalities ... and in denigrating or ridiculing the attempts of other historians who did not agree with him. The choice of Trevor-Roper for the politically-sensitive task of determining Hitler's fate would seem curious if not for the fact that his superior, Brigadier Dick White (later to become Director of MI6), intended that a narrative be crafted that would counter the effects of Soviet insistence that Hitler was still alive. What was required was not the services of a lawyer or a scientist building a legal case from evidence but the services of someone who could build a historical text from odd bits of documents and dubious testimony, hobbled together with an eye towards presenting a single point of view. In other words, the mission objective of Trevor-Roper in Operation Nursery was a foregone one: to disprove Soviet statements that Hitler was still alive. Thus, it had to begin with the premise (presented as fact) that Hitler was dead and had committed suicide in the bunker on April 30, 1945, and then be worked backward from there. No other interpretation or presentation was acceptable. All he had to do was collect enough "eyewitness" testimony—in German, a language he did not understand—that supported (or at least did not contradict) this version of events, and compile them into a neat story that tied together all the loose ends that then would stand as the official version. The official *British* version.

At the same time as Trevor-Roper was conducting interviews of witnesses among prisoners and informants under British control (and being provided with written accounts from prisoners under American control, some of whom he was not permitted to interview personally), the Soviets were doing the same with witnesses they had in their prison camps and interrogation cells. The methods may have been somewhat dissimilar. The Soviets had no problem with torture and what the Americans now call "enhanced interrogation" techniques, especially when it came to the Germans. After all, the Russians lost millions of their people due to Nazi aggression against the homeland. The hatred they had for the Nazis—and for Germans in general—was deep and extensive.

There were several Nazi prisoners whose testimony was deemed of utmost importance to the task of coming to a final evaluation of Hitler's whereabouts, and their testimony was not made available either to Trevor-Roper or to anyone else in British or American intelligence. In fact, no access to these prisoners was provided at all until ten years after the war's end. One might say that the Cold War began with the isolation of these important witnesses from the British and American forces in Germany in 1945. The aura of distrust between the west and the east was already evident in this development of competing narratives concerning the disposition of their mutual enemy, Adolf Hitler.

Operation Myth

> At the end of 1945 new interrogations were carried out to establish the background to Hitler's suicide. His former chief pilot Hans Baur had been questioned. Beria wanted to be sure above all that the dictator was actually dead ... The interrogations of Linge and Günsche ... led the NKVD leadership to instigate the operation codenamed Myth at the beginning of 1946. The goal of the operation was to conduct an 'accurate and strict investigation of all the factors' involved in Hitler's suicide on 30 April 1945.[11]

TWO OF THE MORE IMPORTANT WITNESSES in question were SS Sturmbannführer Heinz Linge and SS Sturmbannführer Otto Günsche, both prisoners of the Soviets. According to the report on Hitler prepared for Stalin by Soviet intelligence and published in 2005 as *The*

---

11 Henrik Eberle, Matthias Uhl, eds., *The Hitler Book: The Secret Dossier Prepared for Stalin from the Interrogations of Hitler's Personal Aides*, New York: Public Affairs, 2005, p. 284

Hitler Book, Günsche was standing outside the door to the antecham-ber in front of Hitler's study when Linge walked up to him and said he smelled gunpowder coming from the room.[12] This was a few minutes before four o'clock the afternoon of April 30, 1945.

Linge went to get Bormann and the two entered the study to find that both Hitler and Eva Braun were dead. Hitler, they said, had committed suicide with a pistol and Eva Braun had taken a cyanide capsule. (It is useful to remember that there has been tremendous confusion over these circumstances, with some accounts saying that Hitler had taken cyanide and then shot himself ... a situation that is extremely unlikely as the potassium cyanide capsules in use were very fast-acting and, *if other reports are to be believed,* Hitler was suf-fering from Parkinson's Disease and the tremor in his hands would have made it virtually impossible to place a gun in his mouth or aim it at his temple and pull the trigger as he was in the throes of cyanide poisoning.)

It is important to point out that there was no report of anyone having heard a gunshot, at least not according to the Soviet report. Other witnesses present in the bunker that day have given contradic-tory statements, and some (those in British and American custody) have insisted they heard a shot fired. As recent tests have shown,[13] this would have been impossible due to the heavy construction of the bun-ker's walls and reinforced steel doors. No one at any distance from the antechamber would have been able to hear a pistol shot coming from Hitler's study and, indeed, the Soviet report makes no mention of any such sound. On the contrary, the Soviet report has guards standing in front of the antechamber door unaware that a shot has been fired. It was only the smell of smoke coming from the thick *fireproof door* that alerted Linge to the possibility that a shooting had occurred.

That means that either the prisoners in American and British cus-tody were lying when they said they heard shots fired, or that the prisoners in Soviet custody were lying when they said it was the smell of gunpowder that was the only clue that someone had used a fire-arm. That *all* the prisoners being interrogated on this point were Nazis

---

12   *The Hitler Book*, p. 270
13   "Hitler's Escape," on *Mystery Quest,* The History Channel, Sept. 16, 2009.

devoted to Hitler—most of whom were also SS officers—would indicate that lying and dissembling over what really happened to their leader would have been (or should have been) expected, not to mention any desire they may have had to put themselves in the most favorable light with their captors. Yet, this is not the only contradiction between the two versions, as we shall see.

The last surviving member of the Führerbunker—Rochus Misch—has himself changed his story several times over the years. Misch, a member of Hitler's elite SS bodyguard (*Liebstandarte SS Adolf Hitler*) as well as a courier and telephone operator in the bunker, initially said that he heard the gunshot; he later changed his story and said that he did not hear it, but that someone else—probably Linge—heard it and spread the alarm. Interviewed for the television series *Mystery Quest* in 2010, he said that he did not hear any gunshot but that he entered the study once the word had spread and saw Hitler's body slumped on the couch and Eva Braun's body next to his. In another, earlier, interview published on Salon.com, he said that he could have been mistaken about the gunshot because "any loud noise echoing through the concrete sounded like a gunshot."[14] More importantly, he doesn't remember how he entered the study where Hitler's body lay: was it with Linge? Or with Günsche? He says he doesn't remember, but according to Linge none other than Martin Bormann opened the door to the study. How could Misch have forgotten the sinister presence of Bormann?

Although both Misch and Linge were in Russian custody for ten years after the war—until 1954 and 1955 respectively—no record of their interrogations by Soviet intelligence has yet to be published, which is exceedingly odd. A brief transcript of one of Günsche's interrogations was made available in *Hitler's Death: Russia's Last Great Secret from the Files of the KGB*, published the same year as *The Hitler Book*. Linge's testimony is referred to several times in that book but is never quoted directly and no transcripts of any of the (presumably numerous and certainly violent) sessions are provided. One is forced to speculate about the reasons for this omission, and it may simply

---

14   Ida Hattemer-Higgins, "Hitler's Bodyguard," *Salon.com*, Feb. 21, 2005 (retrieved June 30, 2011).

be that the original transcripts were lost or, for those of a more suspicious inclination, that details provided by Linge (and Misch) were at odds with the official version. This should not have been a problem for the NKVD and later the KGB, however, who obviously edited the transcripts anyway and could have made Linge and Misch "say" whatever they wanted them to say. So, the omission of the interrogations remains a mystery, albeit only one of many.

One of the Soviet prisoners, SS Brigadeführer Hans Rattenhuber, went even further in his description of what occurred that afternoon. According to his testimony before Soviet interrogators, he claimed that Linge had shot Hitler after the latter had taken poison.[15] According to Rattenhuber, Hitler was worried that the cyanide would not work since he had been taking so many other drugs per the ministrations of the nefarious Dr Morrell (about whom more later). This reasoning, of course, is nonsense but it does go towards Hugh Thomas's speculation that it was, indeed, Linge who killed Hitler although neither with a pistol nor with poison (see below).

It was Günsche and Linge who, according to some accounts (including the Soviet version), were the ones charged with burning the bodies of Hitler and Eva Braun. They first took Hitler—in some versions wrapped completely in a blanket, in others without—outside the bunker and then returned with Eva's body without any blanket or other covering over her blue dress. They poured gasoline over the bodies and set them aflame. This story has been examined and criticized on numerous grounds and we won't get into all of them here but will only highlight significant problems.

One of the leading critics of the Hugh Trevor-Roper account is Hugh Thomas, whose *The Murder of Adolf Hitler*[16] is a good source for many of the inconsistencies between the various eyewitness testimonies (most of which were by SS officers devoted to Hitler, men who could be expected to lie egregiously to the Allies). Thomas published his book in 1995, fully ten years before the Soviet archives on Hitler would be (at least partially) revealed and even further inconsistencies

---

15 *Hitler's Death: Russia's Last Great Secret from the Files of the KGB*, London: Chaucer Press, 2005, p. 195.
16 Hugh Thomas, *The Murder of Adolf Hitler: The Truth About the Bodies in the Berlin Bunker*, New York: St. Martin's Press, 1995

came to light. However, some important and potentially devastating material did surface when Linge was released by the Soviets and was interviewed by the press.

Both Linge's account—and that of Hans Baur, Hitler's personal pilot, released from Soviet custody at the same time—conflicted with Trevor-Roper's narrative in substantial ways. For instance, according to Baur both Hitler and Eva Braun shot themselves; there was no mention of cyanide capsules. Bizarrely, however, the Soviets did not believe that Baur had any useful information and in the end he was placed in a separate facility, away from Günsche and Linge who were charged with writing the document that would become *The Hitler Book*. Even that arrangement was problematic, according to the Russians, for Günsche and Linge fought over what had actually taken place in the bunker on that fateful day. Günsche was characterized as a fervent Nazi who had no desire to be truthful in his account; Linge, however, greeted the task of writing the definitive text on Hitler's death as his "salvation" and was ready to write whatever the Soviets desired.[17] That doesn't mean, however, that he was trusted entirely by the Soviets who planted an informer in his prison cell.[18]

Thus, we have Günsche who is not afraid of lying outright to the Russians and Linge who will tell the truth ... unless, of course, the truth is not what the Russians want to hear, in which case he will amend the story accordingly. Both were SS men. Both were devoted to the Führer. Both presumably had been tortured and subjected to the harshest interrogation methods available to the Soviet secret police who were desperate to learn the fate of Hitler. And this is the source of the Russian version of events.

None of this fazed Trevor-Roper, however, who insisted that the newly obtained access to Linge's version did nothing to contradict his original story. This is perhaps evidence of a particular form of arro-

---

17 *The Hitler Book*, p. 202, Editors' Afterword

18 Thomas, p. 161. Thomas points to many discrepancies between Linge's official testimony and the confidential conversations he was having with a fellow prisoner in the cells who was actually an informer for Soviet intelligence. One of these startling revelations was Linge's "suspicion" that the wound he claimed to have seen on Hitler's temple was "painted on" and that only he and Bormann "knew the truth". (p. 162)

gance among certain academics: Hugh Trevor-Roper was considered (and considered himself) an authority on Nazi Germany and specifically on Hitler and Hitler's inner circle. He had no academic background in German history or politics; he did not even speak or read German. Today, that would have been considered grounds for dismissing his claims to expertise in the field. Certainly no thesis or dissertation would have been accepted from a graduate student in history or international affairs under these circumstances. Then why was he chosen for this delicate task? The only conclusion one can draw is that MI6—which created Operation Nursery—was not interested in an honest, full-blown investigation but only in a story that would sound plausible and which would undermine Soviet propaganda.

We must add to this the evidence of Trevor-Roper's own characterizations of the German psyche as prone to fantasy and hysteria:

> For mythopoeia is a far more common characteristic of the human race (and perhaps especially of the German race) than veracity; and the evidence for this statement has increased formidably since these incidents made it obvious to me.[19]

And later on he references "... the immature Teutonic mind."[20] This type of (unconscious?) stereotyping had to have influenced the final product of his investigation. Virtually nowhere in his book does he treat the subject matter dispassionately. His distaste for his material is evident on every line. It is no mystery to him that Hitler would have committed suicide, for it is consistent with Trevor-Roper's own point of view. He finds witnesses who support this point of view and, when he doesn't, he ignores them or dismisses their inconsistencies with one argument or another. On the one hand he discusses the propensity of the "German race" for myth-making; on the other hand, he accepts the testimony of these same mythopoetic Germans as fact (when it suits him).

Take, for instance, his acceptance of the death scene.

---

19 Trevor-Roper, p. 13
20 Trevor-Roper, p. 196

As Linge and Bormann—according to his version—burst into
Hitler's study, they find Hitler on one side of the couch and Eva Braun
on the other side. Hitler has shot himself through the mouth. Eva has
taken cyanide and she is curled up on the sofa.[21] According to Artur
Axmann, the Hitler Youth leader who was one of the last to leave the
bunker, Eva's head was resting gently on Hitler's shoulder.[22]

One aspect of this scene in particular attracted Hugh Thomas's
contempt: the idea that Eva Braun, after taking potassium cyanide,
would have been peacefully sitting on the sofa next to Hitler. The
effects of potassium cyanide poisoning are far more dramatic than this
tableau would have us believe. There would have been seizures, for
one thing. No one takes a poison capsule of that nature and rests
calmly, waiting for death to arrive. Indeed, this fact—among several
others—lead Thomas to believe that Eva Braun not only did not die
in the bunker at all but that she was enabled to escape and a double
planted in her place.[23]

Before the readers throw up their hands in dismay at this outlandish suggestion, I beg them to recall that there were, indeed, doubles
in use in the entourage around Hitler. One of these Gustav Veler was
even interrogated by the Soviets[24] and another was photographed as a
corpse by the Russian Army who evidently believed the body was that
of Hitler.[25] Videos of this moment have been preserved for posterity,
and can be seen on the Internet. British intelligence knew of these
doubles as well, as revealed in a declassified memo detailing the interrogation of a German prisoner of war, one SS Schütze Obernigg who
was captured in France July 19, 1944. An Austrian, the prisoner had
served at the Obersalzberg area from August 1943 to May 1944 where
Hitler had his country home. According to the prisoner, there were

---

21 Trevor-Roper, p. 230. Yet Linge told the Russians that Hitler had shot himself
in the temple. Trevor-Roper claims that the method of death was reported identi-
cally by three non-witnesses to the event, three secretaries,who themselves heard
it from Günsche and Linge. Thus, the information was second- or third-hand, at
best.

22 Trevor-Roper, p. 46

23 Thomas, pp. 184–188

24 Thomas, p. 161

25 *Hitler's Death*, p. 24

at least two doubles in evidence at the time. One of these worked at the Chancellery in Berlin and wore the same uniform as Hitler. His name was unknown to the prisoner, but was identified as a "ministerial aide." Another double was identified as one Brillmeyer, a "work master" who bore an astonishing resemblance to Hitler except for the way he combed his hair.[26]

The existence of some of these various doubles has been verified and accepted by Soviet intelligence and Veler was referred to by them in *Hitler's Death*.

Additionally, as Thomas cannot accept either the poisoning theory or the pistol shot theory as the cause of Hitler's death, he suggests that the Führer was strangled to death by his adjutant, Heinz Linge.[27] That Linge might have been responsible for Hitler's death would go a long way towards understanding why Linge was so cooperative with the Soviets in coming up with the "smell of gunpowder" story and the shocked entry by himself and Bormann into Hitler's study where both the dictator and his newly-wedded wife were laid out conveniently on the allegedly bloody sofa.

An important point to be made here is that Thomas believes that Hitler did, indeed, die in the bunker but that he did so because he was murdered. His reasoning for this is based on the evidence that was available to him at the time and is the only scenario that accommodated the existing forensic data. He successfully, in my view, obliterates the case for Hitler having poisoned himself, as well as the case that he shot himself with a Walther. What he was left with, then, was the homicide theory.

However, there is one other theory, a theory that Thomas is ready to entertain in the case of Eva Braun and Martin Bormann but not in Hitler's case: and that is the escape theory.

As outlandish as this theory may seem to many, if not most, readers the author prays for a little indulgence at this time as he lays out the possible scenario, one which also satisfies the forensic data (particularly the newly-discovered data brought to light by Dr Nick

---

26 File Inf/2276/C, classified "Top Secret", British intelligence report contained within F01020/3471 Allied Commission for Austria, British Element, Records Section Secretariat, Reference ACA 110/511.

27 Thomas, p. 187

Bellantoni in 2009). One should also keep in mind the fact that MI6—the British intelligence organ responsible for Trevor-Roper's mission to prove the suicide of Hitler—was involved in their own fabrication of death, in this instance the case of Gestapo Hauptsturmführer Horst Kopkow, a man responsible for the murder of approximately 300 Allied agents during the war. Kopkow's knowledge of both German and Russian intelligence nets made him invaluable to MI6 even as the British war crimes investigators wanted him for prosecution. In order to save Kopkow from their colleagues in War Crimes, MI6 faked Kopkow's death and even provided a fake death certificate. Thus MI6 perpetrated a fraud upon their own people, protecting a man who was a major war criminal who sent hundreds to their deaths in the concentration camps. If they were capable of this type of perfidy why would they not collaborate in developing another fraudulent tale, that of Hitler's suicide, especially as Kopkow was being used in the fight against the Soviets and the Hitler narrative was developed with the same purpose in mind?

Kopkow, by the way, lived to a ripe old age before dying of pneumonia in 1996.[28]

The Bunker

By all accounts the situation in the Führerbunker on April 30, 1945 was desperate. Hitler had been advised that his most trusted colleagues were all trying to cut separate deals with the Allies. Air Marshall Göring, the bizarre and corpulent figure in charge of the Luftwaffe, had betrayed his Führer by notifying him that he was now in charge of the Third Reich due to the possible incapacitation of Hitler. Heinrich Himmler, head of the dreaded SS, as well as the Gestapo and the Secret Service, was trying to arrange a surrender with the Allies with Count Bernadotte of Sweden as the go-between; word of it leaked back to Hitler, who was apopleptic with fury. Himmler, after all, had been with Hitler during the Beer Hall Putsch in 1923 and was a devoted follower of the Führer for many years. The Army General Staff was in

---

28 This incident is found in Guy Walters, *Hunting Evil*, New York: Broadway Books, 2009, pp. 225–230.

disarray anyway, due to the famous attempt on Hitler's life in July of 1944: from that moment on, Hitler knew he could not trust his own generals.

He retired to Berlin and eventually to the Bunker in January of 1945. As the bombs and shelling came closer, he was reduced to working and living underground in rather squalid circumstances. Trevor-Roper devotes most of his book to the period before April of 1945, trying to set the stage for what he will claim occurred on April 30. By weaving a dense and elaborate web of stories, memories, and speculations about the last months of the war he hopes to walk the reader through to his own conclusions in the expectation that one will have been so war-weary by this time that one would accept Trevor-Roper's version of events without question. There can be little doubt as to the facts of the war: the military campaigns, the battles lost and won, the number of bombs dropped, the number of casualties ... and this accumulation of facts lulls the reader into a false sense of security, believing that the rest of the tale will be equally factual. It is a clever, but time worn, technique. By the time Trevor-Roper actually gets to the details of April 30 itself, he has only a few more pages left to go. Remember that the purpose of this exercise was to "prove" Hitler's death in the Bunker ... yet a scant thirty-five pages is devoted to the actual circumstances of the death itself.

This extends to his characterization of the thoughts, feelings and psyches of the persons left behind in the Bunker as everyone starts to leave: some to assume new, and virtually imaginary, posts in the defense of Berlin and others to save themselves by heading south towards Berchtesgaden, Hitler's mountain retreat in the Bavarian Alps, where there is a rumor that there will be a rear-guard action against the Allies with the expectation that Germany will be able to retain—or regain—some of its lost glory.[29]

To Trevor-Roper, Hitler is already insane; Eva Braun is ditzy and shallow, little more than a Nazi party girl with barely a thought in her head; Bormann is scheming and insincere; Josef Goebbels, the Minister of Propaganda, remains fanatical to the end and will sacrifice

---

29 The rumors concerning Operation Werewolf and the National Redoubt part of the Nazi "stay behind" operations that so worried the Allies will be detailed later.

not only himself but his wife and six small children as well: their bodies would be found and photographed by the Russian Army. Artur Axmann, the head of Hitler Youth, whose testimony concerning the escape of Martin Bormann was so crucial ... and yet so inconsistent from day to day, providing half-a-dozen different versions to the Nuremberg tribunal alone ... was still regarded as a good source by Trevor-Roper.

There is Bormann himself, of course, and members of his entourage. There is Ambassador Walther Hevel, about whom more later as he leads us directly to Indonesia in astonishing fashion. There are the secretaries: Frau Junge, Frau Christian, Fräulein Krüger.

There are the faithful SS officers and guards. Linge, Günsche, Misch, Schwägermann, Mengershausen, Rattenhuber; a few others. Hans Baur, Hitler's personal pilot. Erich Kempka, Hitler's chauffeur and transport officer.

Ah, Erich Kempka: the man upon whom so much of the suicide story as presented in *The Last Days of Hitler* was based, as Trevor-Roper had no access to Linge or Günsche in 1945. The man who, it was said, carried the lifeless body of Eva Braun up the steps to the Reich Chancellery garden to be cremated.

The man who later claimed he made it up.

Kempka was the single most important source for Trevor-Roper's account of the death of Hitler since Kempka insisted he was there at the time. Kempka told investigators that he was in the corridor outside the bunker when Hitler shot himself. He later changed that story considerably, and told other investigators that he was upstairs and outside the bunker at the time. This was a critical eyewitness, and his testimony was complete deception.[30]

Then there was Hans Baur.

In October of 1955, upon his release from Soviet custody, Hans Baur, Hitler's personal pilot, told journalists that he saw Hitler shoot himself and that Eva Braun shot herself "at the same time".[31] This was

---

30   One of the skeptics is James P. O'Donnell who dismisses Kempka's testimony as a complete fabrication. See O'Donnell, *The Bunker*, New York: DaCapo Press, 2001, p.228–230.

31   *Observer*, October 9, 1955, London; also cited in Hugh Thomas, *The Murder of Adolf Hitler*, p. 98

considered outlandish testimony, of course, for it contradicted everything that Trevor-Roper wrote about the case and even had Eva Braun shooting herself when every other "eyewitness" said she took cyanide.

If Kempka and Baur were lying—and they both changed their stories in critical ways over time—then who was telling the truth? Were there *any* eyewitnesses to the death of Hitler and Braun?

What really happened in the bunker?

SS-MAN HARRY MENGERSHAUSEN (also spelled Mengerhausen in some sources) was a member of the Reich Chancellery guard. In his May 18, 1945 statement to the Soviets while a prisoner he claimed that he was informed that Hitler had shot himself, but did not believe the story until he saw Linge and Günsche carry out the bodies of Hitler and Eva Braun for cremation.[32] He stated that Hitler had been shot through the temple. He further claimed that, aside from Linge and Günsche, no one else witnessed the cremation of the bodies.

Later, when he was released from the gulag in October,1955, he changed his story. Linge's story had the greatest currency at the time, and differed from Mengershausen's considerably. Linge—once released from Soviet captivity—claimed Hitler had shot himself through the mouth.[33] Thus, Mengershausen changed his story once he, too, was released by the Soviets in order to match more closely Linge's account. The Soviets had placed great reliance on Mengershausen's testimony, as is evident from *Hitler's Death*.[34] However, the report prepared for Stalin by Linge and Günsche and entitled *The Hitler Book* contains no mention at all of Mengershausen! In fact, according to *The Hitler Book*, the Führer shot himself through the temple and the famous scene of Eva Braun sitting on the sofa next to him, with

---

32 *Hitler's Death*, pp. 69–81

33 However, a recording has recently come to light with Linge stating that he saw a small wound in Hitler's temple "about the size of a penny." This was a statement given before the Bavarian court on October 25, 1956 during a hearing to declare Hitler officially dead, as reported on January 12, 2010 in the *Telegraph* (UK). Thus, it seems that Linge had reverted to his original story, that Hitler had shot himself in the right temple and not through the mouth … although he expressed doubt about even this possibility to a cellmate as we have seen.

34 *Hitler's Death*, pp. 64–65

her legs curled beneath her and "her lips pressed firmly together", was presented as fact.[35] Although the Soviets insisted that Mengershausen was a credible witness because, they claimed, he led them straight to where the bodies had been burned and buried (including those of Hitler's dog, Blondi, and the Goebbels family) when it came to writing the report for Stalin they omitted his testimony and his presence at the scene completely. This is especially important considering that Mengershausen insisted he was the only one to witness the cremation of the bodies, aside from Linge and Günsche, but *The Hitler Book* has a veritable funeral cortege present at the scene: Bormann, Günsche, Linge, Kempka, SS men Ewald Lindloff and Hans Reisser, SS Sturmbannführer Schädle, Goebbels, Axmann, General Krebs, Werner Naumann (an assistant of Goebbels who will later become involved in a notorious ODESSA-like operation after the war, as we will see), and General Burgdorf[36] ... but no Mengershausen.

This episode alone, with all of its variations, is an example of the disinformation and misinformation that has surrounded all historical narratives of the last days of Hitler. Remember that both *The Hitler Book* and *Hitler's Death* are Soviet records of the testimony of the Nazi eyewitnesses in their prisons ... and they differ from each other considerably. There is virtually no consensus among the witnesses as to what actually transpired. Did Hitler kill himself with a gun, with cyanide, or both? Did he shoot himself through the mouth or the temple? Or, as Rattenhuber claimed, did Linge give Hitler the coup-de-grâce himself? Did Eva Braun shoot herself? Did she take cyanide? If she took cyanide, why did her corpse appear to be so peaceful rather than ravaged by the effects of the poison, effects that include seizures, vomiting, etc.? Who burned the bodies? Who were the first to see the bodies in Hitler's study? Was there smoke, or the sound of a gunshot or gunshots? Was there a smell of cyanide ... the famous "bitter almonds" odor ... or was there no smell at all in the study? Was Hitler wearing new socks or socks that had been darned in several places? (This last goes to the question of a possible Hitler double.) Who witnessed the cremations? When did the cremations occur?

---

35   *The Hitler Book*, p. 271
36   *The Hitler Book*, p. 272

This mass of lies and deception allowed historians to pick and choose their way through the various testimonies and come up with a narrative they liked. No single version could include all the discrepancies, of course, so they dismissed the ones that didn't fit depending on their agenda.

But what of the forensic evidence?

THE ONLY ONES WHO HAD ACCESS TO THE BODIES after the remaining survivors fled the Bunker were the Soviets. They seized the Reich Chancellery and began a systematic exploration of the Bunker and of the surrounding grounds. A unit of Soviet counter-intelligence—the infamous SMERSH—was put in charge of taking possession of Hitler's body (if it could be found) and proving to Stalin that Hitler was, indeed, dead. They found bodies aplenty, but none that could be positively identified as Hitler.

In the Bunker itself, photographs were taken of the sofa where Hitler was presumed to have committed suicide by shooting himself (either through the temple or through the mouth had yet to be determined). It was insisted that the sofa was covered in Hitler's blood, but a problem arises: one very clear photograph of the sofa shows little or no blood at all.[37]

However, SMERSH got a break on May 5, 1945 with the discovery of bodies believed to be those of Hitler and Braun, buried close to the entrance to the Bunker in the Reich Chancellery garden and only partially burned. Strangely, the existence of these bodies was not

---

37 *Hitler's Death*, p. 279 has a blurred photograph of the sofa with what appear to be bloodstains on the left of the photo. However, another photograph—this one taken by *Life* magazine photographer Bill Vandivert in July, 1945—shows very little blood. According to his notes—recently released by *Life*—Hitler had died in the middle of the sofa and fell forward while Eva Braun (who also shot herself in this version) died in the far corner of the sofa and the blood stains on the arm of the sofa were hers. See the *Life* magazine website http://www.life.com/gallery/42032/image/ugc1043592/wwii-inside-hitlers-bunker#index/4 last accessed on July 20, 2011 for Vandivert's notes on the subject taken at the time. This does not mean that Vandivert himself was being dishonest, but that he was reporting the story he heard at the time and presumably from the Soviets. In fact, the Russian photo of the sofa does not match Vandivert's photo at all, but this may be due to the sofa having been stripped of its material by forensic scientists after Vandivert's visit.

revealed at the time: not to Allied intelligence, the media, or to anyone else. It remained a closely-guarded secret of Soviet intelligence for decades, and when the remains of what was claimed to be Hitler's skull was made available for testing the whole house of cards that had been built by Hugh Trevor-Roper and MI6 came tumbling down.

According to the Soviet narrative, SMERSH officials discovered the two bodies of Hitler and Braun on May 5, and a week later their prisoner Mengershausen took them to the precise site where the bodies had been found. This, according to *Hitler's Death*, gave Mengershausen increased credibility and value as a witness.

These bodies were taken and subjected to some form of forensic analysis. Of greatest importance was the state of Hitler's teeth. This would provide virtually the only forensic evidence in the case (DNA testing was unknown at the time). The problem was: who had X-rays of Hitler's teeth for comparison?

This is the beginning of another evidentiary nightmare. In what should have been a simple matter of identification we once again are left with conflicting testimonies, bizarre claims, and hidden agendas.

The Dental Case

We begin with Eva Braun.

According to the Soviet pathologists who examined what they believed to be Eva Braun's corpse there had been extensive damage to the body due to shrapnel piercing the torso in several places. Because there was evidence of haemorrhaging taking place at the sites of these wounds, the body had to have been alive at the time it was struck. Dead bodies do not haemorrhage. Once the heart has stopped beating, blood stops flowing. There could have been post-mortem wounds, but these would not have shown signs of haemorrhaging. This body, however, did show such signs. The body was alive at the time it was struck by shrapnel. Therefore it could not have been Eva Braun's body.

To make matters worse, there was evidence of cyanide poisoning in the mouth of the corpse, extending even to glass splinters from the cyanide capsule. Yet, toxicological tests of the inner organs showed no presence of cyanide in the body. In other words, the only conclusion that could be drawn is that a glass ampoule or capsule containing cyanide had been broken in the mouth of the corpse by ... someone else. Someone living.

Recourse, then, was had to the teeth.

The corpse had an expensive bridge made and this was removed for examination. So far, so good. According to the examination of Fritz Echtmann—a dental technician—by Soviet intelligence Major Vaindorf on July 24, 1947 in a report marked "Top Secret"[38] an unusual gold bridge was created for the right side of Eva Braun's lower jaw to connect two false teeth to two good teeth, and in such a way that the bridge would not show. This was completed in 1944. The following year—in April, 1945 and thus only weeks before her "death"—Echtmann was asked to make another bridge, this time for Eva's upper right jaw. This bridge was completed on April 19, 1945 and delivered to Hitler's dentist, Professor Hugo Blaschke in the Reich Chancellery.

This same bridge was discovered in the burned body with the shrapnel damage and the slivers of broken cyanide ampoule.

However, the bridge could not have possibly been made for the real Eva Braun.

A dental chart prepared by Blaschke after his capture in May of 1945 shows that Eva Braun had remarkably good teeth. In fact, Blaschke's chart bears no resemblance at all to the diagrams of Eva Braun's teeth presented by Echtmann to the Soviets. Further, there is no evidence that the bridge supplied by Echtmann on April 19, 1945 was ever used because there is no record that dental work was being carried out in the Bunker that late in the war with only ten days left before the collapse of the Reich and all hell breaking loose.

Considering the fact that the "Eva Braun" corpse in Soviet possession had died due to extensive shrapnel wounds and not cyanide poisoning, coupled with the fact that the Echtmann bridge was discovered in the mouth of this corpse, can only mean that someone wanted the Russians to believe that the body they had was Braun's ... even though it was not. A paper trail of dental records was prepared to establish a satisfactory identification of an unknown corpse as that of Hitler's long-time mistress.

---

38 *Hitler's Death*, pp. 105–107

The Soviets went looking for Blaschke but could not find him. Instead, they found his dental assistant, one Fräulein Käthe Heusemann, who claimed to be able to draw from memory Hitler's dental records. Amazingly (or perhaps not so amazingly!), this drawing matched perfectly the dental remains found in the putative Hitler corpse; in addition, Heusemann also identified the bridge work for Eva Braun.[39] All of this the Soviets kept in a box along with an Iron Cross and a Nazi Party badge, which certainly would have gone some way towards convincing Heusemann of what she should say.

For her cooperation, Heusemann was taken prisoner by the Soviet Union and disappeared into the gulag for years. Echtmann fared no better, and was released after ten years (during which time he once shared a cell with Mengershausen) and later became one of those (along with Linge and Günsche) who gave evidence before the Bavarian court in the hearing that would declare Hitler officially dead. Later, Heusemann would give explicit written testimony that Blaschke "*had never placed any bridgework in the mouth of Eva Braun*".[40] Heusemann's testimony before the Soviets was given in a state of terrible distress; when she was released, she was able to give a more reasoned and consistent story to investigators. But by that time no one was really listening.

So what of Hitler's teeth?

Actually, Hitler had very few of them. According to all accounts, he had only five natural teeth left by April of 1945. All the rest were metal and in some cases faced with porcelain. His upper jaw was entirely false and was composed of a bridge. His lower jaw had the five natural teeth and the rest were false. This meant that he had substantial bridgework done, and all by Blaschke and Echtmann. What was not so well known was the fact that Blaschke always had Echtmann make duplicate bridges, in case of emergency or if something went wrong during insertion.[41]

---

39 Trevor-Roper, pp. 32–33
40 Hugh Thomas, p. 142; emphasis in original.
41 Hugh Thomas, p. 147

Thus, all of the analysis of Hitler's teeth used to confirm the identification of the corpse that was found buried in the Reich Chancellery garden was really only analysis of the bridgework. In other words,
the Soviet forensic technicians were comparing the *bridgework* they
found in the corpse's mouth with the drawings of the *bridgework* created by the hapless Heusemann; later, in 1972, X-rays were found in
the National Archives in Washington, DC that purported to be those
of Hitler's mouth and which matched the bridgework.[42] As Hitler's
mouth no longer exists, all that is left is the bridgework; but since we
know that duplicates were made, we are left to conjecture whether or
not the corpse that was seized by SMERSH was really that of Hitler,
or that of a man who had Hitler's duplicate bridge inserted—loosely,
as it turns out—into his mouth after death.

Perhaps none of this would have mattered very much had the
Soviets not claimed to have possession of a piece of Hitler's skull, a
claim that was successfully refuted in 2009.

Operation Heel

It was not only the British and the Russians who had intelligence
agendas where Hitler was concerned, however.

In another bizarre revelation concurrent with the declassification
of American intelligence files from the war, we find a tantalizing reference to something called "Operation Heel." Like Operations Nursery
and Myth, this one had to do with Hitler's final days and his possible
escape at the end of the war. Strangely, though, it was created *almost
two full years before April 30, 1945*.

It is to be found in a once-secret OSS memorandum dated September 6, 1943 with the subject line: *"Heel" Campaign*. The memo
was written by Donald V. McGranahan, an expert in sociology and
psychology who had written peer-reviewed articles both before and
after the war. It was addressed to a "Lt. Dolan", who can be none
other than Lieutenant Brooke Dolan, the OSS officer who led several
expeditions to Tibet in the 1930s including one with future SS officer

---

42 Hugh Thomas, p. 150

Ernst Schäfer years before the war began. It was Dolan who—during the war—eventually made it as far as an audience with the present Dalai Lama and who led him to believe that the United States had recognized Tibetan nationhood (which, in fact, it had not). While Dolan's field was Asia, he was nonetheless addressed in this particular memo on a "MO" or "Morale Operations" mission to discredit Hitler in the eyes of the German people by spreading specific types of rumors, gossip, and planting news stories.

In it, suggestions are made to portray Hitler as insane. Some of the descriptions come fairly close to the mark and describe with eerie prescience what Trevor-Roper would say occurred in the bunker in April of 1945. They describe a Hitler increasingly isolated from Germany, the world, and reality itself, who refuses "to see anyone but his personal body guards, lives in a room without windows, and has his food tested before eating it."[43] The memo was written in 1943, before Hitler had retired permanently to the Berlin bunker that was, of course, a "room without windows" and which was soaked in the kind of paranoia and fantasy that the authors of the memo suggested. The purpose of the memorandum was, in the words of its author, "to undermine German respect for Hitler and to widen the cleavage between him and other power elements in Germany." The methodology was "to spread these ideas through rumors and through other concrete operations . . . " In order to be successful, it was recommended "To destroy the Hitler myth and bring der Führer down to the level of an ordinary party leader." The destruction of the Hitler myth was identical to the stated goal of Operation Nursery and Trevor-Roper's report.

The second section of the memo contained suggestions "To picture Hitler as utterly unsympathetic toward the loss of life and the suffering of the individual German." One of these suggestions was to promote the story that "Hitler has declared, 'I will not stop fighting until 10,000,000 Germans have died.' 4 million have gone 6 million to go." The number of 6 million in this context is momentarily arresting as it is, of course, the estimate of the total number of Jewish

---

43 Memorandum of Office of Strategic Services (OSS), from Lt. D.V. McGranahan to Lt. Dolan and Mr. Cushing, dated September 6, 1943, Subject: "Heel" Campaign.

victims of the Holocaust. In 1943 this number was not known and, indeed, there was controversy in the world's capitals as to the very existence of the Holocaust itself. To find it here is startling, to say the least, even though it is otherwise irrelevant.

One of the more fanciful suggestions was to spread the rumor that Hitler was making all of his military decisions based on "star-gazing and occultism" as well as "two Jewish-Gypsy soothsayers."

Another, more apt suggestion, has Hitler refusing "to involve Spain in the war because he has a promise of sanctuary there when Germany is defeated." Spain was one of the destinations bruited about as a possible place to which Hitler would have escaped after the fall of Berlin. It makes sense, as Franco was a fascist and notoriously sympathetic to the Nazi cause. In addition, the Spanish coast was used by Germany during the war for logistical support in an operation known as *Etappendienst*. This was a secret naval supply system that had been established during the first World War and which was then reactivated for service during World War II, in particular as a way of supporting and supplying German U-boats (a program we will come to later on).

In addition the "Heel" memorandum suggests spreading the rumor that "Planes are kept ready at both Munich and Berlin airports for Hitler to flee the country. A special gasoline-carrying plane will allow the fugitives to make only one stop before reaching Japan." Again, this "rumor" would find itself reactivated at the war's end. The persistent story that Hitler had escaped via plane to either Spain or Denmark or some other location while on his way to an ultimate South American destination remained as a possibility for years. That he had escaped via U-boat to either Argentina or Antarctica is another legend that persists to this day in some circles. The idea that Hitler may have wanted to flee to Japan, however, is probably unique to this memo. There is little evidence that Japan would have welcomed Hitler to its shores and, in any event, by the end of the war Japan was having enough of its own problems.

The reason for this digression is to demonstrate that the situation that existed at the end of the war was imagined by intelligence officers years earlier. Now that we know—in Trevor-Roper's own words— that the motivation behind the hastily-assembled report on Hitler's death that he compiled was the intelligence goal of countering Soviet statements that Hitler was alive and in British custody, we can begin to see how this agenda colored the final result: the book that became *The Last Days of Hitler*. But was this final report also the result of a propaganda effort initiated by American intelligence nine months before D-Day, and nearly two years before the fall of Berlin?

How much of that OSS report would reflect the reality of Hitler's "last days"?

CHAPTER TWO

WANDERING GHOSTS

I have not seen any documents providing evidence that this is
the skull of Hitler.
—Alexander Kalganov, Archive Department, FSB[44]

In the midst of all the conflicting testimonies concerning the ultimate fate of Adolf Hitler and Eva Braun, there was a bizarre intelligence operation taking place behind the scenes. This was the mission
of SMERSH—the Soviet counter-intelligence group whose acronym
stands for "Death to Spies"—to secure the bodies of Hitler and Braun
(and, indeed, those of the entire Goebbels family, plus their dogs, plus
General Krebs) and then ... well ... wander around Germany with
them piled in the back of a truck while they figured out what to do.

We have seen that the forensic evidence provided to the Soviets
in the form of the putative corpses of both Hitler and Braun was the
product of a deliberate fraud. Had the Russians merely found some
bodies they believed to be the ones they sought and then later discovered their mistake, this story would not be as compelling. Instead,
they found bodies that were deliberately altered in such a way as to
prove that they were, indeed, those of Hitler and Braun. Had they
merely mistaken some anonymous corpses for those of the Führer and
his mistress there would still be the possibility that the real bodies
would be found one day. Instead, they were presented with corpses
into which Hitler's and Eva's bridges had been carelessly inserted and
this meant the goal of the perpetrators was a deliberate attempt to call
off any further search for the two Nazis. A clever diversion had been
created, one that made the Soviets waste their time and resources.
What, then, was the real purpose behind the hoax?

---

44 Anna Dolgov, "Hitler's Skull Fragment Displayed," Associated Press, April
26, 2000. Note: The FSB is the modern incarnation of the KGB, the Soviet Secret
Police.

There are two possibilities. Either the real bodies had been buried in some secret place by the Nazis and the fake bodies offered up so that the Russians would call off their search; or, and this seems more likely, Hitler and Braun were not dead at all.

The Nazis would not have simply left two look-alikes behind, as-is, because eventually someone would recognize the deception. Instead, the two bodies had to be burned so as to remove any potential for precise visual identification, and then the duplicate bridgework inserted to "prove" their identities. We have seen this before in instances of insurance fraud and in homicide cases where a body is burned beyond recognition in a car—for instance—so that investigators will make the assumption that the corpse is that of the owner of the car while the real owner and perpetrator makes his getaway. Today, however, we have access to means of identification that did not exist in 1945, and this is what eventually exposed the most elaborate and cruel hoax of the twentieth century.

Wandervögel

According to declassified Soviet intelligence files, SMERSH took possession of the bodies and then drove around Germany with them, burying them and then digging them up, burying them again in some other location and then digging them up again, uncertain of what to do with the bodies until they finally settled on the historic city of Magdeburg where SMERSH had a facility.

In the words of the "Report on the Burial of the Corpses of Hitler, Goebbels and Other Persons", and classified Top Secret, dated June 4, 1945:

> In a further search on 5 May, 1945, several metres from the place where the corpses of Goebbels and his wife had been discovered, two badly-burnt bodies were discovered in a bomb-crater; these were the corpse of the Reichschanceller [sic] of Germany Adolf Hitler and the corpse of his wife Braun, Eva. These two corpses were also taken to the 'Smersh' Counter-Espionage Section of the 3rd Assault Army—the city of Buh

(Berlin) ... Because of the relocation of the 'Smersh' Counter-Espionage Section of the Army, the corpses were exhumed and moved first to the region of the city of Finov, and later, on 3 June, 1945, to the region of the city of Rathenau, where they were finally buried.[45]

Then, in the same dated report, special attention is given to the means of burial and the identification of the grave:

The corpses were in wooden coffins in a 1.7 metre deep grave, laid out in the following order:

From east to west: Hitler, Eva Braun, Goebbels, Magda Goebbels, Krebs, and Goebbels' children.

At the western end of the grave there is also a basket containing the bodies of two dogs, one of which belonged to Hitler personally and the other to Braun, Eva.

The location of the burnt bodies: Germany, province of Brandenburg, the vicinity of the city of Rathenau, forest to the east off the city of Rathenau, along the road from Rathenau to Scheetow ... 325 metres from a railway bridge, along a forest road, from a milestone numbered 111 northeastwards 4-side marker bearing the same number 111 ... The grave was filled in and smoothed over and small pine trees were planted on it forming the number 111.[46]

A number of points beg our attention. In the first place, the care taken to keep the corpses of the dogs and carry them around Germany along with the other bodies is somewhat unusual and inexplicable unless it demonstrates the anxiety of the SMERSH operatives lest the dogs one day prove to be invaluable as evidence and no one

---

45 This report is printed in *Hitler's Death*, pp. 110–113. The city of Buh is written in German as *Buch* and is a suburb of Berlin; Rathenau is *Rathenow* and Finov is *Finow* or, these days, *Eberswald-Finow*.

46 *Hitler's Death*, pp. 110–113.

wanted to be the one to tell Stalin that they disposed of them in a ditch somewhere.

In the second place, the almost ritualistic burial arrangement attracts our attention, including the mysterious use of the number 111. While this may just have been for the ease of locating the specific graves at a later date (which they did, in fact, do) one is still struck by the possibility of meaning or significance of the number.

When looking for significance beyond that available to the normal avenues of historical research, one is sometimes tempted to look in obscure and otherworldly places ... at least, until something more concrete comes along. In this case recourse to a book on Kabbalah proved unexpectedly helpful in this regard, for the number 111 can mean anything from "Ruin, destruction, sudden death" to "Common holocaust,"[47] which seems oddly appropriate, especially when coming from a Jewish source! The scene also calls to mind the picture in the Rider-Waite tarot deck of the "Three of Wands" card, which shows three trees standing upright and a man between them, gazing out to sea. The meaning usually attached to this card is "a journey." The author, however, does not imply that the Soviet spies were aware of these associations but only that, sometimes, coincidence has its own contribution to make.

THIS, HOWEVER, WAS NOT THE END of the wandering of the corpses for less than a year later it was decided to dig them up again.

From the SMERSH report entitled "Concerning the Re-Burial of the Remains" dated February 21 and 23, 1946:

> ... on this day, according to orders of the Chief of the 'Smersh' Counter-Espionage Department of the Group of the Soviet Occupational Forces in Germany—Lieutenant-General Comrade Zelenin, we opened up the grave containing the corpses in the vicinity of the city of Rathenau:
> of Reichschanceller [sic] of Germany Adolf Hitler

---

47 Aleister Crowley, "Sepher Sephiroth" in *777 and Other Qabalistic Writings of Aleister Crowley*, York Beach (ME): Samuel Weiser Inc., 1986, p. 17

of his wife Braun, Eva

of the Minister of Propaganda of Germany—Dr Josef Goebbels, his wife Magda Goebbels and their children—son Helmut and daughters Hilde, Helga, Hedda, Holde and [Heide]

of the Chief of the German General Staff—General Krebs

All the corpses mentioned are in a state of partial decay in wooden coffins and were delivered in this condition to the city of Magdeburg, to the headquarters of the 'Smersh' Counter-Espionage Section of the Army and again buried in a grave 2 metres deep in the yard of a building at no. 36 Westendstrasse, near the southern stone wall of the yard, 24 metres due east of the wall of the garage of the house.

The grave was filled in and smoothed over, blending in with the surrounding terrain.[48]

This was to be only a temporary resting place as well, but at least these bodies would stay buried for the next twenty-four years. The wandering of the corpses—from the Reich Chancellery garden, to the suburb of Buch, then to Finow, then to Rathenow, and finally to Magdeburg—had come to an end. A total of five burial sites in nine months. To an outside observer, this peripatetic approach to body disposal makes little or no sense at all.

And all this time, Stalin was insisting to anyone who would listen that Hitler was still alive.

Totenkopf

A portion of Hitler's body that was not buried with him was a part of his skull. This evidence, which consisted of his cranium with a bullet hole in it, was found by SMERSH near where the bodies were discovered in the Reich Chancellery garden. It was immediately assumed that this was a piece of Hitler's skull (just as they had assumed that the

---

48   *Hitler's Death*, pp. 114–116

body in their possession was Hitler's body). This forensic material was transported to Moscow where it was kept in a cardboard box along with Hitler's famous bridgework. Photographs of this skull fragment can be seen in *Hitler's Death*[49] and they have been reproduced since then in many other places. The photos clearly show what seems to be a bullet hole, and this satisfied Soviet intelligence that it was Hitler's (as if a skull with a bullet hole in it was an anomaly in Berlin in 1945!).

If SMERSH was convinced that they had the corpse of Adolf Hitler, and had his skull (or a good piece of it) then why did Stalin keep insisting that Hitler was still alive? In fact, why did the Americans also claim that there was no evidence to prove that Hitler had died in the bunker?

Why do declassified FBI and CIA files indicate that reports of Hitler sightings in Latin America were taken seriously and followed-up as late as the 1960s?

Was it even remotely possible that Hitler had escaped?

To answer that question we have to ask two more: was Hitler healthy enough to leave the bunker, and if so was it possible for anyone to leave Berlin in April of 1945?

Hitler's Health

It has been widely reported that Hitler was suffering from an advanced stage of Parkinson's Disease. However, this was a condition that was never officially diagnosed by a physician at the time. All we have to go on are reports of Hitler's symptoms and erratic medical records kept by various doctors who came and left Hitler's employ over the years and which do little to help clear up any controversy. One of the worst medical professionals attending the Führer was Dr. Theodor Morell, a specialist in patent medicines and general all-around quackery. It was Morell who kept Hitler drugged on a variety of poisons, pain-killers and placebos, and who most likely exacerbated whatever condition Hitler actually had.

---

49 *Hitler's Death*, pp. 114–115

Although rumors of Hitler's Parkinsonism were rampant among Bunker insiders due to the perceived symptoms—trembling hands, stooped posture, fixed stare, difficulty in getting up from a chair or walking very far—there were other factors at work that influenced Hitler's state of being. It is difficult at this remove to state categorically that Hitler's apparently degenerating physical condition was strictly the result of Parkinson's Disease. We would have to subtract the effects of the various drugs he was taking, the 1944 assassination attempt, the stress of the constant bombardments at the end, the realization that the war was being lost, the treachery of his trusted colleagues such as Himmler and Göring, and so much else besides. There was also the question of syphillis.

Another rumor around the Bunker and among insiders such as Himmler was the idea that Hitler had contracted syphillis during his days in Vienna as an impoverished artist. Syphillis is the type of disease that can remain dormant for decades and then suddenly appear. Himmler was eager to get his hands on any documentation that would prove this story, if only to ensure that it was buried as deeply as possible ... or to use it for blackmail purposes should it ever come to that. It seems that no blood test results are available, however, even though Hitler's first visit to Dr. Morell (in 1936) was in the latter's role as a "venereal specialist." It is entirely possible, then, that Hitler believed he had syphillis regardless of any medical evidence, and that Morell might have used that belief to bolster his own position in the Führer's inner circle. Hitler would have been forced to trust Morell with this secret, and Morell would have made as much use of that trust as possible ... short of getting himself killed, for Hitler was known to order the deaths of those he felt were a threat to his image. But if he believed he had syphillis, he would have been loath to take the chance of trusting another doctor with this information which may be why Morell lasted as long as he did. This is probably the only reason we can entertain for the complete faith Hitler seemed to have in this quack, even when other—more traditional and experienced—physicians were available and were occasionally called upon for their specialties; physicians who sized up Morell quite quickly and who were troubled by the influence this man had over the leader of Germany.

A brief description of the more than seventy different medicines Morell was administering to Hitler includes atropine, strychnine, and methamphetamines, as well as various pseudo-medicines as "Septo-Iodine" and "Tonophospan" as well as something called "Testoviron" which was presumably used for erectile dysfunction.[50]

Atropine and strychnine are, of course, poisonous in the right doses. Atropine, a derivative of the Deadly Nightshade plant, can cause hallucinations, dizziness, extreme confusion, and loss of balance. Some of these symptoms are identical to those of Parkinson's. Morell was using atropine in the form of eyedrops for Hitler, since the latter was suffering from impaired vision. If the drops were used continuously over a long period of time—and if the drops were of an incorrect dosage—then the possibility of toxicity cannot be overlooked.

Strychnine comes from the Nux Vomica plant, and is highly toxic. In lethal doses it causes convulsions and rigidity of the abdominal muscles, among other symptoms, and death results from respiratory failure, as the lungs are unable to contract and expand, thus leading to asphyxiation. It appears that strychnine was used to treat Hitler's flatulence in a concoction called Doktor Koster's Antigaspills, in a compound with Belladonna extract.[51] These drugs can cause severe cases of constipation ... something from which the dictator suffered in those last years of his life, which caused Morell to prescribe still other medicines, and so on.

The effects of methylamphetamines are widely known today, and could also have contributed to Hitler's perceived psychotic behavior, including hallucinations, trembling, paranoia, etc. The constant dosing and the length of time (years) that Morell gave Hitler amphetamines suggest a serious addiction; yet, in April of 1945 Hitler grew angry with Morell and even threatened to have him executed.[52]

Thus, we can only safely diagnose Parkinson's Disease in Hitler—long-distance, as it were—if we are able to isolate his symptoms from those of the other drugs he was taking. One thing is known, however,

50   Hugh Thomas, p. 15
51   One of the most detailed analyses of the Morell prescriptions can be found in D. Doyle, "Adolf Hitler's medical care", Edinburgh: *Journal of the Royal College of Physicians*, 2005; 35–75–82.
52   David Irving, *The Secret Diaries of Hitler's Doctor*, UK: Parforce, 2005, p. 219

and that is that Morell flew out of Berlin on April 22, eight days before the end ... which indicates that perhaps Hitler was no longer taking Morell's prescriptions at the time of his presumed death, even though a supply of some of the drugs was left behind and these were presumably—but not definitively—administered by Linge.

In retrospect, Morell's flight from the Bunker just might have saved the Führer's life.

Götterdämmerung

Several important Nazis have discussed the possibility of Hitler's flight from Berlin. One of these was Hitler's favorite commando, Otto Skorzeny.

Skorzeny was the man who rescued Italian dictator Benito Mussolini when the latter had been kidnapped by men loyal to the Italian king. It was a daring rescue attempt, with Skorzeny using gliders and parachutes to rescue the Fascist from the top of a mountain in a surprise attack. He was a man who understood military operations and commando action, and knew what was possible and what was not.

Just as importantly, it would be Skorzeny himself who would play a pivotal role in the creation and maintenance of the Nazi underground after the war.

Interviewed by author Glenn B. Infield, Skorzeny had this to say about Hitler's possible escape:

> "It was entirely possible for the Führer to leave the bunker by a subterranean passage under the Reich Chancellery ... climb to street level on the Hermann Göring Strasse, cut across the Tiergarten at the Zoo Station area near the Adolf Hitler Platz and follow the railway lines to the Reichssportfeld. He could then have crossed the Scharndorfestrasse, traversed the Piechelsdorf Bridge, and walked to the Havel. He then could have been picked up by a seaplane that would have landed on the river."[53]

---

53 Glenn B. Infield, *Skorzeny: Hitler's Commando*, New York: St. Martin's Press, 1981, p. 121

The fact that a seaplane did, indeed, land on the River Havel the night of April 29 or April 30 before taking off a few minutes later, only adds some credibility to Skorzeny's educated guess.[54] Further, no one knows where Skorzeny was on April 30, 1945 for he is next seen on May 2 sitting in his personal train on a siding in Austria. This is important for another reason, for one of his visitors on that train was SS Oberführer Josef Spacil, the SS officer in charge of finances.[55] Spacil is a name to conjure with, for he told Allied investigators essentially the same story after his capture: that Hitler had escaped Berlin:

> Spacil claimed that Hitler had not died in his bunker. Under cover of darkness, disguised as a civilian, he was secretly transported out of Berlin in a small plane. A partially cremated body double had been left behind to fool the Russians.[56]

This story is important for several reasons. In the first place, it corroborates Skorzeny's version (but that could have been because Spacil and Skorzeny had met only days before Spacil's capture by Allied forces and thus had time to coordinate their stories). In the second place, the story of Hitler's partially cremated remains was not general knowledge outside a small circle of insiders which include either the Bunker inhabitants themselves who were complicit in this hoax, or the Soviet agents who found the planted body. Also, the presence of Skorzeny in Austria might possibly indicate complicity in Hitler's presumed escape for, as we shall see, Austria was one of the stops on the Ratline and a possible transit point for the subject of this book.

---

54 According to Infield, p. 121. See also Günther Ott, "Unternehmen Reichskanzlei", in *Jet & Prop*, 04/1995: Zweibrücken, Verlag Heinz Nickel p 43–50; and the interview with Capt. Ernst Koenig which reveals an escape plan for evacuating Hitler and his entourage by air from the Wannsee and Havel, in Nick Fielding, "How I prepared the Nazis plan for great escape to Greenland" in *The Times*, London, Dec. 28, 2003.

55 *Skorzeny*, p. 122

56 Sidney D. Kirkpatrick, *Hitler's Holy Relics: A True Story of Nazi Plunder and the Race to Recover the Crown Jewels of the Holy Roman Empire*, New York: Simon & Schuster, 2010: p. 213

In the third place, Spacil was one of those faceless bureaucrats who nevertheless knew where all the other bodies were buried. Spacil's job was overseeing the financial arrangements that emanated from the death camps. All those gold rings, jewelry, confiscated art, and confiscated currency from the victims of the Holocaust were under his supervision and disbursement. He was an important person to know in the last days of the Reich, and traveled tirelessly between various locations in Germany and Austria to ensure that the vast Nazi wealth would not fall to the Allies. It would be Spacil who, once captured, would eventually lead the Allies to some of the treasure that was hidden by the Nazis in the last months of the war. It would also be Spacil who was well aware of the vast counterfeiting operation undertaken by the Nazis, with a view to destabilizing the British Pound and other currencies.

This trafficking in illicitly-obtained funds was one of the cornerstones of what would become the Ratline: the escape route used by the Nazis (and most especially the SS) to the Middle East, North America, Latin America, Australia and ... as the author discovered by accident one warm tropical evening ... Asia.

ODESSA

One of the problems facing any responsible historian or investigative journalist attempting to present a coherent narrative of the wholesale escape-and-rescue operation of Nazis after the war is the looming spectre of ODESSA. Promoted by professional Nazi-hunter Simon Wiesenthal as a fact, ODESSA was most likely a term that covered a wide range of various mechanisms and independent operators and not the single, monolithic organization popularized by the Frederick Forsythe novel, *The ODESSA File*. The idea of ODESSA as a powerful international brotherhood of former SS officers has been exploded, which means that anyone researching and writing about the Ratline has to confront the fiction in order to uncover the facts.

However, that does not mean that underground networks created specifically to help the Nazis escape did not exist. In fact, the truth is much more shocking than the fiction.

In the last days of the war, as the Russians advanced inexorably on the Reichstag and eventually the Reich Chancellery itself, the rats began deserting the sinking ship. Notable escapees from the Bunker included Martin Bormann, Artur Axmann, and the SS officers Linge and Günsche, among many others. They were able to make it successfully to various points in Berlin, and Axmann made it as far as southern Bavaria. Linge and Günsche were captured by the Soviets, as we have seen, as were Baur and Mengershausen. Bormann's fate remained something of a mystery, however, and rumors of his survival were legion; a story we will get to later on in this investigation.

Throughout Germany, high-ranking SS officers were seeking ways to avoid capture and almost certain incarceration, if not execution. The SS had been declared a "criminal organization" and many of them had, indeed, committed what can only be considered war crimes or crimes against humanity. As early as 1944—after the D-Day invasion of June, 1944 when it became obvious that the war was lost—pragmatic Nazis such as Bormann were quickly and efficiently creating an exit strategy. This strategy involved the movement of gold and other currencies out of Germany and eventually out of Europe.

The number of Nazi personnel who were involved in this project, as well as the bewildering array of Nazi organizations they represented, was impressive. While much attention has been focused on recognizable names such as Martin Bormann there were other individuals and groups with a vested interest in making sure that enough money was expatriated from Germany and its wartime possessions to enable a flow of war criminals relatively unimpeded by considerations of politics, visa documentation, or arrest warrants.

Some of these individuals included those that were well known to Allied intelligence but who were not household names to the rest of the world. One of these, identified by Argentine investigator Uki Goñi, was Carlos Fuldner.[57] Fuldner was a native of Argentina of German heritage who became an SS officer and who, later, wound up working for the SD (*Sicherheitsdienst* or Foreign Intelligence) depart-

---

57   Uki Goñi, *The Real Odessa: How Perón Brought the Nazi War Criminals to Argentina*, London: Granta Books, 2002. The story of Carlos Fuldner is to be found on pages 63–71, and again on pages 140–141.

ment of the SS, presumably under SD chief Walter Schellenberg. Without delving too deeply into Fuldner's long and chequered career we can focus on one or two aspects of his involvement in the story of the Ratline.

Fuldner was a con man, and in the last months of the war a con man is precisely what the Reich needed. With dual Argentine and German citizenship, he was able to cross borders almost effortlessly. As someone who had committed fraud in the past and who even went so far as to embezzle SS funds at one point, Fuldner had abilities that the Nazis would eventually find quite useful as their government degenerated into a criminal or rogue state. It is worthwhile to point out that Argentina stayed neutral during most of the war, but that did not mean that Argentina was truly neutral in any ordinary sense of the word. The large and influential German community in Argentina made sure that political and government sentiments and policies (especially immigration) were staunchly pro-Nazi and anti-Semitic. Some of the most virulent anti-Semitic tracts ever published came out of Argentina in the 1940s and, indeed, many Argentines felt themselves to be more European than "Latin American", a phrase they viewed as a pejorative.[58] By staying out of the conflict, Argentina was actually more useful to the Third Reich. Its shipping was not vulnerable to attack from either side in the war and thus Argentina was able to sell its beef and other products abroad with relative impunity. It was also able to conduct dialogue with both sides, enabling the Reich to use its influence to ensure that Argentina would remain a useful partner in the war and also its aftermath.

Fuldner's brief was to help ensure that relations between Argentina and the Reich remained solid and that networks were formed and maintained that would enable the movement of men and money to Argentina via Italy and Spain. Franco's Spain was an essential element in the early days of the Ratline, for Franco himself was a Nazi-sympathizer who had gone so far as to send a division of 20,000 troops—the famous "Blue Division"—to help Hitler fight the Russians on the

---

58 During the author's own investigation in Buenos Aires in the 1990s, he was told on several occasions that Argentines considered themselves European and should not be confused with Latin Americans who were, in their estimation, "Indians."

Eastern front. The Nazis used Spanish ports as support bases for their U-boat traffic, the *Etappendienst* or "Stages Service". Established by the future Admiral Dönitz during the First World War, the Etappendienst was brought back to life in the Second World War as a vital part of the Nazis' U-boat strategy. When the war was over, the men who were involved in the Etappendienst remained behind to serve as a kind of fifth column to support the flight of their fellow Germans out of Europe and to safer harbors.

Fuldner's role in Spain was murky. Allied intelligence could not completely understand what he was up to in Germany and Spain, but suspected that he was working for German intelligence in some capacity involving finances and the movement of money. He is said to have served with Franco's Blue Division on the Russian front, and also to have obtained a position with Sofindus (short for Sociedad Financiera Industrial), a Spanish-German conglomerate that at its peak controlled more than 50 ships and 10 agricultural enterprises, and which was run from Berlin by SS Oberführer Johannes Bernhardt. Bernhardt himself wore a black SS uniform replete with the Spanish Falange insignia, explicit testimony to his involvement with Franco's regime. This also implies a discrete connection with the Etappendienst and, with the war coming to an end in the spring of 1945, we find Fuldner arriving in Madrid in March of that year to start working on his real career achievement: the establishment of the Ratline's Spanish component. It is worthwhile to note that the Allies had computed the amount of gold coming into Spain from Nazi Germany during the period of the war as more than *122 tons* (conservatively; other estimates put it at more than 200 tons). These calculations were based on records obtained from Sofindus and from trucking manifests out of Germany to Spain. The final disposition of this gold is unknown, but it would have been worth more than US$100 million in 1945 dollars.[59]

By December of 1947, then in Genoa and with credentials provided by President Juan Perón of Argentina, Fuldner was able to create

---

59   For official Allied estimates of the gold brought to Spain see for instance "Preliminary Draft: Memorandum on Gold Acquisitions by Spain During the War," August 6, 1946, prepared by Otto Fletcher, RG 59, Records of the Legal Adviser, Records Relating to German Assets, 1942–1959, Box 18, National Archives, Washington DC.

a complex but efficient machinery for the movement of SS officers and other war criminals out of Europe and to Argentina, including the architect of the Final Solution: Adolf Eichmann. While Nazis already had been on the run by mid-1945, it would not be until Perón's election to the Argentine presidency in 1946 that the large-scale escape of war criminals to South America would begin in earnest.

The first documented case of a war criminal fleeing to Argentina was that of the French aeronautics engineer Emil Dewoitine. Dewoitine designed jet aircraft for Germany and Japan as well as for Spain during the war, and was wanted by the French authorities. Using a Spanish passport, he was able to flee Europe for the safety of Argentina in May of 1946. By the following August, he had already developed a jet plane prototype for the Perónist regime, to much fanfare. The person who helped him escape was Cardinal Antonio Caggiano, an Argentine clergyman who helped set up the Spanish end of the Ratline along with assistance from French and Belgian Nazis.[60]

Knowing all this, would it have been possible for Hitler to have escaped and, if so, how and when and where?

IF WE ACCEPT THE IDEA that he escaped Berlin by plane (a theory that is by no means certain), where did he wind up in the immediate days after the fall of Berlin?

One of the scenarios that has been suggested[61] is that the small seaplane that landed in Berlin on April 29 or April 30 then took off for Denmark. The passenger(s) was then taken aboard a U-Boat and made for the open sea. While we know that planes did take off and land in Berlin at the very end of April—famed pilot Hanna Reitsch's plane did just that—it was an extremely dangerous undertaking. Soviet batteries were constantly sweeping the skies over Berlin and although Hanna Reitsch did make it out of Berlin it is doubtful (although possible) that she had Hitler on board.

---

60   Uki Goñi, *The Real Odessa*, London: Granta Books, 2003, p. 93–99

61   See, for instance, the AAP report "Sentence on Pilot: Claims He flew Hitler Away" in *The Sydney Morning Herald*, Feb 9, 1949 for a summary of the testimony of Luftwaffe Capt. Peter Baumgart who insisted he flew Hitler and Eva Braun to Denmark in April, 1945 from where he believed they boarded a submarine.

A more likely escape route would have been to the south, to the area around Berchtesgaden where, indeed, Artur Axmann eventually did appear, safe and sound. This escape route would still have been physically arduous not to mention dangerous. It was also a target for Allied forces who were aware of the importance of the region to the Nazi high command, many of whom—like Göring—had houses in the vicinity. It was also the location of the legendary National Redoubt, where it was believed the Nazis would organize a post-war operation against the Allies. Had Hitler repaired to his famous retreat it would have been only a matter of time before the most wanted man in Europe was apprehended.

The one place that remained relatively secure for the Nazis, however, was the Alpine region between Austria and Italy known as the Tyrol.[62] Accessible from southern Bavaria in a straight line south of Munich, it was a notorious link on the Ratline from Germany and Austria to the Italian port city of Genoa. This area was known for its smugglers and for a multi-cultural environment that was both German and Italian; the Tyroleans were used to the trafficking of humans as well as of goods. It would have been possible for Hitler to have remained in the Tyrol for years before finding it necessary to move along the line to Genoa. Indeed, several Nazis on the Allies' most-wanted list did just that.

The families of Martin Bormann, Heinrich Himmler and Josef Mengele—among many others—found refuge for a while in the South Tyrol. Others—war criminals like Erich Priebke, the SS officer implicated in the massacre at the Adreatine Caves[63] in Italy—wound up in hiding there for quite some time before fleeing to South Amer-

---

62   The author's own maternal line originated in the Tyrol, and while his mother's family was nominally Italian her grandparents spoke German as well as Italian.

63   On 24 March 1944, Hitler approved retaliation against the Italian civilian population of Rome for a partisan attack the previous day which saw the deaths of more than forty Nazi policemen of the Police Battalion Bozen. Bozen is a town in the South Tyrol known in Italian as Bolzano and, indeed, the battalion was composed of ethnic Germans from the Italian Tyrol. Priebke himself carried out many of the gruesome murders, which involved bringing the victims into the unused quarry ten at a time and shooting them individually in the back of the head at close range, resulting in the deaths of more than three hundred in this manner. Hitler himself authorized the reprisal.

ica. Many French collaborators fled to the region after the collapse of the Vichy regime, some with entire families and their possessions on wagons. Eastern European fascists and Nazis also used the South Tyrol as a convenient—and congenial—way-station on their escape route.

The area was well-known to Bormann and Hitler and, indeed, Hitler himself was an Austrian by birth who came from the town of Branau-am-Inn. There had been rumors that the Führer had established some sort of Alpine redoubt in the Tyrol, but that was never proven although recently declassified documents make it clear that such a Redoubt was at least in the planning stages by the end of the war. However, the close association of the Tyrol with Hitler had been made and the Allies were aware of the possibility that Hitler would manage to find refuge in an area he knew well.

From the South Tyrol there were several possible avenues of escape out of Europe. One of these led to Genoa, the seaport on Italy's northwestern coast, but this was not used immediately after the war due to the large Allied presence in the region. Another route led to the southern coast of Italy, to Bari on the Adriatic, a port popular with traders, fishermen and smugglers from Greece and West Asia.[64] These were logical points of egress and, once the Allies stopped looking aggressively for war criminals in 1947, it became fairly easy for former SS officers and their families to mix with the huge rush of displaced persons and other emigrants trying to find a home or safe haven abroad. Indeed, there was even a Jewish Displaced Persons (DP) camp in Bari at the end of the war.

While more focus has been directed at the port of Genoa—for that was the exit point for ships traveling to the Americas—the eastern

---

64 A recent (January, 2010) case involved a Greek trafficker—Alexandros Lepesiotis—with an Afghan teenager stuffed in a suitcase in the back of his car, a Peugeot 207 with Greek license plates, and another in the trunk. The two teenagers had been hiding in the car since the ferry left Greece for Italy and were discovered by Italian border control officers and Lepesiotis arrested. Intriguingly, Hollywood actor Sterling Hayden—as OSS officer "Jack Hamilton"—used Bari as his base for undercover operations against the Nazis and the Ustashe in Yugoslavia during the war, operations that were severely hindered by British forces who considered Yugoslavia their own theater of operations. See the declassified OSS file on Sterling Hayden.

coast of Italy was useful for anyone traveling to the eastern Mediterranean or the Middle East. In those days of tremendous confusion in the immediate post-war period, it would not have required the organizational capabilities of an ODESSA in order to effect an anonymous flight abroad, especially if money was no object and especially if the currency in question was gold (since Reichsmarks would have been worthless, and other currencies—such as the British pound—had been famously counterfeited by the Nazis).

Thus, there were several routes available to the Nazis and it is only a matter of conjecture at this point, which one would have been used by Hitler. The possibility of a flight to Denmark (or to another country with a sea coast, such as Spain) cannot be discounted, even though the Denmark story has been justifiably criticized. Hitler would have had to travel in tremendous secrecy, in such a way that there was no possibility of capture. Many of his associates and henchmen did manage to escape that way, of course, but Hitler had to have been the most easily recognizable person on the planet by that time. He would have had to change his appearance considerably. As he was most famous for his Charlie Chaplin-style moustache, that would have had to go. Without it, there is a good chance that he would not have been immediately recognized ... especially if no one had been looking for him after the widely disseminated report by Trevor-Roper in September of 1945 confirming his death.

If he was indeed, as sick as has been suggested then there would have been steps taken to accommodate his illness while simultaneously maintaining his cover. Would anyone have seriously challenged an old man in a wheelchair? Perhaps being accompanied by a nurse or a doctor? All that was necessary was that the ruse be maintained at least until the "patient" was safely aboard a plane or a vessel that would take him to sanctuary.

At a time when there were so many casualties of the war, so many persons with wounds, or crippled, or missing eyes or limbs, one more hospital case would not have been challenged very deeply particularly if the "victim" in question were an old man in a wheelchair. By the end of the war Hitler was only fifty-six years old, but according to those who knew him in the Bunker he had aged considerably since the July, 1944 assassination attempt. Add to that the symptoms so suggestive of

Parkinson's Disease (and it is important to remember that his condition was a state secret and not known to the general public) and you have an excellent candidate for pity and mercy. Such a stateless person, with no identity documents, would have been an ideal candidate for the International Red Cross passport as well: a travel document that was being issued with somewhat reckless abandon and with little or no supporting identification documentation required ... except, in certain cases, identification provided courtesy of the Roman Catholic Church.

Such a stateless person would have been able to find another home, anywhere on the planet, particularly if they had the blessing of the Vatican itself.

CHAPTER THREE

THE MONASTERY ROUTE

I had no idea how one went about finding a bishop at the Vatican.... 'Are you on the way to see Hudal?' I said yes, but that I didn't know where to find him.... The Bishop came into the room where I was waiting and he held out both his hands and said, 'You must be Franz Stangl. I was expecting you.'[65]

Bishop Alois Hudal (1885–1963) was a central figure in the escape route used by the Nazis, and a devoted National Socialist who wrote a book defending Nazism and praising it as an ideological adversary to Communism. He was an Austrian, born in Graz.

Franz Stangl (1908–1971), also an Austrian, was the commander of the extermination camps at Sobibor and Treblinka, responsible for the deaths of 900,000 people. Bishop Hudal personally arranged his International Red Cross travel documents[66] and his escape to Syria, from where Stangl eventually made it to South America before being arrested and extradited to West Germany to stand trial. Decades after the war's end he was found guilty of mass murder, and died six months later of a heart attack.

Hudal also arranged the escapes of Gustav Wagner (1911–1980), Stangl's deputy commander at Sobibor who later died in Brazil, as well as SS-Hauptsturmführer Alois Brunner (1912–1996?) responsible for the deaths of nearly 150,000 Jewish prisoners in the gas chambers and who some believe is still living in Syria, as well as Brunner's immediate superior SS-Obersturmbannführer and architect of the Final Solution, Adolf Eichmann (1906–1962) and so many others ... with the assistance of Msgr. Krunoslav Draganovic.

---

65 Gitta Sereny, *Into that Darkness: From Mercy Killing to Mass Murder*, London: Pimlico, 1995, p. 289

66 Gerald Steinacher, *Nazis on the Run: How Hitler's Henchmen Fled Justice*, Oxford: Oxford University Press, 2011, p. 251

THE NAME KRUNOSLAV DRAGANOVIC in the Indonesian diary was the most significant discovery of the entire investigation. In 1970, very few individuals were aware of who Draganovic was, or of his connection to the Vatican and the escape route used by the Nazis called by military intelligence the "ratlines."

Draganovic was a monsignor in the Roman Catholic Church, and a Croat who was a supporter of the vicious Ustashe regime led by Ante Pavelic (1889–1959) and, indeed, helped Pavelic obtain the Red Cross passport he would need to escape to Argentina. The Ustashe were fascists and Nazis, extremely anti-Semitic, anti-Communist and also anti-Eastern Orthodox. They were Catholic, and numbered Catholic clergy not only among their membership but also in the violence associated with the Croatian concentration camps. These crimes did not matter to men like Bishop Hudal or Draganovic, or to a number of other Catholic clergy who formed an important element of the ratlines known as the "monastery route."

In July of 1946, American intelligence became aware of the monastery route and a U.S. State Department official wrote a memo (only declassified in 1985) identifying the major players and associating it directly with the Croat Ustashe movement. Dated 12 July 1946, the subject line is: "Alleged Vatican Protection of Jugoslav War Criminals."

It reads, in part:

> 1. At No. 7 Via Carlo Alberto, Rome, in a building under extraterritorial Vatican jurisdiction, are located the COLLEGIUM ILLIRICUM and the COLLEGIUM ORIENTALIS.
>
> 2. The Ustasche of PAVELIC'S Independent Croat State formerly championed the theory that the Croats are not Slavs, but are of Gothic origin. Subsequent to the fall of Nazism this theory was repudiated, and [censored] the COLLEGIUM ORIENTALIS is engaged in advancing the theory that the Croats are of Persian origin.
>
> 3. Both theories, that of the Gothic and that of the Persian origin of the Croats, are supported by the Vatican which wishes to strengthen Croat separatist tendencies and to assure their support of the Vatican-inspired "Catholic State" which

is projected to include CROATIA, BOSNIA-HERZEGOV-
INA, DALMATIA, SLOVENIA, CARINTHIA, ISTRIA
and the JULIAN MARCH linked to AUSTRIA.

4. This same separatist tendency, is evident among the
Slovenians, too, and the "Strazar" Party supported by the
Jesuit Academy at No. 6 Via Borgia, Rome, is its princi-
pal propaganda organ. The Academy is headed by Father
PRESEREN himself of Slovenian origin, a member of the
Supreme Directorate of the Jesuit Institutions. Hesitation of
Slovenian People's Party leader Dr. Mih KREK to join the
Jugoslav Central Committee in London, despite his strongly
maintained position regarding the necessity for the creation
of a democratic Jugoslav Federation, is surely to a great extent
based on a knowledge of what is taking place in the Croat San
Girolamo degli Illirici Foundation in Rome and in the Jesuit
Academy.

5. In Austria, following their withdrawal from Jugoslavia with the Germans, the members of the NEDIC and the
Dimitrijo LJOTIC Quisling organizations, and the Monte-
negrin Separatists proceeded to draw up a deed with Croatian
Ustascha organs by means of which they hoped to obtain Vatican sponsorship with a view to escaping possible war-crimi-
nal prosecution. Such Vatican sponsorship was accorded the
Ustascha, chiefly in order to assure their silence regarding the
atrocities committed by Clergy-led Croats who had indulged
in a ruthless program of extermination of Jews and Orthodox
Serbs.

The Collegium Orientalis, mentioned above, was the headquarters of Bishop Alois Hudal in Rome. It was at the Collegium Orientalis that Franz Stangl met Bishop Hudal. The San Girolamo degli
Illirici Foundation was the Roman headquarters of Father Krunoslav
Draganovic.

It is evident in the State Department memo that there was considerable rationalization among these clergymen concerning the racial
identity of the Croats, since the Nazis had deemed the Slavs to be an
inferior race. If the Croats were Slavs, then they were but a half-step

above the Jews and the Gypsies and suitable only for slave labor at best; but if they were Persian, then they were Aryan. (After all, the word Iran means "Aryan").

The Croats were largely Catholic, and the idea of a Catholic bulwark against Communism was something that had wide appeal. This concept was mirrored in Argentine fascism, which saw itself and its role in the world in identical terms. Thus it should come as no surprise that there was a natural alliance between the Croats and the Argentines, through the intermediary of churchmen like Draganovic and Hudal. They saw their enemy as Communism, and their natural allies in the fight against the Communists were the Nazis.

Hudal had written a book on National Socialism[67] that was well received by the Nazi high command. Although the Third Reich was suspicious of the Church—and, indeed, were intent on eventually replacing Christianity with their own form of neo-Paganism—they understood that it was better to have the Church on their side, at least for the duration of the war. Politically it meant that the Church would not officially condemn the Third Reich, thus assuring a certain degree of cooperation from both the clergy and the laity. Militarily, it meant that Catholics would have no qualms about joining the German army and that they would be less likely to offer resistance to the Nazis, at least not on ideological grounds. In addition, the Reichsconcordat signed on July 20, 1933 by Cardinal Secretary of State Eugenio Pacelli with Franz von Papen on behalf of Hindenburg essentially left the German Catholics at the mercy of the Reich at a time when Hitler had just been named Chancellor and was on his way to becoming Germany's dictator. While ostensibly designed to safeguard German Catholics, what it did in essence was acknowledge the Reich's authority vis-à-vis the Church in Germany. It reduced the ability of the German church to criticize the Reich and effectively neutralized the opposition.

It was within this tense atmosphere of 1930s Europe that bishops like Hudal and clergy like Draganovic could openly support the Nazi regime. The Concordat gave their praise of the Nazi Party a degree of

---

67 Alois Hudal, *Die Grundlagen des Nationsozialismus* ("The Foundation of National Socialism"), Leipzig: Günther, 1936. A copy of this book was presented to Hitler by Hudal, with the inscription: "To the architect of German greatness."

legitimacy they might not otherwise have enjoyed, and it freed them to focus their attention on resisting and defeating Communism, seen as the true enemy of both the Church and the State. There was no official censure of pro-Nazi bishops or priests by the Holy See; had there been, the plight of Catholics living under the Third Reich would have been imperiled. So it was the "lesser" of two evils: turn a blind eye to the horrors of the Holocaust so that the Catholics of Germany would remain safe and out of danger. Meanwhile, some Catholic clergy and laypeople did their best to save as many Jews as possible; but it was not official policy and had to be done quietly.

The man who signed the Reichsconcordat with Germany—Cardinal Eugenio Pacelli—became Pope Pius XII: the wartime pontiff who did not raise his voice against the Nazis but who did, once the war was over, turn his energy and attention to the defeat of Communism, a strategy that fit well with that of the pro-Nazi clergy under his administration and which contributed mightily to the obscene scenario of clergymen helping war criminals accused of the most hideous atrocities to escape justice.

Much has been written about Pope Pius XII and what is perceived as his support—tacit or implicit—of the Nazi regime. The Catholic Church has been criticized for this by any number of historians and observers, and the Vatican has usually fought back, insisting that the allegations are without merit. The fact remains, however, that the Nazi war criminals most famous, most wanted, most notorious were protected and aided in their escape by a series of Catholic priests, bishops, and cardinals throughout Europe and North and South America. Whether or not this was "official" policy, it most definitely took place and there was no policy—official or otherwise—to stop it.

While many high-ranking clergy were pro-Nazi—and not just in their sentiments but in the actions they took to promote Nazism and to defend its perpetrators—that does not mean that the Vatican itself was pro-Nazi; but from the point of view of the laity, of the people who filled the pews on Sunday and who looked up to their priests as men of God, it could only appear as official policy. A churchgoer in Zagreb or Sarajevo would come away with the clear perception that the Church supported Nazism in all its manifestations. Photographs of Roman Catholic priests, bishops and cardinals standing shoulder to shoulder with men in the uniforms of the SS or the Ustashe, giving the "Heil Hitler" salute, could only be construed as evidence of tacit approval.

It is a luxury for historians to parse the documents and deconstruct the speeches and analyze the treaties and the wars in an effort to identify trends, affiliations, and responsibilities; but the history of the world from the point of view of those who suffer is fundamentally different from the point of view of the comfortable and the powerful. The suffering deal with the *experience* of history—the blood. The powerful deal with the data of history—the documents. The truth, if it can be discovered, lies somewhere between the two.

This is especially true when documents are released piecemeal due to classification, "national security" concerns, etc. The story slowly unfolds, over the course of years and decades, and as it does it changes. If one dies before the whole story is revealed, one has lived one's whole life with a lie and under the illusion that what one knows is true.

This issue is central to this book, this research. There is no doubt that lies were told about the death of Hitler; there is no doubt that lies were told about the culpability of persons in the Allied governments concerning the flight and protection of criminals such as Eichmann and Barbie, Rauff and Stangl. But this information has only been coming to light since the mid-1980s, long after the end of the war when we thought we already knew the "truth." These deceptions extend to those perpetrated by the Catholic Church at the same time, concerning these same criminals, and for the same reasons. As the governments of the United States, the United Kingdom, and Russia begin to come clean regarding what actually took place in the weeks and months after the end of the war in Europe, the role of the Church is similarly exposed.

One of the most revealing statements concerning American intelligence cooperation with the monastery route is contained in a document dated July 12, 1948 from Paul E. Lyon and Charles Crawford, both Special Agents of the CIC 430th Detachment in Vienna. The subject line reads; "Rat Line from Austria to South America" and contains unequivocal proof of the involvement of the US military in

Draganovic's operation. Declassified in the 1980s, it can be seen as the "smoking gun" in the wider implementation of the monastery route to include U.S. military and intelligence personnel.

It is worthwhile to quote the memo in length in order that the reader realize the scope of the project:

2. Through the Vatican connections of Father Draganovic, Croat, DP Resettlement Chief of the Vatican circle, a tentative agreement was reached to assist in this operation. The agreement consists of simply mutual assistance, i.e., these agents assist persons of interest to Father Draganovic to leave Germany and, in turn, Father Draganovic will assist these agents in obtaining the necessary visas to Argentina, South America, for persons of interest to this Command.

3. It may be stated that some of the persons of interest to Father Draganovic may be of interest to the Denazification policy of the Allies; however, the persons assisted by Father Draganovic are also of interest to our Russian ally. Therefore, this operation cannot receive any official approval and must be handled with minimum amount of delay and with a minimum amount of general knowledge.

4. On 3 July 1948, these agents contacted the Austrian representative of Father Draganovic in Salzburg, as prearranged. Through the assistance of CIC Salzburg, transportation was obtained and the representative was escorted to Bad Reichenhall, Germany, where he was to meet the German representative of Father Draganovic's organization. However, due to unforeseen circumstances, the German representative did not appear. The Austrian representative was escorted back to Salzburg to await developments.

5. On 4 July 48 these agents received a telegram from the U.S. contact in Rome (Fred Martin) that the German representative was arrested while crossing the German/Austrian border on or about 1 July 48. It was the desire of the agents to go to Bad Reichenhall, Germany to make the necessary investigation, however due to transportation difficulties, this was not deemed advisable.

6. The status of subject rat line is not settled at this time, however it is felt that with CIC connections in Germany, these agents can assist the German representative and continue their progress as outlined above.

NOTE: It is suggested to the Chief, 430th CIC Detachment, USFA, that a reassignment of jeeps be made, and that two detachment jeeps be assigned to headquarters. These jeeps could be stationed and utilized by Land Salzburg and Land Upper Austria but be prepared to move upon call from representatives of CIC headquarters. In this manner most of the difficulties in obtaining transportations for such operations can be avoided. Also the responsibilities for incorrect use of said vehicles, i.e., police violations, utilizing Government vehicles for pleasure, will be the responsibility of the driver and not the Land Section to which the jeep is originally assigned.

It is believed that in this manner considerable time, personal difficulties, and personality differences could be avoided and assist in the speedy completion of similar missions.

A number of things can be discerned from this memo. In the first place, the decision to assist Draganovic was made as early as July of 1948, even though CIC memos from 1946 and 1947 expressed a certain degree of alarm over his operation. Further, CIC placed transportation and other services at the disposal of the Ratline. And finally CIC kept the entire operation secret from the Russians, who were looking for many of these individuals for war crimes in the Soviet zone and, indeed, the entire operation would not receive "official approval" and would be handled with a "minimum amount of delay and a minimum amount of general knowledge." It was a black op, an intelligence operation conducted without *official* approval.

The pact had been made. American military intelligence colluded with the Vatican to assist Nazi and Ustashe war criminals in their escape to South America. The Ratline ran from Austria (and specifically Salzburg, where we will find the Pöch couple at this time) to South America, with the American military providing logistical support.

Some of the clergy involved at one time or another in the "monastery route" include, in addition to Hudal and Draganovic, Msgr. Don Giuseppe Bicchierai, the secretary to Archbishop (later Cardinal) Ildefonso Schuster of Milan, and Archbishop Siri of Genoa. According to Simon Wiesenthal, Msgr. Bicchierai arranged for SS Standartenführer Walter Rauff (and others) to "stay covertly in the convents of the Holy See"[68] prior to their escape from Europe. During the 1948 election campaign in Italy—in which there was a danger of a Communist takeover—Bicchierai worked with the CIA to frustrate attempts by the Italian Communist party to seize control of the government, an effort which possibly involved Walter Rauff as well.

Rauff—the SS chief in Milan during the last years of the war—had been working with future CIA Director Allen Dulles in the well-documented Operation Sunrise while Dulles was chief of the OSS in Berne, Switzerland. Operation Sunrise was an arrangement between Dulles, the SS and the Wehrmacht that ensured that the German surrender to the Allies in Italy would take place in a gentlemanly fashion. It was a strange agreement, one that afforded the SS in particular special treatment at the hands of Dulles and the OSS. Dulles had understood early on that the "real enemy" was Soviet communism, and by enlisting the aid of SS officers as well as the generals of the Wehrmacht he felt he could contain that threat more successfully. Walter Rauff was one of the beneficiaries of this arrangement, regardless of the fact that it was Rauff who invented the Einsatzgruppen's mobile gas chambers—specially fitted vans that had the carbon monoxide exhaust piped directly into the back of the van holding the victims—that were used to kill more than 100,000 Jewish prisoners before the gas chambers and crematoria at the camps were built.

Walter Rauff was a war criminal by every known metric, yet both the Church and American intelligence collaborated in his escape from justice. Rauff eventually wound up in Chile, where the mass murderer lived out the remainder of his days in peace and with the moral sup-

---

68 Jonathan Levy, *The Intermarium: Wilson, Madison and East Central European Federalism*, Boca Raton: Dissertation.com, 2006, p. 38. See also Gerald Steinacher, *Nazis On The Run: How Hitler's Henchmen Fled Justice*, Oxford: Oxford University Press, 2011, p. 193–4

port of the significant German community in that country as well as the dictator Augusto Pinochet, and former Chilean Ambassador Miguel Serrano who conducted a Nazi-style funeral service for Rauff in Santiago when the latter died there in 1984. He was not the first war criminal to use the monastery route of the Ratline, nor would he be the last.

The total number of war criminals who used the monastery route remains unknown, but there is ample evidence for some of the most notorious. We also have documentation concerning the flight of many other persons for whom the Allies may not have had accurate dossiers in the months and years after the war, such as the Ustashe officers who fled en masse to South America, courtesy of Draganovic, or the thousands of Ukrainian Waffen-SS who wound up in both North and South America after the war. Many of these men may have been minor functionaries, lowly guards or bureaucrats, pushing the paper that would send hundreds if not thousands to their deaths; others were merely following orders in the Nazi structure of *Führerprinzip*: the Führer Principle in which every man had a leader—a Führer—above him whose orders had to be followed immediately and without question. The fact that they had to flee, however, does indicate a certain level of culpability in war crimes.

Take the Ustashe for example.

The Independent State of Croatia was formed as a puppet government of the Third Reich. In 1929 the Ustashe (a form of the Croatian verb "to rise up") had been conceived as a Croatian liberation movement against the Yugoslav state which was seen as heavily biased in favor of the Serbian population, but by 1941 it included not only present-day Croatia but parts of Bosnia as well. The Kingdom of Yugoslavia itself had come into existence after World War One, comprising several different ethnic groups including the Serbs, Croats, Slovenes and Montenegrins in much the same way Czechoslovakia was formed out of two disparate ethnic groups, the Czechs and the Slovaks[69]. As in the case of Czechoslovakia (not to mention Iraq, with Sunni, Shiite

---

69 It is worthwhile to mention that the leader of the "independent" Slovak government during World War II was the pro-Nazi Monsignor Tiso, a Roman Catholic priest.

and Kurdish groups all in a single, artifically-created, country designed by academics and spies after World War One) the various ethnicities did not always relate in harmonious fashion. In the case of Yugoslavia, there were ancient disputes and disagreements. The Croats were largely Catholic and Muslim; the Serbs were Eastern Orthodox. Thus the Ustashe was formed to emphasize a homogenous racial identity—Croat—with both Catholic and Muslim manifestations.

Its undisputed leader was Ante Pavelic, a vicious fanatic and political assassin, who counted among his foremost supporters priests and bishops of the Roman Catholic Church. One of these, Archbishop Stepinac, was beatified by Pope John Paul II and is on his way to becoming a saint of the Church even though his wartime record is spotty and his support for the Ustashe and for Croatian independence was never in doubt.[70] Jewish groups have praised Stepinac for having saved some Jews from the Holocaust, and for bravely standing up to the Ustashe regime when it came to the atrocities being committed against the Serbs and the Jews; yet it seems the real interest of the Church in canonizing Archbishop Stepinac is in the clergyman's reputation as an anti-Communist who was arrested, convicted and imprisoned for war crimes by the Yugoslav government. This is evidence of another kind of problem when it comes to understanding history.

If one is a supporter of Stepinac's canonization, one is automatically considered pro-Fascist (or a dupe of Fascists) by the Left. If one criticizes his canonization, then one is automatically considered a Communist (or a Communist dupe) by the Right. Skepticism is fine for analyzing historical events; cynicism, though, is an obstacle and colors the results, especially when a simplistic, dualistic approach is taken.

---

70   There is even an Archbishop Stepinac High School in New York, created in 1948 with the blessings of Cardinal Spellman. The author attempted to obtain a list of its alumni from the school's website but that information is locked to outsiders. One has to be an alumnus oneself, and prove it, before being admitted to what is surely an innocent roster in any other school. For comparison purposes, the author visited the website of his high school alma mater—Christopher Columbus HS in the Bronx—and was able to access the list of alumni freely and without a password.

For instance, the Ustashe believed in a Catholic *and* Muslim Croatia, oddly enough by today's either/or standards. The Ustashe saw Croatian Muslims as essentially pure-blooded Croats who converted to Islam in order to preserve the state under Ottoman rule. Serbs, however, as well as Jews and Gypsies (both Roma and Sinti) were seen as inferior races only deserving of extermination, and the Serbian Orthodox Church as a tool of the oppressive Yugoslav regime.[71] To that end, the Ustashe created its own death camps, among them the notorious Jasenovac concentration camp.

Jasenovac had been created as a forced labor and death camp by the Ustashe for mostly Serbian prisoners as well as Jews and Gypsies. There is controversy over the total number of victims slaughtered at Jasenovac, but most authorities agree that between 65,000 and 100,000 Serbs and others met their fate at that camp, with hundreds of thousands of others sent from Jasenovac to the death camps at Auschwitz and elsewhere. During most of the period of Ustashe rule over Jasenovac, the camp was run by a Franciscan priest, Fr. Miroslav Filipovic (1915–1946).

Filipovic, like his colleague Draganovic, was interested in the conversion of Serbian Orthodox Christians to Roman Catholicism ... by force. In addition, he subscribed to Ante Pavelic's dictum that one third of all Serbs should be deported, one third forcibly converted, and one third killed. He participated in massacres of the Serbian population—men, women and children—along with his close associate, Fr, Zvonimir Brekalo, another priest. He and Brekalo would engage in contests of killing Serbian children with their bare hands [72] ... the same hands with which they would consecrate bread and wine into

---

71 By comparison, in the Ukraine the Ukrainian Orthodox Church was seen as pro-Nazi, as was the Russian Orthodox Church and its American headquarters in New York City. This was because both these churches were under the control of the Communist government in Moscow; they naturally assumed that their best chance for independence was siding with the Nazis who were at war with Russia.

72 Details on the atrocities committed by Fathers Filipovic and Brekalo can be found in various sources, such as *Lazar Lukaji : Fratri i ustaše kolju* (*Friars and Ustaše Do the Slaughtering*), Belgrade: 2005 and in Viktor Novak, *Magnum Crimen: Pola vijeka klerikalizma u Hrvatskoj* (*Half a Century of Clericalism in Croatia*), Zagreb (1948, n.p.) and Beograd: RO "Nova Knjiga" 1986.

the Body and Blood of Jesus Christ. They saw themselves as Crusaders, with all the impious slaughter that term has acquired over the centuries.

Filipovic was eventually executed for his crimes, hanged while wearing his Franciscan habit. But it would be hasty to conclude that this was an isolated incident of one or two psychotic priests.

The Golden Priest

We need not speculate about Draganovic, or the connection between the Catholic Church and the Ratline, because the details of this arrangement are detailed clearly in a number of declassified American intelligence documents that date from 1946 to 1956, and later. Thus, there can be no ambiguity concerning this unsavory situation.

It began with the realization—by the US Army intelligence group known as the Counter Intelligence Corps or CIC—as early as 1946 that there was a network of Croatian priests assisting the leaders of the Ustashe movement in their escape from Europe. The priests were not merely individual clergymen engaged in this network on their own accord. These were men who were connected directly to archbishops, cardinals, and the Vatican itself. They drove around Rome in limousines with CD—*corps diplomatique*—license plates, and as such were untouchable. They had audiences with the Pope. And they were in direct contact with the government of Argentina and most especially with the newly elected President of Argentina, Juan Domingo Perón.

But the main operator of the monastery route at this time was Draganovic himself, who seemed to have been placed in that position even before the end of the war. The declassified intelligence files contain a lot of background information on Draganovic, beginning with his childhood in Croatia and extending through his association with church hierarchy as well as the Ustashe movement. These documents conclude with revelations concerning Draganovic's work for American intelligence and in particular with the CIA. It would be well to begin with a brief analysis of the information contained in these documents, for they will help us to understand their relevance to the Pöch material.

Krunoslav Draganovic was born and raised in the town of Travnik. He had two brothers, one of whom became a member of the Croatian Embassy in Berlin during the war, the other who was involved with a business enterprise in Zagreb. Draganovic himself was attracted to the priesthood and went to Sarajevo to complete his education in theology and philosophy. While there, he came to the attention of Archbishop Ivan Saric who saw great potential in Draganovic, sending him off to Rome courtesy of his Vatican connections.[73]

Archbishop Saric (1871–1960) was a zealous Croatian nationalist who considered Serbs and Jews as vermin worthy only of slaughter. To that end, once the Independent State of Croatia was formed, he wholeheartedly supported the forced mass conversions of Serbs to Roman Catholicism and the murder of those who resisted or refused. It was alleged, though not proven at the time, that Saric was also involved in the seizure of property from the Sephardic Jews of Sarajevo in collusion with the local police and Ustashe forces. He praised Croatian leader and war criminal Ante Pavelic repeatedly in print and, when the war was over, fled with Pavelic to Spain. This was Father Draganovic's mentor in the Church.

In 1943, Saric sent Draganovic to Rome with the archives of the Independent State of Croatia to the Monastery of San Girolamo as the Croatian legation escaped to northern Italy. While there, Draganovic established something called the Bratovatina Relief Association: an organization designed to aid in the escape of Ustashe war criminals. He set up an operation that issued identity cards under false names and arranged for travel out of Europe ... tickets that were paid for by the International Relief Organization (I.R.O.), the International Committee of the Red Cross (I.C.R.C.), etc. At the same time, he ran what can only be called an intelligence network that extended from the POW camps where Ustashe were held prisoner, from sources still active in Yugoslavia, from sources in Trieste and Rome, and throughout the Croatian communities of Europe, passing the information

---

73 All the above details are from a CIC HQ document dated February 12, 1947, "Subject: Father Krunoslav DRAGANOVIC, and signed by CIC Special Agent Robert Clayton Mudd.

back to the "Central Direction" of the Ustashe in Buenos Aires, Argentina. In a 1952 memo that was only declassified by the CIA in February, 1998, Draganovic is classed as a "dangerous and uncompromising extremist."

To quote from a memo written by C.I.C. Special Agent Robert Clayton Mudd on February 12, 1947:

> Many of the more prominent Ustashi war criminals and Quislings are living in ROME illegally, many of them under false names. Their cells are still maintained, their papers still published, and their intelligence agencies still in operation. All this activity seems to stem from the Vatican, through the Monastery of San Geronimo [sic] to Fermo, the chief Croat Camp in Italy. Chief among the intelligence operatives in the Monastery of San Geronimo [sic] appears to be Dr. DRAGA-NOVIC and Monsignor MADJARAC.[74]

As if to emphasize the danger of this operation, Mudd goes on to name dozens of Croatian Ustashe officials living in the monastery at the time (1947). These officials include the Croatian Deputy Minister of Foreign Affairs, the Minister of the Croat State Treasury, the Corporations Minister, the Minister of Education, a general of the Ustashe Air Force and the Commander-in-Chief of the Air Force. Virtually the entire Ustashe government made its way to Draganovic's monastery safe house in Rome while they waited for the false papers and the tickets they would need to leave Europe and head for Argentina. Some, like Archbishop Saric and Ante Pavelic, would head for Spain first, where they were guaranteed a measure of safety by the Franco regime as well as the support of the Nazi spy network that was left behind after the end of the war, a network run by SS officer Carlos Fuldner, among others. But Pavelic is known to have left Europe from Genoa aboard the *SS Sestriere* which arrived in Buenos Aires on November 6, 1948, according to a declassified US Army intelligence

---

74   Robert Mudd memo, already cited, paragraph number 8. The author has been unable to further identify Monsignor Madjarac.

report dated December 2, 1948. The same memo reports that Pavelic traveled under an assumed name and with International Red Cross documents, after having stayed at the monastery run by Draganovic.

Mudd's memo goes on to analyze the reasons why the Vatican would support so noxious a regime as the Ustashe, even after the war:

> DRAGANOVIC's sponsorship of these Croat Quislings definitely links him up with the plan of the Vatican to shield these ex-Ustashi nationalists until such time as they are able to procure for them the proper documents to enable them to go to South America. The Vatican, undoubtedly banking on the strong anti-Communist feelings of these men, is endeavoring to infiltrate them into South America in any way possible to counteract the spread of Red doctrine. It has been reliably reported, for example that Dr. VRANCIC has already gone to South America, and that Ante PAVELIC and General KREN are scheduled for an early departure to South America through Spain. All these operations are said to have been negotiated by DRAGANOVIC because of his influence in the Vatican.

Draganovic appears in many intelligence memos dating from about 1946 to the 1960s. His operation was successful and deep: it had functionaries in Austria, Italy, Spain, Yugoslavia, Germany, and of course in Argentina. In the beginning, he was only interested in helping Ustashe war criminals escape justice, whether they were major war criminals with the blood of hundreds or thousands on their hands, or minor figures who aided and abetted, and collaborated, with the Ustashe and the Nazis. In later years, he was approached by American intelligence and use was made of his networks by the newly-formed CIA to infiltrate Communist-bloc espionage networks and to help specific Nazis to escape to South America: Nazis that were of use to intelligence operations or who had to be protected from arrest and possible public exposure.

Eventually, even the CIA had had enough of Draganovic and he was "burned" in spy parlance: he was cut off from the Agency and made persona non grata. There were suspicions that he was a double agent for the Soviets, and there was irritation at his constant demands for money and privileges. Finally, the CIA calculated that Draganovic cost more than he was worth.

The "Golden Priest" as he was known then, inexplicably defected to Yugoslavia where he lived out the rest of his life. To this day, no one knows for sure why this fanatic Nazi, anti-Semite and anti-Communist, would willingly go over to the enemy. There has been speculation that he was kidnapped by agents of the Yugoslav regime; others insist that his "conversion" was genuine. The only thing for sure is that we will never know or understand what motivates men like Father Krunoslav Draganovic.

The number of Catholic clergymen involved in this operation is bewildering. A complete list is impossible to obtain, but there are literally hundreds of names already available. This was well known to American intelligence at least as early as 1946, before the major elements of the monastery route were even in place. These were not merely men who felt a pang of conscience and were willing to help Nazis and Ustashe who might have been wrongfully accused of war crimes; this list also includes men who were directly involved in the atrocities themselves, such as the Franciscan friars running the death camp at Jasenovac, or the priests forcing Serbs to convert to Catholicism or die. It also includes the men who blessed these operations, and who urged their followers on to greater and greater levels of depravity and hatred, men like Archbishop Saric or Archbishop Hudal.

One possible scenario has been put forward as the reason why Pius XII looked the other way when the monastery route was in full operation under his nose, and that is that he did not want the Ustashe in particular to be arrested and tried in open court for it would reveal the mortal sins committed by his clergy in the name of Jesus Christ. It would erode the Church's credibility in the world and give the Communists a heavier weapon to use against it. So the atrocities were swept under the rug, and the torturers and murderers were allowed to go free.

In addition, many Nazis—including SS officers—were invited to convert to Catholicism in order that they might be able to make use of the escape networks. This was considered a great accomplishment, having these butchers piously queue up before the baptismal font in order to save their lives. The Church believed it saved souls during that process, and that was more important than what the men had done in their "previous" lives. The Church was merely being merciful.

As Archbishop Alois Hudal wrote, in a book published in 1976: "I felt duty bound after 1945 to devote my whole charitable work mainly to former National Socialists and Fascists, especially the so-called "war criminals."[75]

AND A PROTÉGÉ OF ARCHBISHOP SARIC—Father Franjo Kralik—wrote the following in 1941:

> Love has its limits. The movement for freeing the world from Jews is a movement for the renaissance of human dignity. The all wise and Almighty God is behind this movement.[76]

LOVE HAS ITS LIMITS, but evidently not when it came to rescuing Eichmann, Josef Mengele, Ante Pavelic, Franz Stangl, Klaus Barbie and so many others who were the beneficiaries of the Church's love.[77]

And this network—this notorious underground ecclesiastical system of safe houses and escape routes—was the one used by a mysterious "German doctor" in his flight to Indonesia. The implication is obvious: Dr. Georg Anton Pöch and his wife were people who would have been arrested and imprisoned by the Allies. They were war criminals. Father Draganovic arranged their papers and the money necessary for them to flee Europe.

But there is no record of the couple's war record, they were not Ustashe, their names appear on no list, and they sought the most remote area of the world from Europe they could find. Even Argentina was not safe, even though Mengele, Eichmann, Barbie, Stangl, and

---

75 Alois Hudal, *Römische Tagebücher* ("Romam Diary"), Graz: Stocken, 1976, p. 21 and cited in Goñi, p. 231

76 Franjo Kralik, "Why Are the Jews Being Persecuted?" in *Katolicki Tjednik* (Catholic Weekly), Sarajevo, 1941.

77 Ironically, one of the monastery route operations had the name Caritas, which is Latin for "charity." It was under the direction of Cardinal Montini, the Vatican's Secretary of State under Pope Pius XII. Montini would later become Pope Paul VI.

Rauff all made it to Argentina in the first years after the war. The only conclusion that can be drawn is that this couple was in greater danger than even the "architect of the Final Solution", the "Angel of Death of Auschwitz," and the "Butcher of Lyons."

So who were they? And how was their escape across multiple continents and time zones financed?

And why did the address of the German Archaeological Institute appear in the Pöch diary?

CHAPTER FOUR

THE LAND OF LIVING DANGEROUSLY

Nazi Germany typically laundered looted gold and non-monetary gold by re-smelting it and casting it into bars that were hallmarked with black eagle swastikas, numbered in keeping with standard practice of the Reichsbank. This gold was moved to banks in Switzerland, Sweden, Portugal, or Argentina. Japan used the same techniques, moving gold through Swiss banks in Tokyo, Portuguese banks in Macao, and banks in Chile and Argentina. When gold was physically moved to those countries it was carried by large cargo submarines.[78]

One of the least reported of all the individuals who were with Hitler in the Bunker on April 30, 1945 was Walther Hewel (1904–1945?). Although history remembers Bormann, Goebbels, Eva Braun, General Krebs, and even Linge and Günsche, Hewel is rarely mentioned except occasionally and in passing[79]. It is an odd omission, particularly since Hewel seemed to have been one of Hitler's closest friends and associates from the earliest days of the Nazi Party. In fact, Hewel's own membership number in the NSDAP was even earlier than Hitler's.

---

78   Sterling and Peggy Seagrave, *Gold Warriors: America's Secret Recovery of Yamashita's Gold*, New York: Verso, 2005, p.52. This comprehensive volume details the movement of gold that was stolen from Asian banks, companies and individuals by the Japanese during World War Two. While focusing on the Pacific theater of operations, it nevertheless offers a valuable insight into the process, and the shipping of gold to Latin America and Spain certainly had a positive effect on the financing of the Ratline.

79   An exception in the literature is that of David Irving, the controversial historian of the Nazi era who has become a Holocaust denier. His book *Hitler's War* contains numerous references to Hewel, derived from Hewel's diary which was obtained by Irving from Hewel's widow.

Hewel was only eighteen at the time of the Beer Hall Putsch: Hitler's failed attempt to take control of the state in Munich in 1923. Hewel marched with Heinrich Himmler under the swastika banner, and was later arrested with Hitler for treason and served time in Landsberg Prison, the same prison where Hitler would write *Mein Kampf.* Hewel was an intimate of Himmler, Rudolf Hess, and all the old comrades around the Führer since the beginning of the Nazi experiment. And he was present in the Bunker in the last days, as well.

Yet, few historians speak about him.

THE REASON FOR THIS STRANGE OMISSION is unknown, but it does lead us into some interesting territory for after his release from Landsberg Prison Walter Hewel went on to establish Asia's only real Nazi Party organization ... in Indonesia.

Hewel was born on January 2, 1904 in Cologne. His father was the owner of a factory that made cocoa, but he died when Hewel was only nine years old. His mother was the Baroness von Lindenfels. At the age of eighteen, Walther entered the Technical University of Munich to study mechanical and industrial engineering, but it was a short-lived education due to his participation in the Beer Hall Putsch.

By 1925, however, Hewel—released from Landsberg where he functioned as a kind of valet for Hitler—began working for a Hamburg firm involved in import-export and a year later wound up in England where he eventually got a job with a company called Anglo-Dutch Plantations of Java Ltd.

Beginning with his sojourn in England, Hewel—a committed Nazi and true believer—was active in promoting Nazi ideals. Encouraged by Rudolf Hess to form alliances with British fascists, he then went on to create an active Nazi Party in Indonesia starting in March of 1927 and remained in Java until called back by Hitler at the end of 1935 to serve as an ambassador to Spain and then as a special advisor to Nazi Foreign Minister Ribbentrop (who was hanged at Nuremberg). The positions in Spain and in Indonesia are suggestive, since they would form an important—but largely unrecognized—leg of the Ratline.

While in Indonesia, Hewel formed Nazi Party units throughout

Java: in Jakarta (then known as Batavia), Bandung, Medan, Padang[80], Semarang, Makassar ... and Surabaya. In fact, Hewel was known to the Bunker inhabitants as "Surabaya Wally."[81] That there was a Nazi Party in Surabaya is interesting, because it leads us eventually to the deeper mystery of Hitler's possible escape.

Hewel would remain in Dutch-controlled Indonesia for nine years, during which time he saw the Nazi Party in that country grow and expand, largely among the ex-patriate German and Dutch communities in those cities. It may come as a surprise that the Netherlands provided the largest number of volunteers for the Waffen-SS out of all other countries in Europe. Even Prince Bernhard—the father of Queen Beatrix of the Netherlands—was briefly a member of the Nazi Party in the 1930s as well as of the SA. (the "Brown Shirts" paramilitary wing of the Party) while at university, although he later fought against the Nazi invasion of his country during the war. In Indonesia, the Dutch Vaderlandsche (Fatherland) Club of Medan helped to financially support the Nazi Party there using money raised from plantation sources, and its membership was eventually subsumed into the Dutch Nazi Party.[82] This would have been exactly the type of activity for which Walther Hewel was responsible.

There was a small Nazi Party in the Netherlands itself for years before the invasion, and it held only a few seats in the Dutch parliament. After the invasion, there was a power struggle between the

---

80 There is a photograph of the Nazis in Padang circa late 1930s in the Munz Collection of the Archive of Australian Judaica at the University of Sydney and reproduced in Jeffrey Hadler, "Translations of Antisemitism: Jews, the Chinese, and Violence in Colonial and Post-Colonial Indonesia," *Indonesia and the Malay World*, Vol. 32, no. 94, November 2004. The photo shows a large, swastika-emblazoned banner in the rear of a hall with approximately 23 persons in attendance; nine are women. In addition, the Munz Collection contains approximately 80 more photographs of Nazi Party events in Medan, Semarang, Malang, Menado ... and Padang and Surabaya. (Hadler, p. 302)

81 James P. O'Donnell, *The Bunker*, Cambridge MA: Da Capo Press, 2001, p. 313

82 Jeffrey Hadler, "Translations of Antisemitism: Jews, the Chinese, and Violence in Colonial and Post-Colonial Indonesia," *Indonesia and the Malay World*, Vol. 32, No. 94, November 2004, p. 302

Germans (who wanted to annex the country) and the Dutch Nazis who wanted autonomy. The Dutch lost their bid, and the Netherlands became an outpost of the Third Reich, with the murderous Seyss-Inquart as its Governor-General. While student demonstrations against the invasion and against the Nazis were famous—and brutally suppressed—many in the Dutch intelligentsia were sympathetic to Hitler and to the ideals of the Nazi regime (as was Prince Bernhard, briefly). Therefore it would not be surprising to learn that elements of the Dutch expatriate community in Indonesia would have flirted with the idea of joining the Nazi Party there.

Once Hitler came to power in Germany in 1933, he began to take steps to form his own government, and to do that he surrounded himself with people who did not necessarily have the requisite experience in political matters but who were reliable from an ideological point of view. One of these was Joachim von Ribbentrop, a man roundly despised by most who knew him but who was trusted completely by Hitler since Ribbentrop studied the Führer obsessively and knew what buttons to push, and when. Ribbentrop held various posts under Hitler, all concerning foreign affairs. He created various institutions, some of which were designed ostensibly to improve Anglo-German and French-German relations, but which were used by Hitler to manipulate foreign affairs in a somewhat more cynical manner.

One of the men called upon by Hitler to work with Ribbentrop in these endeavors was Walther Hewel. Hewel had, by that time, spent nearly a decade in Indonesia, was also familiar with China and Japan as well as the United States, and was recalled personally by Hitler to work in Spain and, later, to assist in the Anglo-German projects (since Hewel had a good command of English and had spent time in England, unlike Ribbentrop). We have very little information as to what Hewel was doing in his position with Ribbentrop, and he is usually dismissed as a kind of clownish personality—a characterization that is at odds with his background, his education and experience, and his devotion to the Nazi ideal. As one of the last men to leave the Bunker, he is believed to have committed suicide a few days after Hitler by simultaneously biting down on a cyanide capsule and shooting himself in the head (the same improbable fiction promoted as Hitler's means of death).

One historian[83] believes that Hewel worked for the *Abwehr* (Germany's military intelligence operation, under the command of Admiral Canaris until 1944) while in Spain, and this connection with Spain is tantalizing. Canaris, like Dönitz, had been a U-Boat commander during the first World War. He spoke fluent Spanish and was instrumental in developing a close working relationship between Franco and Hitler. His admiration for Hitler soured early on, however, and he began to conspire against the Führer and was eventually arrested for treason and hanged by the Nazis in the last days of the war.

This meant that the Abwehr would come under new management in the form of Walter Schellenberg when the Abwehr was merged with the SD in 1944. Canaris's network of agents in Spain (those considered above reproach and not tainted by their relationship with the presumed traitor) would have taken orders then from Schellenberg's group. This meant that Germany's military intelligence operation was removed from military control and placed under Schellenberg, and thus under Himmler and the SS, thereby effectively becoming an arm of an ideological entity rather than the Wehrmacht. This is important, for it means that the work of the agent network in Spain could be diverted to matters that were non-military in nature: such as creating escape routes for the SS or finding ways to transport gold and other valuables out of Europe. We have already seen that the Etappendienst was established by Admiral Dönitz to supply the U-Boats out of Spanish ports, and that money-men such as Carlos Fuldner were active in Spain in the last days of the war with only one purpose in mind: to create an escape channel for men and money out of Europe and to safe havens around the world.

What is perhaps not so well known is the fact that Nazi U-boats were seen not only in Europe and along the coasts of North and South America both during and after the war, but also as far away as Indonesia.

THE NAZIS AND THE JAPANESE had formed a political alliance against their common enemy, the United States. However, that alliance was formed only after much resistance by the German military and

---

83 O'Donnel, *The Bunker*, p. 313

members of the foreign policy establishment who saw China as their natural ally in Asia in a relationship that dated back to the First World War. It was only after tremendous effort by men like Ribbentrop— and Hitler's inspiration for ideas like *lebensraum*, the geo-politician Karl Ernst Haushofer (1869–1946)—that a more aggressive approach to Nazi-Japanese relations bore fruit.

While Japan extended its authority over most of East Asia from Korea and China to the Philippines, Singapore, Malaya, Indochina and Indonesia, it had virtually no direct contact with the armed forces of Germany. It did, however, control important natural resources in those territories—like rubber, tin and other commodities—that were essential to the war effort in Europe. Rubber, in particular, was necessary for the production of tires and other components of tanks, trucks, jeeps and aircraft parts, and rubber was abundant in Malaya and Indonesia, areas under Japanese control.

Thus, a system was established whereby the Germans would transport jet engine technology, machine tools and raw materials the Japanese did not have—such as uranium[84]—in exchange for rubber, tin, tungsten, and whatever else was needed by the German war machine. The method of transport was the U-boat. The port of call was Penang on the western coast of Malaya, with the first such shipment arriving on July 15, 1943 via German U-boat U-511. The submarine was actually a gift to the Japanese Navy by Adolf Hitler himself, in return

---

84 The Japanese were involved in their own attempt to create an atomic weapon, and the two projects of which we have any information—the Ni-Go and the F-Go projects—were evidently not successful. However, a German U-boat (U-234) carrying more than 500 kg (about 1,200 lbs) of an unspecified type of uranium oxide was captured by Allied forces in the Atlantic in April of 1945 before it could reach Japan. There is some controversy over whether this uranium would have been used to create a bomb, or would have been used in the development of aviation fuel. In 1946 claims were made (by a former US Army investigator) that a primitive atomic device was exploded by Japanese scientists at or near the Korean city of Konan in August 1945, but these claims have been dismissed by historians. Had the US believed that Japan was imminently capable of producing an atomic bomb, however, this might have gone some way towards justifying President Truman's authorization of the attacks on Hiroshima and Nagasaki, particularly in light of the V2 rocket technology and parts shipped to Japan in the last days of the war.

for a Japanese submarine shipment of desperately-needed war materiel on Japanese sub I-30. Thus we have the rather bizarre image of Nazi U-boats bearing the swastika on their conning towers sailing into Asian ports halfway around the world from Germany.

The Asian U-boat bases represented the only occasion in the entire war when the Germans and the Japanese actively cooperated militarily. German U-boats would refuel in the Indian Ocean on their way to and from Malaya, out of range of British bombers, in an operation that was conducted quickly and efficiently. The submarines themselves had been outfitted more as cargo ships than as engines of destruction, and towards the end of the war they were carrying V-2 rocket components to the Japanese. There has been much speculation that the Japanese were working on their own version of the atomic bomb at the time and, had they managed to build the V-2 rocket using German blueprints and parts, they would have had not only the bomb but also an effective delivery system.

As the British grew in strength in Asia in 1944, and using India as a base, they began to bomb Penang in order to disrupt the U-boat traffic from Europe and also to deny the Japanese that important port that controlled the sea lanes in the Melaka Straits. At that time the decision was made to move the base to Indonesia, to Batavia (now Jakarta), as well as Surabaya, and the shipments carried on as before.

Aside from the Nazi U-boat presence, in 1943 a Gestapo team arrived in Indonesia to coordinate their activities with the Japanese and against whatever Dutch resistance there was in the archipelago. The Netherlands had been invaded in 1940, and the Dutch in Indonesia were cut off and without any support or resources from their homeland. The Japanese had promised Indonesians their independence from Holland if they would support Japan in its project of wiping out Dutch resistance, and future Indonesian leaders like Sukarno were cooperating with the Japanese for that oldest of reasons: "The enemy of my enemy is my friend."

The Gestapo then began rounding up whatever Jews they could find, for arrest and imprisonment. This is an important part of the historical record, for it shows that the zeal with which the Nazis persecuted the Jews was not confined to a European or even a Western context but extended to the Jews wherever in the world they could be found. They were hardly a threat to the Third Reich in Japanese-occupied Indonesia, but nevertheless the Gestapo felt it necessary to conduct their own Holocaust in that tropical, Asian country thousands of miles from the concentration camps of Poland. The Japanese themselves did not understand this attitude towards the Jews—saying that they were at war with countries and not with races[85]—but tried to cooperate the best way they could, essentially humoring their German colleagues. Jewish men were separated from Jewish women and put into separate camps for the duration of the war. This occurred most notably in Surabaya, which had a large Jewish population[86] as well as a Nazi Party branch.

Thus, we have a documented Nazi presence in Indonesia going back to the 1920s (long before Hitler came to power in Germany) and which does not disappear until the end of the war in the Pacific, for the Nazi U-boats that were stranded in Indonesia after the German surrender were commandeered by the Japanese for their own use. That meant that U-boat crews were also stranded in Indonesia and many found themselves unable—or unwilling—to return to Germany.

Many U-boat crewmen discovered Indonesia to be a relatively congenial berth after the rigors of submarine warfare on the losing side. Although they were taken prisoner by the Allies once Japan surrendered, some managed to escape and others were charged with guarding the Dutch against the Indonesian rebels. Some became active in the Indonesian revolt against the Dutch, who returned to Indonesia in force after the Japanese surrender. Several died in Indonesia and are buried in what has to be one of the strangest cemeteries in the world, Eight Hundred Statues.

KNOWN AS *Arca Domas*, which translated from the Sanskrit means "eight hundred statues", this cemetery is located south of Jakarta in the region of Bogor, near the village of Cikopo. It had been part of a tea plantation owned by two German brothers, Emil and Theodor Helfferich ... and therein lies a tale.

---

85   Jeffrey Hadler, "Translations of Antisemitism," p. 303
86   As an interesting aside, Xaviera Hollander—the author of the best-selling *The Happy Hooker*—was born in 1943 in Surabaya to German and Jewish parents. See Hadler, p. 304

Emil Helfferich (1878–1972) was a Nazi Party member and an intimate of high-ranking Nazi officials, including Heinrich Himmler. Emil had spent decades in Java as a pepper trader in the first years of the twentieth century, from 1899 to 1928. He returned to Germany at the age of 51 to take up important positions in the Weimar Republic, including becoming chairman of the Hamburg-Amerika shipping company (which became HAPAG and then HAPAG-Lloyd) as well as chairman of Esso Oil (of which 94% at that time was owned by Standard Oil of New Jersey). In November of 1932, he was one of the co-sponsors of the Industrialists Petition to President Paul von Hindenburg insisting that Adolf Hitler be made Chancellor of Germany. Much against Hindenburg's wishes, Hitler was made Chancellor in January of 1933, only two months later, with the all-important backing of German bankers and industrialists like Helfferich.

He was one of the members of the *Freundeskreis Himmler* (or "the Friendship Circle of Himmler") along with Oswald Pohl (the SS general in charge of the concentration camps and also of Himmler's mystical castle, Wewelsburg; hanged at Nuremberg), Hjalmar Shacht, Ernst Schäfer (of the SS-Ahnenerbe and the leader of the SS-Tibet Expedition), Otto Ohlendorf (mass murderer of Jews in the Ukraine, who was hanged at Nuremberg), Wolfram Sievers (chief of the SS-Ahnenerbe who was hanged at Nuremberg), and many others.[87] As one can see, it was an organization composed of wealthy industrialists as well as high-ranking SS officers ... and men later accused of some of the worst crimes of the war.

Hjalmar Schacht (1877–1970) for instance, was the main organizer of the Industrialists Petition to Hindenburg to name Hitler as Chancellor. He was also President of the Reichsbank and chief economist for the Third Reich. He grew disillusioned with Hitler in the late 1930s, and repudiated anti-Semitism, The Führer eventually dismissed him in 1943 and, after he was believed to have been involved in the assassination plot against Hitler in July, 1944, he was imprisoned at Flossenberg Concentration Camp and then at Dachau. Eventually de-nazified by the Nuremberg tribunal, he went on to form his

---

87 See *Freundeskreis Himmler: Friedrich Flick, Emil Hellferich, Oswald Pohl, Hjalmar Schacht, Hans Fischbock, Karl Rasche*, Bucher Gruppe, Books LLC, 2010.

own bank and became an economic advisor to ... the Government of Indonesia.

For his own part, Helfferich managed to convince the Allies that he was not a war criminal, even though he was one of those who helped put Hitler in power and who maintained a long relationship with Himmler. His brother, Theodor (1872–1924), was Vice Chancellor of Germany and Secretary of the Interior during World War I, and was responsible for the development and construction of the first German submarines. He was killed in a train wreck in Switzerland in 1924 at the age of 52.

Thus, the two Helfferich brothers were important figures in German politics, industry and finance with Emil Helfferich, an intimate of Himmler, Schacht, and Hitler as well as a chairman of Esso Oil and the Hamburg-Amerika shipping company. These were the brothers that owned the tea plantation at Bogor that was turned into a cemetery for the Nazi U-boat crew. It was Emil Helfferich who built the monument at the cemetery to the famed Admiral Graf von Spee, who died in the Battle of the Falkland Islands on December 8, 1914 and who dedicated the cemetery:

DEM TAPFEREN DEUTSCH-OSTASIATISCHEN GESCH-WADER 1914
("To the Brave German East-Asian Squadron 1914")

And:

ERICHTED VON EMIL UND THEODOR HELFFERICH 1926
("Erected by Emil and Theodor Helferrich 1926")

THE GERMAN EAST-ASIAN SQUADRON was the armada commanded by Admiral Graf von Spee in a battle with the British Navy, in which he lost his life and those of thousands of his fellow sailors. Although the monument says Emil and his brother Theodor erected it, Theodor was already dead by this time. The monument is designed in a Javanese style, and boasts a statue of Ganesha on one side and of Buddha on the other.

During World War II, the tea plantation—then under the owner-ship of one Albert Vehring—became a logistics support area for the U-boats, supplying food and other materials for the more than forty German submarines that were operating in the area. Once Germany surrendered, some of the crew members—notably under the command of U-219 commander Walter Burghagen—fled to the plantation and became civilians ... at least until they were captured by the British and then placed in prison camps run by the Dutch. Some escaped, and others died of disease or from attacks by Indonesian guerrillas who mistook the Germans for their Dutch opponents.

Later, the monument and its surrounding grounds became the *Deutscher Soldatenfriedhof* or German Soldiers Cemetery. Ten U-boat crew members are buried there, with headstones in the shape of Iron Crosses. To this day, the German government quietly finances the maintenance of the cemetery is and occasionally, surviving crew members make the pilgrimmage to Arca Domas to visit the graves of their old comrades. In fact, one of these "old comrades"—Hans-Joachim Krug, first officer of U-219 under Walter Burghagen—was the techni-cal advisor to the film *Das Boot* (1981).

The reason for taking so much time with these seemingly dispa-rate personalities and events is to demonstrate the extent to which Indonesia and Nazi Germany were linked ... at the highest politi-cal and military levels. While much attention has been paid to the role South America and the Middle East played in the escape of Nazi war criminals known as the Ratline, this aspect of the project—the Asian theater—has been largely, if not completely, ignored. But we have clear and unequivocal evidence that (a) the passage to South-east Asia by U-boat was not only possible, but an integral part of the Nazi effort to source important war materiel, (b) that those closest to Hitler's inner circle—men like Walther Hewel, Hjalmar Schacht and Emil Helfferich—had close connections to Indonesia, in some cases lasting for a decade or more, and (c) since so many war criminals did manage to escape, it stands to reason that some would have made it as far as the former Dutch colony whose raw materials were so vital to continuing the war, and where European and Asian armed forces met both in combat and cooperation.

With the end of Dutch hegemony in the region, it would be seen that Indonesian revolutionaries like future president Sukarno had demonstrable pro-Nazi sympathies. But was Indonesia an environment conducive to the type of anti-Semitism so typical of the devoted Nazi? Had there ever been any Jews in Indonesia? Was Indonesia a fertile ground for anti-Jewish conspiracy theories, such as the Jewish-Masonic global conspiracy to rule the world made famous by the *Protocols of the Elders of Zion*, the legendary turn-of-the-century hoax that so influenced Hitler and the Nazis?

Would Indonesia have offered a congenial sanctuary for a rabid Nazi war criminal?

To UNDERSTAND HOW INDONESIA might have become a haven for a Nazi war criminal, it is helpful to see how another country (far removed from the conflict of World War II) became identified as a "safe house" for evil men. One of the reasons Argentina became so famous as a sanctuary for Nazis after the war was the attitude of the Argentine government towards immigration. Argentina had long considered itself more European than Latin American, and looked across the Atlantic for its cultural roots. A visit to Buenos Aires in the 1990s, for instance, made one think of Paris or Vienna in the 1930s. Surnames were often Italian, French or German, and it is a fact of history that future president Juan Domingo Perón had trained with Italian fascists during the Mussolini era and had developed a fondness for fascist ideology. Perón was a populist leader, in many ways like both Mussolini and Hitler, who had an obsession for military dress and the machismo of the career soldier. The Perónist regime also railed against foreign influences, particularly from North America, and saw itself as a bulwark against Communism. In the native Catholicism of Argentina there was a political rapport with the Vatican as well: and the dream of some Argentines was to create a kind of fascist-Catholic nation, purged of "other elements" and a safe haven for anti-Communist fighters and sympathizers. There was a strong anti-Semitic movement in Argentina which came into its own once Perón was elected; prior to that time there had been Jewish migration to Argentina from Europe, but by the mid-1940s this had slowed to a trickle as Nazis and former SS officers found themselves in control of the Immigration Department and the immigration policies of Argentina, with Perón's blessing and support.

A further comparison could be had with Croatia which also combined ardent Catholicism with a hatred of Communism and Jews. As Croatia fell to the Communists under Tito, Argentina became the de facto leader of the Catholic anti-Communist alliance ... aided and abetted by a large contingent of Croatian Ustashe refugees.

We have some parallels, then, with Indonesia during the same period. While Indonesians as a rule never identified with Europe the way Argentina did, they had a similar political position vis-à-vis capitalism and the superpowers, especially the United States. There was also a nascent fascist movement in Indonesia that sought to recover the ancient glory of the Majapahit empire.[88] The Japanese, however, enraged them with their insistence that Muslims face Tokyo when they prayed instead of Mecca,[89] thereby alienating the religious leaders whose support was necessary in order to bring the population in line with Japanese military and economic goals.

As World War II came to an end in the Pacific with the surrender of the Japanese in August of 1945, the Dutch attempted to retake their colony in the East Indies. The Japanese had quickly given the Indonesians their independence on their way out of Indonesia, but the Dutch did not accept this development. A revolutionary struggle began between the Indonesians and their former Dutch colonizers that went on for nearly five years (with the Dutch constantly breaking treaties and truces and ignoring international agreements to which they had been signatories) before Indonesia formally won its independence.

One of the leaders of the revolt against the Dutch became the first president of Indonesia, Sukarno (1901–1970). As with many

---

88 It is too long to go into here, but reference can be had to a number of books on the subject of Indonesian fascism, including the history of the Partai Fascist Indonesia (PFI), the Partai Nasionl Indonesia (PNI), and similar groups; most recently Wilson, *Orang dan Partai Nazi di Indonesia: Kaum Pergerakan Menyambut Fasisme*, Jakarta: Komunitas Bambu, 2008.

89 George McTurnan Kahin, *Nationalism and Revolution in Indonesia*, Ithaca NY: Cornell, Southeast Asia Program, 1952, p. 111

revolutionary leaders of the twentieth century, Sukarno was basically a populist. He strove to unite the many disparate peoples living on the thousands of islands in the archipelago into a single nation with a single language, flag, and central government.

Sukarno, however, also had a pragmatic approach to politics. While he had been actively pro-Japanese (and moderately pro-Nazi) during the war, as his administration progressed he was seen to identify more and more with Communism—particularly Chinese Communism but also accepting military and other aid from the Soviet Union—a position that made the West nervous especially as the French were being defeated by Communist forces in Indochina, and India, Malaya and Singapore had won their independence from Great Britain. By 1948 China had become a Communist nation under Mao, and the Korean War had started in 1950, which would split that country into a Communist North and a capitalist South. The colonial powers were losing their territories in Asia, and it seemed as if it was only a matter of time before the entire continent—with the possible exception of Japan—became Communist.

But Indonesia is a predominantly Muslim nation. While the Chinese presence in that country was blamed, often unfairly, for being pro-Communist and contributing to the development of the Communist Party of Indonesia (PKI), and while Sukarno was blamed for conspiring with the Communists during the famous " Year of Living Dangerously" in 1965, the idea that Indonesian Muslims would embrace completely the atheistic ideology of Communism was unrealistic. Sukarno wanted Indonesia to become a secular state, however, and was more afraid of the colonial powers returning to invade and subjugate Indonesia than he was of any implications of atheism. To Sukarno—as well as to many populist leaders of the post-World War II era—Communist revolution meant resistance to what they perceived to be the excesses and basic unfairness of capitalism, especially as capitalism had been visited upon the developing nations as a form of repression and enslavement and not as a means of development.

This position was not too far removed from that of the Nazi Party, which also saw capitalism in negative terms, associating it with Jewish bankers and their perceived attempt to control the world through economic imperialism. The left wing of the Nazi Party was decidedly more socialist than nationalist, but in the end the Nazis saw Communism as another ploy by the "Jewish-Masonic conspiracy" to control the world (reiterating the fact that Karl Marx himself was Jewish), and the left wing of the Party was effectively silenced through brutal purges by the time the war started.

A revolutionary in Southeast Asia could see the Nazis in a somewhat more sympathetic light than would a European. For leaders like Sukarno, the Nazis (and the Japanese) represented the enemy of the superpowers: Russia, Great Britain, and the United States as well as their old colonizers, the Dutch. While the Aryanism of the Nazis would never gain ground in a country like Indonesia with so many different cultures and indigenous languages and religions (arguably none of which would have been identified as "Aryan" by the Nazi ideologues), the anti-Semitism of the Nazis played on the paranoia of a people just coming into their own after centuries of European dominance.[90]

Thus, the situation in Indonesia in the 1940s and 1950s must be seen in the light of the local political environment rather than as an extension of the European and Western conflicts of the same time period. Communism was seen as a movement that repudiated all the existing power structures of state, church, banks, and culture. It reflected a desperate desire to break free of the rule of an elite class "by any means necessary" and to re-establish indigenous rule and custom in all areas of life. As Sukarno matured in office, he would condemn his own support of the Japanese invaders, particularly in the use they made of Indonesian slave labor and the rape of the raw materials of that country to fuel the Japanese war effort. But during the war he was flown to Tokyo where he was feted as the country's natural leader, and where he made his famous statement: *Amerika kita setrika, Inggris*

---

90 Sukarno was replaced by Soeharto in 1967 who ran the country until the Reformasi movement of the late 1990s—fueled by the Asian Economic Crisis of 1997—toppled his regime and replaced it with a democratic form of government. Soeharto famously blamed his fall from power on a worldwide Zionist conspiracy; similar sentiments were being echoed by the Malaysian Prime Minister, Mahathir Mohammed who blamed the economic crisis on the Jews.

kita linggis ("Let's iron[91] America, let's bludgeon the British") as a call to arms for his compatriots to support Japan and work in its service.

He had always flirted with Communism, even before the war broke out, but he anticipated and welcomed the Japanese entry into the war as a means of dislodging the European powers from Southeast Asia. While the Cold War seemed to many Westerners a black-and-white situation with good guys in America and Western Europe and bad guys in Russia, China and the "East", to the developing nations the choices were not so simple. They were forced to resist the influence of the Western powers as a source of exploitation and repression in the colonies that now declared their independence, and so they turned to the dubious embrace of the revolutionary governments of China, Cuba and the Soviet Union.

In the 1950s, Sukarno was struggling to keep his country in one piece while fending off attempts by fundamentalist Islamic parties as well as the army itself to fracture the delicate balance of powers. In 1953, there were rebel groups and anti-government forces forming in West Java and in Aceh, such as Darul Islam which agitated for an Islamic state. The first free elections would be not be held until 2 years later.

It was into this chaotic political environment that a mysterious European man and his wife landed at Jakarta, on January 6, 1954.

They had been on the run since April 30, 1945.

---

91 In the sense of "flatten."

CHAPTER FIVE

THE GERMAN DOCTOR

"Some say that Hitler is still alive, others say that Hitler is dead ..." said Esih.
"Does Esih want to meet Hitler?"
"Of course, I do. But it doesn't seem possible," replied Esih.
The German looked at Esih and smiled.
"Well, this is Hitler," he replied, patting his chest.[92]

On the 6th of January, 1954 a ship arrived at the port of Jakarta with two European passengers, a man and a woman, who had been on the road for nearly nine years. A copy of the man's immigration document shows his name to be Pöch, a German citizen with passport number 2624/51 issued in Rome on September 28, 1951 and valid until September 27, 1956. His place of birth was listed as Przemysl, and his year of birth was 1895. His parents were Josef and Emma Pöch, both deceased.[93]

His Indonesian citizenship paper—issued on December 20, 1967—gives his full name as "Dr. Med. Georg Anton Pöch" with a birthday of November 1, 1895, in Przemysl, Austria.[94]

The author of a book on Pöch entitled *Hitler Mati di Indonesia* (or "Hitler Died in Indonesia") claims that the mention of Przemysl as being in Austria is an indication that Pöch was lying about his identity since that city is in Poland.[95] Actually, in the year 1895 (when Pöch states he was born) Przemysl was indeed part of Austria and remained so until after the First World War when the Austro-Hungarian Empire

---

92 Ir. KGPH. Soeryo Goeritno, *Hitler Mati di Indonesia*, Jakarta: Titik Media, 2010, p. 98. The translations from the original Bahasa Indonesia are my own.
93 *Hitler Mati di Indonesia*, p. 42–43
94 *Hitler Mati di Indonesia*, p. 70
95 *Hitler Mati di Indonesia*, p. 67

was dissolved.[96] However, it would seem that Pöch could not have claimed *German* citizenship in any case; that was definitely a deception, unless he had been a member of the SS or of the Nazi Party, in which case, under the rules of the Third Reich, his German citizenship would have been automatic ... and he would have been subject to arrest, interrogation, and possible prosecution.

Further, based on the evidence of one Dr. Sosro Husodo, Pöch did not have medical training at all, yet he is listed as a Doctor of Medicine in his citizenship document. In fact, by the time Dr. Sosro met him in 1960 on the remote island of Sumbawa, Pöch was running the largest hospital on the island. Famous as "the German doctor", he was considered strange: a no-nonsense person, who seemed to have military background or training, he was energetic, domineering, and impatient. Dressed always in the white coat of his profession, he had no qualms about making house calls or even, at times, dispensing medicine for free for those in need.[97]

Yet, he was close to no one and stayed away from general social visits. While he would attend formal functions connected to the hospital, he avoided close contact with the Indonesians themselves.

It is this same Georg Anton Pöch—the "German doctor"—who, many claim, was in reality Adolf Hitler.

THE RESEARCH FOR THIS STORY WAS EXHAUSTING and often unrewarding. That is not because the information on Pöch in Indonesia was thin, but because there is almost no record of the real Pöch's activities in Europe during the War and nothing for the period immediately after. As the author began to trace the name and the background of this mysterious individual he came up against brick walls of silence. If Pöch was truly Pöch and not—as Sosro and others have claimed—

---

96   As an example, my grandfather—who was Slovak—entered the United States at Ellis Island in the first decade of the twentieth century, but his citizenship was listed as "Austrian."

97   For this and for most of the description of Pöch in Indonesia, I rely upon recently published accounts such as *Hitler Mati in Indonesia* and Solomon Group's *Melacak Garis Keturunan Hitler di Indonesia* ("Tracing the Lineage of Hitler in Indonesia"), Yogyakarta: Pustaka Solomon, 2011, as well as other sources where noted, as well as interviews with surviving witnesses.

Hitler, then Pöch was still someone who should have been arrested and brought to trial for war crimes.

For the original Georg Anton Pöch was a Nazi medical officer who asked to work on Jewish prisoners in the concentration camps of the Netherlands.

The Camps

> The Jews are not Dutch for us. They are an enemy with whom we cannot agree upon cease-fire or peace ... We will hit the Jews wherever we find them, and those who side with them shall have to bear the consequences.
> —Reichskommissar Arthur Seyss-Inquart, March 12, 1941[98]

Holland was host to four specific camps: Amersfoort, Vught, Westerbork and Ommen. Amersfoort began as a transit camp but evolved into a work and prison camp. Vught—although generally known as Kamp Vught—was officially called Herzogenbusch Camp and was also generally a transit camp for those Belgian and Dutch prisoners on their way to the death camps such as Ravensbrück. Westerbork was another—perhaps the most famous—of the transit camps. Originally built by Dutch Jews to house German Jews fleeing from the Nazis, after the invasion it was commandeered by the Nazis as a transit camp for Dutch Jews and Gypsies (Roma) who were being sent to Auschwitz, Sobibor, and Treblinka (among other destinations). In all, more than 100,000 Dutch Jews, 5,000 German Jews and more than 400 Roma passed through Westerbork on their way to the Polish concentration camps. Anne Frank was one of the Dutch Jews held prisoner at Westerbork before she was sent to Auschwitz on September 3, 1944 on one of the last trains to leave the camp.

Ommen, the last of the four Dutch camps, had an unusual pedigree. Before the war, it had served as a cult center for the group around Krishnamurti: the guru "discovered" by Bishop Leadbeater of the

---

98   *Rede van den Rijkscommissaris Rijksminister Dr. Seyss-Inquart geheouden op Woensdag 12 Maart 1941 in het Concertgebouw te Amsterdam voor het Arbeitsbereich der NSDAP in de Nederlanden (n.p., n.d.)*

Theosophical Society. Their last meeting was held at Ommen in September of 1939, only months before the German occupation. Once the Nazis invaded the following year, it was decided to use the existing facilities at Ommen as a detention center for Dutch Jews and other "undesirables."

One of the Dutch SS guards—Herbertus Bikker , known as "the Butcher of Ommen"—was sentenced to death by a Dutch court, but the sentence was commuted to life in prison. On December 26, 1952 Bikker and several of his SS comrades (including the infamous Klaas Carel Faber, one of the most wanted Nazi war criminals and another member of the Dutch SS as well as of a Sonderkommando unit charged with the assassination of prominent Dutch citizens who opposed the Nazi regime; his brother Peiter Johan Faber was executed for war crimes in 1948) escaped prison in the Netherlands and went over the border to Germany. Although Bikker and Faber were Dutch according to the Führer Edict of May, 1943 anyone who was a member of the Nazi Party or of the SS was automatically considered a German citizen, and thus both Bikker and Faber escaped extradition since their crimes were committed in the Netherlands and not in Germany. Using this loophole, Bikker managed to live peacefully in Germany for the next 50 years until he—like Erich Priebke, among others— boasted to a reporter of his exploits in the camps and particularly of his execution in cold blood of a Dutch resistance fighter. At that point, it was impossible not to arrest Bikker and he went to trial—in Germany—in 2004. However, due to Bikker's alleged ill health, the trial did not proceed. Bikker died peacefully at home four years later, in 2008. Faber's case is still pending, but it is believed that he, too, will die of old age before there is any criminal proceeding against him.

It is important to note that many of the guards and Waffen-SS assigned to the camps were Dutch nationals: persons (men and women) who were supporters of the Nazi regime and its racist ideology. It is an episode in the history of the Netherlands that many Dutch citizens are confronting only now. Until a few years ago, the iconic image of non-Jews protecting Jews from the Nazis—such as in the case of Anne Frank—was the operative narrative. In fact, many non-Jewish Dutch citizens did speak out against the Nazis and did assist in hiding Jewish families from the occupiers. Yet, the Netherlands had the highest proportion of any European country of its Jewish population deported to the death camps during the war, and the highest proportion of its citizens who became members of the Waffen-SS and other Nazi organizations.

The Anthropologists

February 28, 1944

Dear Party Comrade Bormann,

We have cleaned up the Jewish question in the Netherlands, insofar as now we only have to carry out decisions that have already been formulated. The Jews have been eliminated from the body of the Dutch people and, insofar as they have not been transported to the East for labor, they are enclosed in a camp.

Reichskommissar Arthur Seyss-Inquart

On September 29, 1943 the last Jews were found and brought to the Dutch camps. After that date there were no Jews left in the Netherlands except for those already in prison or in hiding. There were constant raids on homes and businesses by the SS until 1944, as the last remaining vestiges of Dutch Jewry were identified and shipped to Auschwitz.

However, until that date there was much work to be done. Measurements to be taken. Blood and other biologicals obtained. Photographs processed. Data collected. The prison camps and transit camps were gold mines of anthropological material. For anyone conducting a study of the differences between Ashkenazic and Sephardic Jews, places like Westerbork and Ommen were ideal. The added benefit of a captive population of Roma would only make the prospect of studying the prisoners even more attractive.

Along with the predominantly Ashkenazic Jews of the Netherlands there was a sizeable population of Portuguese, or Sephardic, Jews in Amsterdam. With both of these "racial types" so easily available, it was an opportunity that Georg Anton and Hella Pöch could not pass up. As friends of the Reichskommissar for the Netherlands—fellow Austrian Arthur Seyss-Inquart—they had unfettered access to the Jewish prisoners.

Hella Pöch was easily the more famous—and more experienced— of the two. She had been married to the father of modern Viennese anthropology, Rudolf Pöch (1870–1921), who made use of prisoners of war for his anthropometric research during World War One. Rudolf Pöch was also one of the first anthropologists to make use of the modern inventions of the motion picture camera and audio recording equipment in the field. Some of his films and recordings— especially of the Bushmen of Southern Africa—have survived to this day. He also visited Indonesia and Australia, from 1904–1906. But there is much more to this story than this simple recitation of facts would suggest.

The Pöch Alliance

In May of 2008 there was a flurry of controversy during a workshop in Vienna concerning the legacy of Rudolf Pöch. Organized by Maria Teschler-Nicola, Director of Anthropology at the Natural History Museum in Vienna, the workshop was acutely nomenclatured "Archival Horizons: Landscapes of knowledge and borders of perspective within the multimedia estate of anthropologist and explorer Rudolf Pöch." It was intended to be a celebration of Pöch's contribution to the field of anthropology, but it quickly turned into a condemnation of his bizarre practices in the field; practices that included grave-robbing and the mutilation of corpses. In what would become an eerie precedent for Nazi *Rassenkunde* ("race science"), Pöch had begun a collection of human bodies and skeletal material for exhibits in Europe, exhibits that would reflect the growing preoccupation of German and Austrian anthropologists with the idea of racial "purity."

The authors of a book on the rapacious practices of European anthropologists in Africa were invited to participate in the workshop. Ciraj Rassool and Martin Legassick had written *Skeletons in the Cupboard: South African museums and the trade in human remains, 1907–1917*[99]. It is a sobering account of the way in which anthro-

---

99 Martin Legassick and Ciraj Rassool, *Skeletons in the Cupboard: South African*

pologists literally stole corpses from their graves, in some cases fresh graves, in order to expand or deepen museum collections in South Africa and abroad. These were bodies of indigenous Africans—notably the Khoisan of Southern Africa, composed of the Khoe and San tribes, the latter often referred to as "Bushmen"—and in Pöch's case in particular, they were collected illegally and transported in barrels or drums, in some cases after their heads had been severed from their bodies and their limbs mutilated in other ways to make it easier to fit in the barrels (packed in salt) and ship them out of the country and back to Austria.

This was not the end of the story, however, for these corpses were then subjected to further indignities. In some cases, plaster casts were made of the bodies and these were then painted and hair and animal skin applied, to serve as models in museum dioramas. As the bodies decayed and became less amenable to study, they were macerated—the flesh removed from the skeletons—and the skeletons retained for further investigation and display.

According to workshop organizer Teschler-Nicola, Pöch had collected "80 skeletons, 150 skulls and made 50 casts. He saw 1000 Bushmen who spoke 10 different languages, and measured the bodies of 300."[100] Teschler-Nicola then located two of these remains in the private collection of Emil Breitinger (1904–2004), an anthropologist who had pro-Nazi sympathies during the war.

When Rassool and Legassick introduced this evidence at the workshop there was general shock and dismay. What had begun as a celebration of the accomplishments of the man generally considered the founder of the "Vienna School" of anthropology, ethnology, morphology and anthropometrics was cast in the light of a racist who looked upon the bodies of dead Africans as just so much "material" for his research. That Pöch had conducted these disinternments without any kind of official permit from the South African government only

---

museums and the trade in human remains, 1907–1917, Cape Town (South Africa): South African Museum, 2000.

100   Ciraj Rassool, "Human Remains, the Disciplines of the Dead and the South African Memorial Complex," a talk given at Museum Africa, Johannesburg, 8–9 July, 2011 at the Politics of Heritage Conference sponsored by the University of Michigan.

further reinforced the idea that he was some kind of ghoulish grave-robber.

This would not be the end of Pöch's outrages, however. When World War I began, he had the idea that the prisoner of war camps would be an excellent source of "material" for his racial studies, for these prisoners came from all parts of Europe and even the East. Like a young boy in a candy factory, Pöch ran amok in the camps, taking measurements and photographing candidates for his race studies.

To understand the rationale behind this, one has to become familiar with the ideas on race current in the German-speaking academic world at the time. The basic concept was that there were only a handful of "pure" races. Other ethnic groups represented admixtures of these "pure" races. Take the example of the primary colors: red, blue and yellow. Mix red and blue together and you get purple. Mix red and yellow together, and you get orange, etc. Thus, secondary colors are created from mixtures of the primary colors. The idea of race was quite similar. One had to examine a subject and attempt to discern the mixture of races present in their anatomical structures, etc. extending even to the genetic. This same approach would be taken by the Third Reich when it came to identifying the *Mischlinge*: the mixed Jewish and Aryan persons. Just as the color orange implies the presence of red and yellow, certain anatomical characteristics would imply the presence of "tainted" Jewish blood.

Rudolf Pöch died in 1921 at the age of 51, leaving the chair of anthropology that he created at the University of Vienna vacant. By that time, however, he had married Hella Schürer von Waldheim, a young, 28-year old assistant 23 years his junior. Hella Pöch (1893–1976?) became involved in creating paternity tests, ostensibly for determining paternity in general civil cases in the courts. This type of research, however, would have other applications once the Reich had been established. Until then, however, Hella Pöch devoted herself to a wide range of race studies, including her well-known survey of the Volhynian population of Ukraine.

This was an attempt to isolate an ethnic group from a region that had been heavily populated by German immigrants. Her focus was on the "pure" Volhynians, i.e., those who were not German, Jewish, or Ukrainian. Her methodology included family surveys, a system taught to her by her late husband. Parenthetically, after the German invasion of Ukraine in June of 1941, there were massacres of the local Jewish and other populations in order that Germans from the Reich, as part of the Lebensraum program, could colonize the region. One wonders what part Hella Pöch's fieldwork in Volhynia contributed to the identification of the ethnic groups to be exterminated, for her perspective was on determining that the Volhynians were members of an "Asiatic" race, and thus not Aryan.

The *Journal* of the American Medical Association for June, 1934 has a brief article in which Hella Pöch is mentioned as one of the presenters at a joint session of the Gesellschaft für Rassenkunde (the Society for Race Science) and the Anthropologische Gesellschaft (Anthropology Society) of Austria, in a program entitled "Composition of the Jewish Population in Vienna, from the Standpoint of Anthropology."[101] Pöch based much of her report on the methods devised by her late husband and used during his Bushmen research in Africa as well as his work in the prisoner of war camps during World War One. The thrust of the conference was to present the findings of the participating anthropologists that the Jews seemed to represent "at least seven distinct racial types, and possibly three more". This conference took place in 1934, a year after Hitler came to power in Germany but still long before Anschluss made Austria part of the Greater German Reich. This political climate gave rise to an unintentionally sardonic remark in the JAMA report that "Since scientific research may still be carried on in Austria unhampered by politics, which is an impediment in Germany, the results of such a discussion should be interesting." How a study of Vienna's 200,000 Jews in terms of racial "types"—based on Rudolf Pöch's blatantly racist method of collecting African corpses, robbing graves of their bodies—could be seen as "unhampered by politics" is perhaps a greater characterization of the place and time than anything that could be said in its defence.

Although Hella Pöch was still a little careful in pre-Anschluss Austria, she was not so careful when it came to the Reich. According to historian Brigitte Füchs, Hella Pöch was deeply involved in questions

---

101   From the "Foreign Letters" section of the *Journal of the American Medical Association*, August 4, 1934, p.356–357.

of race science since the 1920s, when she conducted an anthropological survey of 850 people in order to prove the "Nordic" character of the Austrian population.[102]

The years 1934–1938 saw Hella Pöch traveling frequently to Germany where she nurtured good relations with the *Rassenpolitischen Amt der NSDAP* (The Race Policy Office of the Nazi Party). By the time Anschluss made Austria part of the Reich, Hella Pöch was already well established in her field as a bona fide race scientist.

AT SOME POINT SHE MARRIED Georg Anton Pöch (date unknown) and moved with him to Salzburg. The strange coincidence of her marrying two men named Pöch would not have escaped the reader; but the author must confess he has no explanation for this. The two men do not appear to have been related, but until further investigation is completed we must assume that they were simply two men named Pöch.

Georg Anton Pöch was a physician rather than a pure anthropologist like his wife, but he accompanied her to the Netherlands and together they applied to their friend Seyss-Inquart for permission to use the camps as the raw material for their dubious study of Sephardic and Ashkenazic Jewish prisoners.

Prior to the war, both Georg Anton and Hella Pöch had published articles in peer-reviewed journals (some of them in English) concerning the epidemiology of disease, and inherited racial traits, among other things. For instance, Georg A. Pöch published—with the American Charles N. Leach of the Rockefeller Foundation—"A Diphtheria Immunization Campaign in Austria" in *The American Journal of Public Health* (February, 1935), while Hella Pöch delivered "A Contribution to the Muscular Anatomy and Certain Racial Distinctions of Bush Natives" to the Anthropological Society of Vienna, in Salzburg, in September of 1926.

By 1940, however, the situation had changed considerably. Germany had invaded the Netherlands, the war was on, and anthropologists had to make a living somehow. The Pöch couple went to Seyss-

---

102 Brigitte Füchs, "Hella Pöch," in Keintzel and Korotin (ed.s), *Wissenschaftterinnen in und aus Österreich: Leben-Werk-Wirken*, Vienna: Böhlau Verlag, 2002, p. 587–589

Inquart and asked to be allowed to examine the Sephardic Jews then at the Ommen transit camp. The idea was to take blood and other biological samples from the imprisoned Jews to conduct racial comparison studies with samples from the more numerous Ashkenazic populations of Central and Eastern Europe. The Reich Ministry of Education approved the project by March, 1941 and 6,000 Reichsmarks earmarked for the study, with more financial aid coming from Seyss-Inquart himself.[103]

The Pöch couple was excited about the potential for determining racial characteristics specific to Sephardic Jews. It would become a useful tool for extending the reach of the Nazi bureaucracy to encompass another sub-set of the Jewish "racial type." If there were considerable differences between the Ashkenazic and Sephardic types, that meant that the racial profiling that had been taking place to date throughout the Greater German Reich and its occupied territories was missing some important variables.

The Nazis were determined to do whatever they had to do to eliminate the Jew from Europe (as Seyss-Inquart's own statements to that effect make very clear) as well as from the rest of the world (as revealed by the Gestapo action in Indonesia as well as the determined efforts of the Argentine immigration authorities to forbid Jewish immigrants from landing in their country). To those who would deny the Holocaust, it is a simple matter of reading what the Nazis themselves had to say about their intentions towards the Jews (and the Gypsies, homosexuals, etc.) and the actions they took to eliminate the Jewish people from society, government, culture, and science and not only in Europe but around the world, in as much as they were able to do so. In order to be effective in this program, it was necessary to isolate as many ethnographic and anthropological variables as possible for racial markers. Heretofore, all the emphasis had been on the Ashkenazic Jew, which was the type most familiar to those living in Germany and Austria. The Sephardic Jew, with origins in Spain, Portugal and the Middle East, was less well known and thus it was important

---

103   See Brigitte Füchs, *"Rasse", "Volk," Geschlecht: Anthropologische Diskurse in Oesterreich 1850–1960,* Frankfurt: Campus Verlag, 2003, p. 291–292

to identify them as quickly as possible for isolation from society and eventual elimination from Europe.

Unfotunately for the Pöch couple, the deportation of the Jews from Ommen took precedence over their research project. It was evidently more important to kill the "material" than to study it. That did not deter them, however, for they had other—even more ambitious— projects in mind, such as asking leave to inspect all the large German prison camps for suitable research "material." Again, they approached their friend Seyss-Inquart for support and again he gave his blessing, but by that time the war was making increasing demands on both the camps and the Wehrmacht itself.

If it seems strange that anthropologists—scientists, after all, and in the case of Hella Pöch one of the most celebrated in her field— should be working for the government, one only needs to remember one of the twentieth century's most popular fictional academics: Indiana Jones.

In the first Indiana Jones film, the rugged archaeologist is approached by US military intelligence in the years leading up to World War II to find the Ark of the Covenant before the Nazis do. The idea that an academic, and an archaeologist (not a specialist in armaments or aerospace technology), would willingly work for the military never bothered the general viewing public who made *Raiders of the Lost Ark* one of the highest grossing films of its time. Yet, this is an issue that is controversial today for the Pentagon does have such a program currently in place. Known as Project Minerva, it is a program whereby the US military gives grants in the millions of dollars to American anthropologists to study terrorism. Minerva has come under fire from the American Anthropological Association who sees it as a dangerous mingling of military and academic agendas. After all, one tends to tell the person writing the checks what that person wants to hear. At best, it results in bad science and tainted research; at worst, it contributes to a skewed perspective on one of the world's most serious—yet least understood—modern problems: that of international terrorism. It is a conundrum looking for a practical as well as an ethical solution.

FAILING IN THEIR EFFORTS TO USE the concentration camp system as their personal anthropometric laboratory, it is not clear what the Pöch couple did next, or where they spent the rest of the war years (in the Netherlands? Back in Austria? Elsewhere in the occupied territories?) but the next time we run across them it is in Austria and it is 1946.

The Mysterious Dr. Pöch

Dr. Sosro Husodo is an Indonesian medical professional. In the year 1960 he was part of a famous enterprise known as "Project Hope." This fact is almost casually mentioned in the few available articles on Sosro—all in Bahasa Indonesia, the official language of the archipelago—but no clarification is ever offered. As it was the pivotal role of Hope that led to the discovery of Pöch, we shall look at it briefly here.

Project Hope was a highly touted American medical mission that took the form of an ocean-going vessel that called at Southeast Asian ports in the 1960s. The author clearly remembers Project Hope from grade school classroom discussions and presentations at the time (the author even remembers making a donation to the Project Hope fund, as did his classmates, after the presentation). A film on the project won the Academy Award for Best Documentary Short Subject in 1961, and can be viewed on Project Hope's website today.

The first voyage of the SS Hope began on September 22, 1960, leaving the port of San Francisco bound for Indonesia. It carried a staff of medical professionals (doctors, nurses, and technicians) as well as much-needed equipment and medical supplies. It opened an orthopaedic clinic in Indonesia, and treated thousands of people for cancer, leprosy, and various infections as well as malnutrition, all without charge of any kind. It called on Indonesian ports and invited hundreds of local medical personnel on board for training as well as to form cross-cultural links that would enable the American doctors to more effectively interact with local customs and practices.

One of these local medical professionals was Dr. Sosro Husodo.[104] A graduate of the Faculty of Medicine at the University of Indonesia,

---

104 Most Indonesians have only one name; the use of a first name and a surname

he worked in the towns of Bima (on the island of Sumbawa) and Kupang (a town on West Timor) before visiting the city of Sumbawa Besar with the SS Hope on its 1960 maiden voyage.

Sumbawa is an island to the east of Bali and Lombok. Aside from Sumbawa Besar, its biggest towns are Bima and Dompu. The native population of Sumbawa is divided into two distinct ethnic groups with their own languages but these days Bahasa Indonesia (the official state language of Indonesia) is widely spoken. The Sultan of Bima ruled the island until the Japanese occupation, and there is today an Heir Apparent to the throne of the Sultan who has not yet been installed. Both Islam and Hinduism contributed to the culture of Sumbawa, and there was a significant Roman Catholic presence on the island as well.

Sumbawa Besar is not Jakarta. It is not even Bandung, or Kuta in Bali. And in 1960, the isolation of Sumbawa island from the center of political and economic power in the nation's capital was even greater than it is today. Communications with Java and with the world at large would have been difficult; transportation even more so. Today, most visitors pass through Sumbawa from the relaxed tropical paradise of Bali to the west on their way to the unspoiled beauty of Flores island to the east, stopping only briefly in Sumbawa waiting for either a boat or a ferry to take them the rest of the way to see the fabled Komodo dragon in its natural habitat on Flores and nearby Komodo island. Balinese looking for work on Timor may also pass through Sumbawa. The point to be made is that, to the outside world, Sumbawa is a transit point and not a destination.

Yet, when Dr. Sosro Husodo landed in Sumbawa Besar in October of 1970 as part of Project Hope's mission to bring modern medical care and technology to this Indonesian backwater, he found to his surprise a "German" doctor in residence at the island's largest hospital.

Dr. Sosro and several of his colleagues visited the doctor, intrigued by the appearance of this foreigner in such a remote locale. After all, according to the statistics current at the time and mentioned in the Project Hope documentary film, there was only one doctor per every

---

is not common. Thus, the doctor's name is often given as Sosrohusodo rather than Sosro Husodo, but common usage allows both versions.

100,000 people in Indonesia in 1960 and in some areas only one doctor for every 500,000 people. Therefore a doctor, and a foreign one at that, merited some attention.

He was introduced as Doctor Pöch, and the impression that Dr Sosro had was that the man was German, and with an equally German wife; but Sosro had another impression as well: that the man knew very little about medicine and yet was running the largest hospital in Sumbawa Besar.

Pöch appeared to be a man in his sixties. He had trouble with his left leg, which dragged, and a tremor in his left hand. Sosro assumed it might be Parkinson's Disease, which would not have been unusual for a man of his age, although he argeed the symptoms could reflect another disorder entirely.

Sosro visited Pöch several times over the next few years. In October of 1960, he seemed to be living with a woman and a small boy of about 7 years of age. The woman was called "Gerda" and the boy's name was given in Sosro's memoires quite specifically as "Frank G. Spisak."

There is no indication as to why this boy's name should have been given so precisely. In fact, there is no more information in Sosro's account of the boy except to say that he and "Gerda" left for the United States shortly thereafter, i.e., in October or November. Then, the following month—November of 1960—"Gerda" is replaced by another woman, here named "Helena"[105] who can thus be identified with Hella or Helena Pöch.

The reason this is important is that there was a real Frank G. Spisak, and he was a convicted serial killer in Cleveland, Ohio charged with killing three persons and wounding others in a spree lasting several months in 1982. There would be no point in mentioning this fact, except for the strange coincidence that Spisak was a neo-Nazi who committed his crimes in order to spark a race war between Blacks, Jews and Whites, and who quoted Hitler and wore a Hitler mustache during his trial in 1983. A strange, seemingly demented cross-dresser

105 Ir. KGPH. Soeryo Goeritno, *Hitler Mati di Indonesia*, Jakarta: Titik Media, 2010, p. 76–78. As mentioned, most of this account of Pöch in Indonesia is taken from this source, unless otherwise indicated.

and Hitler-worshipper, Spisak was finally executed in 2011 after serving the longest time of any American prisoner on death row.

How could there be two individuals with the exact same name and middle initial, both associated with Hitler, on opposite sides of the world? According to Sosro's account, the boy in Sumbawa Besar was about seven years old at the time (1960). That meant that he would have been born roughly 1953. The convicted serial killer Frank G. Spisak was born on June 6, 1951. They were thus contemporaries.

Did Sosro see the future Hitler devotee and murderer in a small house on an Indonesian island in 1960?

LATER, SOSRO WOULD WRITE OF DISCUSSIONS between the mystery woman and Pöch; another woman—Sulaesih—would add considerably more detail. According to Sosro, Pöch defended Hitler and the Nazi Party. He denied the reports of mass murder at Auschwitz. When Sosro was asked to give his opinion about Pöch's trembling left hand, Sosro said it might be Parkinson's to which Pöch vehemently objected. The mystery woman—in this case Helena—offered the explanation that he had banged his hand on a table in a violent manner when hearing of the defeat of the German Army outside Moscow, and that his hand had never been the same since then.

A few years later, Sosro learns that Helena Pöch has also left Sumbawa. Georg Anton Pöch winds up converting to Islam and taking the name Abdul Kohar.

And takes another wife, the Sundanese woman Sulaesih.

The Pöch Diary

It is thanks to Sulaesih (known as "Esih" for short) that we have more detail concerning the mysterious "German doctor," for she not only shared her experiences with Dr. Sosro, she also provided him with some papers that were left behind when Pöch died in 1970. Among them was a kind of diary, some of which was in an obscure form of German shorthand which Sosro went to some lengths to get translated. It contained information concerning a network of persons around the world who were involved in helping Nazi war criminals escape justice.

It contained information on the Ratline.

It is important to note that this diary was written no later than January, 1970 for that is when the enigmatic Dr. Pöch died. While this story did not make the Indonesian press until 1983 at the latest, when Dr Sosro wrote an article on Pöch voicing his suspicions about him, the specific condition of the diary makes it doubtful that it was a later forgery. Written in the old Gabelsberger form of shorthand (that had to be translated by specialists in Germany) it contained details that no one except a beneficiary of the Ratline would have known as early as 1970. It was this diary—and the name Draganovic written in its pages—that got the author involved in the investigation. Had it not been for that written record, he would have never given the fanciful tale of Adolf Hitler escaping to Indonesia a second thought.

Further, we are well aware of the existence of forged Hitler diaries. The self-proclaimed expert on Adolf Hitler—Hugh Trevor-Roper himself—was famously conned by an individual who claimed to have such diaries, diaries that were later proved to be forgeries. But the important thing to remember about the Pöch diary is that it does not pretend to be a Hitler diary at all; it is, rather, a record of an escape from Germany to Italy and from there eventually to Indonesia. It is not signed "Hitler" nor does it in any way offer specific evidence that its author is indeed the Führer. The reasons behind the conclusion by Sosro and others as to the real author of the Pöch diary will be made clear as we proceed.

The diary—or notebook—is a small, 9 cm (about 4 inches) x 16 cm (about 6 inches) brown book about 44 mm (an inch and a half) thick. Inside the front cover there is the legend "JR KepaD No. 35 637" and "35 638", each number marked with a biological symbol for Male and Female, respectively. The author has not been able to decipher the legend "JR KepaD" but the numbers are presumably a means of identification for both Pöch and his wife.

A clearer statement is found inside the book which, when translated, reads:

"Escape Organization. Mr. and Mrs. Oppenheim replacement. Krüger. Sardegna Roma 79 A/1. Expenses for travel to South America (Argentina)."

This gives us somewhat more to work with. In particular, the name of Krüger is suggestive of an Argentine-Nazi network that was revealed recently by investigator Uki Goñi. Known as Vianord, this travel agency—which never handled any tourists—was set up by Carlos Fuldner, already mentioned as the SS officer assigned to Spain in 1945 to set up one leg of the Ratline. Vianord was based in Buenos Aires, but had "offices" in Switzerland and elsewhere in Europe. Its mission was to provide the necessary documentation and bookings for Nazis fleeing prosecution.

One of Vianord's most infamous clients was SS officer Josef Schwammberger. Responsible for the atrocities committed at a concentration camp in the town of Przemysl in Poland—the same Przemysl that was stated as his birthplace on Pöch's immigration documents—Schwammberger was high on the list of most-wanted Nazis. It was Vianord who came to the rescue, and the man running Vianord in Buenos Aires was former Swedish SS officer Hans-Caspar Krüger.[106]

It is not known whether the Krüger in the Pöch notebook is the same as the one at Vianord, but the specific mention of his name in association with travel to Argentina would imply that they were the same person, and Vianord was in operation at the time of the Pöch flight to Argentina (which would take place in 1951). Further, the name Oppenheim recalls one Clemens Oppenheimer, also in Buenos Aires, who provided immigration documents for Arthur Wiederkehr, a Swiss lawyer involved in extorting huge sums of money from Jews wishing to escape Nazi Germany during the war. Wiederkehr and his Nazi colleagues ran this operation through Spanish and Argentine embassies and consulates in the Netherlands (where Pöch had been working) and Spain. Indeed, one of Wiederkehr's contacts in the Third Reich was none other than the "architect of the Final Solution," Adolf Eichmann.[107] In his escape at the end of the war, Eichmann would later benefit from the services of Krunoslav Draganovic and the Catholic Church, as we shall see presently.

---

106 Uki Goñi, *The Real Odessa*, p. 273–274
107 Uki Goñi, p. 56–58

The address given above—Sardegna Roma 79 A/1—is a little startling, for it is the address of the building that houses the *Deutsches Archäologisches Institut,* the German Archaeological Institute, and the building at Via Sardegna 79 in Rome is one of the oldest archaeological organizations in the world which was founded in the early nineteenth century in Rome. It would make perfect sense that someone like Pöch (and especially his famous anthropologist wife) would have contacts there stemming from his wartime and pre-wartime activities. Reference to the Institute's own website shows that there is no mention of the organization's activities during and immediately after the war, an omission one will come across again and again when researching the escape routes used by the Nazis. In this case, the presence of this address in the Pöch diary lends it further credibility as a legitimate German document rather than a later forgery, for this address and its associated Institute would not be general knowledge outside a very small circle of academic experts and would not have been something Dr Sosro would have known; certainly, in the unlikely event he had heard of the Institute, he most certainly would not have had its address in Rome nor thought to include it in the diary if he had. In fact, the Institute will lead us to another—far more notorious—organization, the SS-Ahnenerbe, as well shall see in a later chapter.

This was not the only address, however, for on another page one comes across two of the most infamous addresses on that part of the Ratline known as the "monastery route": Via Albaro 38 in Genoa, and Via Tomacelli 132 in Rome. Both addresses are specifically linked in the diary to the name of Krunoslav Draganovic, the Roman Catholic monsignor who was the administrator of one of the most sinister operations of post-war Europe.

As we have seen in Chapter Three, Draganovic—a Croatian priest of the Catholic Church—was part of a larger group of Catholic clergy that included bishops and cardinals who were instrumental in assisting hundreds (if not thousands) of Nazi SS officers and other indictable war criminals to escape. In fact, underneath the Genoa address in Pöch's diary is the one word "Vatican."

In the antique Gabelsberger shorthand, there is found the following intriguing testimony:

"Short Description of the Individual Pursuit by the Allies and
the Local Authority in the year 1946 in Salzburg. We both,
my wife and I, in 1945 in Salzburg."

This is consistent with information that Georg Anton Pöch was the
medical officer of the Salzburg Gau. Hella Pöch was on the board of the
Vienna Anthropological Society throughout the war until 1945, so it
is possible that—after their Netherlands adventures—the Pöch couple
wound up back in Austria if, indeed, they ever left. In Salzburg when
the war ended they were eventually questioned by the CIC (the Counter Intelligence Corps of the US Army which was, at the time, the only
military agency involved in actively hunting Nazi war criminals).

But the question remains: why? Why did the Pöch couple find it
necessary to evade the Allied authorities in Salzburg and eventually
flee to Italy and escape Europe altogether? The author has been unable
to find their names on any of the lists of wanted Nazis, war criminals,
Nazi scientists, etc. that were in the hands of the CIC. Recourse to
recently declassified CIA and FBI files from the war years similarly
was fruitless. There is virtually no record at all of these two individuals, except in the annals of the Viennese anthropologists and "race
scientists." Among all their colleagues, the Pöchs were "unwanted."
Yet, there seems to be a wall of silence surrounding them in Europe.
Even the Rudolf Pöch Institute in Vienna claims to know nothing
more about his wife, Hella Pöch, even though she was a prominent
member of the Vienna Anthropological Society and still bore her husband's familiar and unmistakable surname, and even though they have
it on record when she died (possibly for legal reasons; as the widow
of Rudolf Pöch it is possible she had an interest in his estate; proving
her death might have released her assets as well as those of Rudolf
Pöch, but since the Institute does not respond to repeated inquiries
we may never know the truth). And Georg Anton Pöch? If we trust
the available records and archives, he might as well have never existed
after April, 1945. In fact, he barely existed before then. It seems his
only claim to fame in those days was his marriage to the indefatigable
Hella.

A tantalizing clue follows in the next few sentences of the Pöch
diary:

"My wife had to deal with the CIC a total of five times, sometimes at home and sometimes at CIC offices.... I was accused of falsifying information and of war crimes, concerning the death of Jews in Camp Macorr."

Unfortunately, there is no record of a "Camp Macorr" anywhere in Europe and, indeed, the name appears to be a corruption of another name, the corruption perhaps due to the Glasberger shorthand that might have not been up to the task of recording foreign names. If the camp in question was in Poland or in one of the occupied territories there is every reason to believe that its name was garbled in translation. There were thousands of camps and sub-camps during the war, so it is entirely possible that further research will reveal the identity of this place.[108]

Why would the Pöchs be accused of war crimes and specifically of the death of Jews in a concentration or extermination camp? If they were anthropologists, how would they have been culpable of mass murder? Unfortunately, as we will see, many of their anthropologist colleagues were capable of just such activities and several of them were arrested, charged, convicted and in some cases executed for them.

Further along in the diary we read:

"The thing that damned me and my wife were documents revealed by the government Chancellery office according to a report by Mr. Von Kruz, a despicable human being."

It is impossible to tell to what documents Pöch refers, but they were enough to implicate *both* Georg Anton *and* Hella Pöch in the murder of Jews in the camps. The name "von Kruz" is an unlikely one. There is no record of a von Kruz or a von Kurz or even a Kruze or Kruise with either the CIC or in any other capacity. Von Kruz means, literally, "of the Cross" and often is used in conjunction with Johann von Kruz or "John of the Cross," a famous Catholic saint. The author has tried several different variations of the name and still

---

108   It is possible that Macorr is a garbled form of Maribor, a POW camp in northern Slovenia/southern Austria.

comes up empty. It is entirely possible that the name was a kind of inside joke at someone else's expense, perhaps a way of designating a particularly religious interrogator. It is also possible—and difficult to establish at this remove—that the "von Kruz" was not one of the Allied interrogators but someone who wrote a report for the Reich during the war, complaining about the Pöch couple. We will not be able to identify this person until more records are forthcoming from the Vienna Anthropological Society, the Rudolf Pöch Institute, and/or the wartime files of the German government itself.

According to the diary, the Pöch couple survive the five CIC interrogations and eventually make their way to Graz where they wait for six weeks before going on to a place identified only as "J". There is no indication as to how long they spent in Salzburg, except that it was from 1945 to—at least—1946.

The letter "J" is not the only enigmatic reference in the diary. The complete list of letter designations runs:

B S G J B S R

Dr Sosro believed that these letters stood for Berlin, Salzburg, Graz, Jugoslavia, Belgrade, Sarajevo and Rome, respectively. This is not entirely a fanciful conclusion, as it is clear from the diary that the Pöchs were first in Salzburg and then in Graz[109], and that they eventually wound up in Rome. That accounts for three of the seven letters in the proper order of the escape route. We may be tempted to assign the first "B" to Berlin or even Berchtesgaden (although there is no evidence that the Pöch couple was ever in either place), in which case we only have to identify the remaining three letters, and this is where the difficulty lies.

Jugoslavia (or Yugoslavia) was Communist-controlled territory in those days. Belgrade and Sarajevo both would have been deep within that zone. It sounds as if it would have been suicidal for any Nazi—let alone Hitler—to enter Yugoslavian territory at that time. Yet, even the notorious "Angel of Death" of Auschwitz, Josef Mengele, ventured into the Soviet zone for several weeks during his escape from the Allies

---

109   Graz was in the British Zone of Occupation at the time.

"in the late summer and early fall of 1945" as described in the official OSI report on Mengele,[110] an adventure that would have lead to certain death if he had been captured by the Russians, for it was the Russian Army that liberated Auschwitz and was witness to the horrors that were perpetrated there.

Strangely, however, a letter appeared in the declassified FBI files on Hitler that insists that the Führer himself was in the same region as the Pöch couple, if we are to believe Dr. Sosro's account.

The letter is dated "At the end of May, 1948" from Cavalesso (i.e., Cavalese), Italy.[111] In it, the writer claims that Hitler was living in a small hamlet called Bobovo, which was located in the Ponikva region of Lower Styria (today, east central Slovenia), about 47 kilometers southwest of Maribor (Marburg). The directions in the letter for reaching the hamlet were quite specific, allowing for differences in spelling ("Ponikva pri Žalcu" was spelled "Ponikva pri Jelsah", for instance). The writer claimed that Hitler was living there quietly, and that there was some rumor about him traveling to or from South America.

What makes the letter compelling is the fact that it was written in German but sent from Cavalese, Italy, which immediately brings the Ratline to mind. Cavalese is only a few kilometers south of Bolzano in the Italian Tyrol where major elements of the Ratline were located and through which many war criminals would pass.

The letter was originally addressed to the CIA, but it was forwarded for some reason to J. Edgar Hoover. It was translated into English, but the German original was also attached to the file. The unnamed forwarder of the letter remarked that the writer was either not German or not an uneducated German due to several spelling errors; further, the fact that "Stati Uniti" was used for "United States" made the forwarder believe that the author was an Italian.

This was a case of over-analyzing the data. A person living in northern Italy in that particular place might well have been an Italian of German ancestry or an Austrian or even some other nationality

---

110 Office of Special Investigations (OSI), *In the Matter of Josef Mengele: A Report to the Attorney General of the United States*, October 1992: Washington DC, p. 64
111 The letter has no file number that the author can find, but can be located in the FBI's declassified file on Hitler beginning on page 157 of the first volume.

who had a good working knowledge of German. It actually goes to support the provenance of the letter as having come from someone with an insider's knowledge of the Ratline.

The letter does not seem to have been followed up, but for some reason the author of the letter did not think it strange that the most wanted man in Germany would have been hiding in Slovenia, in Communist-controlled Yugoslavia. This random letter from the FBI file may actually go a long way towards supporting Dr. Sosro's contention that Pöch wound up in Yugoslavia for a while.

The author can only conjecture as to the reasons for the Pöchs to go to Yugoslavia (if, in fact, that is what the letters represent). Belgrade (also known as Beograd) is in Serbia and Sarajevo in Bosnia. There seems no logical reason for a Nazi fleeing from the frying pan to dive into the fire, for Serbia was the enemy of Croatia; the former were largely Eastern Orthodox and the Croatians were Catholics who— when they were in a position of power during the war—forced many Serbians to convert to Catholicism before shipping them to the death camps or actually slaughtering them outside the very churches where they had been forced to convert. Fr. Draganovic would have been no help to the Nazis in Serbia, unless he had underground contacts there from the war (which, of course, he claimed he did to the CIC) ... but why would they go to such hostile territory in the Communist East when Italy was much safer and so close, across the Tyrolean Alps where the rest of the fleeing Nazis would find themselves?

Yet, the evidence does seem to point in that direction. To go from Salzburg to Graz was definitely counter-intuitive for someone escaping the Allied forces. Graz was close to the border of Slovenia, one of the states that made up the former Yugoslavia, and far to the east of the Tyrol where most of the escaping criminals were hiding, waiting for their false identity papers. The mysterious letter to the CIA concerning a Hitler sighting in the Ponikva region of Slovenia reinforces this idea. The Pöchs were going in the opposite direction from safety and if they did, indeed, wind up in Belgrad and Sarajevo they were headed not towards Genoa and a boat to Argentina, but towards Greece, Turkey and the Middle East. The hard way, through Communist controlled Serbia and Bosnia.

Bosnia is at least partly understandable, as during the war it was part of the Croatian Independent State, which was a Nazi puppet regime. Draganovic was a Croatian priest and was helping many of his countrymen escape the Communists by sending them to South America. And there was a large Muslim presence in Bosnia, which, due to the recruiting efforts of the Grand Mufti of Jerusalem, had fielded a Muslim SS Division during the war, the famous Handschar Division also known as the 13th Waffen Mountain Division-SS and the 1st Croatian Division-SS. But after the war, the directionality of flight for the Nazis was from Bosnia and Croatia to the west; not the other way around. Had the Pöchs continued on their way south and east, they would have had a much longer and much more dangerous excursion ahead of them before they reached sanctuary somewhere in Syria, Palestine or Egypt. They would have had to deal first with Yugoslav partisans who were fierce opponents of the Nazi regime; then, as Yugoslavia was declared a Socialist Republic in January of 1946, they would have had to deal with a government that was similarly hostile. While the Allies in the west—the British, French and Americans—were just as eager to imprison Nazi war criminals, the general consensus among the Nazis themselves was that it was far better to be captured by those enemies than by the Soviets who would show them no mercy whatsoever.

There would have had to have been a compelling reason for the Pöchs to decide on the eastern route to safety rather than follow their compatriots to the west, to the Tyrolean Alps and from there to Verona and on to Bari or Genoa. The situation on the Italian border was ridiculous: in some towns, Nazi troops and even SS officers still wore their uniforms in the street and in some cases were charged with keeping order. There was a huge influx of displaced persons to northern Italy from Austria, and the prison camps and DP camps could not accommodate the large numbers of refugees. It was easy to escape these makeshift camps once apprehended, and there was a flourishing market in the border towns in forged identification papers ... made even easier for the SS who had contacts in an underground network of safe houses and sympathetic ethnic Germans.

However, things were not that easy for the Pöchs in Salzburg. Pöch writes that things were relatively quiet for most of 1945 and 1946, until a "Jew" insulted his wife by coming to their apartment and telling her that they should have left Salzburg long ago, that there was an article in the local Communist newspaper[112] that attracted the attention of the CIC to their case. It was then that the CIC accused Pöch of lying about his Nazi Party membership. What is intriguing is the question of how there came to be an article in a local newspaper that would have implicated the Pöchs in anything, particularly exposing their possible membership in the Party. Further, if the article was in a "Communist" newspaper, then it makes even less sense for the Pöchs to escape to Communist-controlled Yugoslavia, of all places.

In any event, and leaving aside the question of whether the J, B and S really refer to Jugoslavia, Belgrade and Sarajevo (or to other towns in Slovenia), years later the Pöchs eventually make it to Rome. The Pöch diary states, "On the first day of December, we had to go to R to receive a letter and a passport that enabled us to leave Europe." Pöch is not specific as to the year, but it must have been December 1, 1950 for he will receive passport number 2624/51 in Rome, dated September 28, 1951.[113]

As he had the address of the Draganovic safe house in Genoa in his notebook, we can surmise that the Pöchs then made the trip from Rome to Genoa sometime after September 28, 1951 and boarded a ship bound for Argentina. Genoa was an important link not only in the ratlines but also for a wide variety of refugees and displaced persons seeking a better life in the New World. The underground network of Nazi supporters, however, usually managed to mix Nazi escapees among the regular refugees on the ships and to provide them with the all-important entry visas for Argentina, without which they would have not been able to disembark in Buenos Aires.

Pöch had the name of Krüger in his notebook, as well as the information that he was going to Argentina, so the author tentatively assumes that Vianord, the Nazi front organization booked his passage. They would have disembarked in Argentina sometime in late 1951 or early 1952, depending on how quickly they were able to get a berth.

But something went wrong in Argentina.

---

112 Probably *L'Unita*, a popular Communist paper of the time.
113 The passport number is also problematic, for the ICRC passports were not numbered in this fashion.

IT IS IMPOSSIBLE TO KNOW at this remove what prompted Pöch to leave Argentina where there were so many other Nazis—famous Nazis, wanted war criminals—leading relatively peaceful lives there and in other countries in South America. Why did the Pöchs feel they could not stay anywhere on the continent?

Why did they choose the absolute furthest destination available to them?

Why was Argentina not safe enough?

ALONG WITH THE BRIEF ACCOUNT of the escape from Austria and—via Yugoslavia?—to Rome and then to Genoa and Argentina, there is almost nothing else that can tell us where the Pöch couple was located between the years 1951 and 1954 when they finally arrived in Indonesia. However, there are indications that they were in contact with a far-flung network of fellow travelers. The diary was also an address book (and one that is being withheld from publication by its current owner) containing—according to Dr Sosro—the names and addresses of hundreds of "foreigners" living in countries around the world. Some of those countries include Pakistan, Argentina, Italy, South Africa ... and Tibet.

Tibet, of course, attracted the attention of a generation of Europeans (and especially Germans and Scandinavians) in the first half of the twentieth century. The SS mounted an expedition to Tibet in 1938, as recounted in the author's *Unholy Alliance*. Photographs and videotapes of this expedition have been made available recently by the Bundesarchiv and can be found online. Heinrich Harrer—author of *Seven Years in Tibet*, which became a film starring Brad Pitt—was an SS officer who fled a British POW camp at the outset of the war and found himself across the border in the Forbidden Kingdom, befriending the young Dalai Lama. Tibet was a siren song for the German archaeologists working for the SS-Deutsches Ahnenerbe, the "Ancestral Heritage Research Foundation" of the SS, which accommodated many crank academics and mystics in the employ of Heinrich Himmler. Wolfram Sievers—the chief of the SS-Ahnenerbe—would be executed at Nuremberg; some of the "academics" under his command were involved in heinous experimentation on living prisoners in the concentration camps, including at least one anthropologist—Bruno

Beger—who was a member of the SS-Tibet Expedition and who later was involved in the selection of human skulls from camp prisoners for a museum of anthropology. Beger himself was arrested and imprisoned for a short time, but managed to live out his days peacefully in Germany, dying only two years ago as this is being written. He considered himself a friend of Tibet—and of the Dalai Lama—until the end of his days.

In fact, there was a direct connection between the SS-Ahnenerbe and the German Archaeological Institute which has only recently come to light,[114] a connection that leads us back to the Pöch diary and its enigmatic reference to the Institute's address as part of the "escape organization."

Thus we have to ask ourselves, in light of all the foregoing information, how did the Ratline work? What was it? What were its components?

And whom did it serve?

Most importantly ... could the Ratline have managed to save the most wanted war criminal of the twentieth century?

---

114   See, for instance, Klaus Junker, "Research under dictatorship: the German Archaeological Institute 1929–1945" in *Antiquities*, June, 1998.

ABOVE: *Adolf Hitler. Please note the jawline and ear shape. Comparison with those of Pöch are suggestive. (See last page of this photo-insert.)*

BELOW: *Hitler and Eva Braun at the Berghof with Hitler's dog, Blondi. According to the Trevor-Roper report, all three died at the Berlin bunker in April, 1945.*

ABOVE LEFT: *Otto Skorzeny, who would organize the Ratline in Spain with the help of Spanish dictator Federico Franco.*

ABOVE RIGHT: *Hans Ulrich Rudel, another key figure in the Ratline. Together with Skorzeny, he would remain in charge of Nazi financial support for escaping war criminals.*

BELOW: *This photo shows Skorzeny standing to the right of Italian dictator Benito Mussolini, whom he has just rescued.*

RIGHT: *Admiral Karl Doenitz, former submarine commander during World War One who helped establish the Etappendienst network in Spain, and who later became Hitler's appointed successor as leader of the Reich.*

BELOW: *Admiral Doenitz inspecting a U-Boat and crew in June of 1941. U-Boats would become essential elements of the Asian Ratline.*

BOTTOM: *The arrest record of Admiral Doenitz. He spent ten years in Spandau Prison for war crimes and was later released, to die peacefully in 1980 of a heart attack.*

ABOVE: *Josef Mengele, the Angel of Death of Auschwitz. Escaped to Brazil.*

BELOW: *Adolf Eichmann, Architect of the Final Solution. Escaped to Argentina.*

ABOVE: *Martin Bormann, Hitler's second in command. Believed to have escaped to Paraguay.*

BELOW: *Franz Stangl, Commandant of Treblinka. Escaped to Argentina.*

ABOVE: *Emir Al Husseini, the Grand Mufti of Jerusalem and pro-Nazi agitator, with Adolf Hitler in Berlin.*

BELOW: *Al Husseini inspecting the troops of the Muslim SS-Handschar Division, composed of Bosnian Muslim troops.*

ABOVE: *Heinrich Himmler with Franco in Spain.*

BELOW: *The Condor Legion, Nazi troops in Spain to support Franco.*

ABOVE LEFT: *Monsignor Krunoslav Draganovic, the Catholic priest who set up the Austrian-Italian segment of the Ratline and who later worked for American intelligence, including the CIA.*

ABOVE RIGHT: *Nuntius Pacelli with his pro-Nazi assistant, Father Robert Leiber. Leiber was Bishop Hudal's direct connection with the Pope.*

BELOW: *The famous photograph of the signing of the Concordat between the Vatican and Germany. Eugenio Pacelli, the future Pope Pius XII, is shown seated at the head of the table.*

TOP LEFT: *Georg Anton Pöch on the occasion of his marriage to Sulaesih.*

TOP RIGHT: *Pöch and Sulaesih along with unidentified Indonesians.*

ABOVE: *The gravesite in Surabaya of Georg Anton Pöch.*

RIGHT: *Walter Hewel, "Surabaya Wally," Hitler's close friend and confidant from the days of the Beer Hall Putsch.*

Chapter Six

The Ratline

A U.S. State Department Report on Nazi gold (the Eizenstat Report) of 2 June 1998 . . . contains a chapter entitled "Ustasha Gold." It was that gold that made the "Rat Lines" possible, that is the escape routes for Ustasha and Nazi criminals at the end of the Second World War . . . [115]

The movement of men out of Europe was not the only commodity transported courtesy of the monastery route. The elaborate Vatican-OSS escape mechanism cost money. Papers had to be forged, fugitives moved across borders, housed and fed, officials paid off, overseas ocean travel arranged. While the Nazi priests like Draganovic, Saric and Hudal were true believers, committed to the cause, the rest of the operation required the services of hundreds of support personnel in more than a dozen countries[116] whose loyalty was measured in dollars and pounds rather than slogans.

Often, these funds were in the form of gold bars, various international currencies, diamonds, and artwork—paintings, manuscripts, rare books, furniture, and sculpture—stolen from museums and private collections all over Europe. A considerable amount of these resources was stored at various churches and monasteries along the escape route. Some of them were even stored at the cathedral of Archbishop Stepinac, as well as in churches and monasteries in Italy, Austria, Germany and Spain.

---

115 Dr. Milan Bulajic, "Jasenovac—work camp or the system of Ustasha camps of genocide?" in the *Second International Conference of Jasenovac—System of the Croatian Ustashe genocide camps (1941–1945)*, Banja Luka (Bosnia and Herzegovina): 2000, p. 47
116 These countries included (but were not limited to) Austria, Germany, Yugoslavia, Italy, Spain, Switzerland, the UK, Portugal, Argentina, Chile, Brazil, Syria, Egypt, and Turkey, as well as the United States, Canada and Mexico.

Some of these funds went to fill the coffers of Perón in Argentina. While the Argentine president was pro-Nazi in sentiment, he was not above taking as much as he could from the Nazi loot to help finance the Ratline on his end. It was up to Draganovic (and SS officer Carlos Fuldner) to ensure that the money flowed as easily to Buenos Aires as did the war criminals themselves.

Again, none of this is speculation. Documents declassified since the mid-1980s (the time of the Klaus Barbie revelations, the hunt for Josef Mengele, and the famous "Hitler Diaries" hoax) show in some detail how this operation worked. In fact, it was the Barbie episode that more than anything else brought the monastery route—and the complicity of US intelligence—to world attention.

Barbie had been chief of the Gestapo in the French city of Lyon, where he was known as the "Butcher of Lyon" for his cruelty in the interrogation and execution of Jews and French partisans (resistance fighters). Draganovic arranged his escape and, indeed, Draganovic himself, signed his forged International Red Cross papers—in the false name of "Klaus Altmann." But before Barbie left Europe for South America and his eventual sanctuary in Bolivia, he worked for the CIC as an intelligence agent. In fact, American intelligence admitted that Barbie is the only Nazi war criminal whose escape it aided. Although intelligence agents insist that they had nothing to do with him after he arrived in South America, the documents tell a different story. Barbie was so well protected in Bolivia that he eventually became head of that country's secret service, at the same time that he was running arms[117] throughout Latin America and financing assassination squads, in concert with Nazi forger and convicted murderer Freddy Schwend

---

117 Barbie's involvement with the German munitions firm Merex AG—a firm wholly-owned by the Gehlen Organization which was itself part of the West German BND (secret service) and a collaborative effort with CIA—is well-documented. Along with Freddy Schwend, Barbie also coordinated arms deals with Gemetex, another German arms supplier. Between the two of them they arranged deals with the governments of Chile, Paraguay, Bolivia and Peru, at times using Hans Rudel as a go-between. With Skorzeny, they also sold arms to Spain. And by "arms" one has to include tanks and rockets. See Linklater, et. al., *The Nazi Legacy: Klaus Barbie and the International Fascist Connection*, New York: Holt, Rinehart & Winston, 1984, p. 237–240.

(see below). Indeed, more than anything else the Barbie case demonstrates that the need to pursue Nazi war criminals transcends motives of revenge and justice for the unspeakable atrocities of the Second World War: rather, it is clearly a very real and pragmatic need to isolate these unprincipled actors from the stage of global politics. One historian has even suggested that Klaus Barbie had a role in the creation of the Joe McCarthy phenomenon in the United States in the 1950s: that secret American intelligence reports were leaked by Barbie to the anti-Communist Senator and firebrand.[118]

The above-mentioned Eizenstat Report prepared by the Under Secretary of Commerce, Stuart E. Eizenstat and released in May, 1997 seemed to exonerate the CIA from charges of actively aiding or abetting the escape of Nazi war criminals, but it was an exercise in semantics and as such it was blasted by various members of the US government as well as by historians and journalists who had lived with the material for decades. A General Accounting Office investigation on Nazis and their collaborators working with Allied intelligence admitted that the difficulties inherent in conducting this type of investigation at CIA made their conclusions rather open-ended. According to the GAO Report, while the investigators were "not denied access to any documents requested ... intelligence agencies often assign projects innocuous names which do not reflect the projects' purposes and, therefore, we cannot assure that we requested all relevant projects' files. ... we cannot be completely sure that we have obtained all relevant information or that we have identified all Nazis and Axis collaborators assisted by US agencies to immigrate to the United States."[119]

Between the GAO Report and the Eizenstat Report, much was revealed but much more remained concealed. They show that the actions of the so-called "neutral" countries were critical in supporting the Nazi regime, both during and after the war. That meant that Switzerland, Spain, Portugal, Turkey and Argentina—among other

---

118 Peter Dale Scott, "Why No One Could Find Mengele: Allen Dulles and the German SS," in *The Threepenny Review*, No. 23, Autumn 1985, pp. 16–18
119 United States General Accounting Office, Comptroller General of the United States, *Nazis and Axis Collaborators Were Used to Further U.S. Anti-Communist Objectives in Europe—Some Immigrated to the United States*, GAO/ GGD-85-66 (Washington, DC: GAO, 1985, p. 6–7

nations—were financially involved with Nazi swag even after 1945. While Switzerland is, perhaps, the most famous culprit in the case of the missing Nazi gold, other countries were enthusiastically hording and transporting the Reich's ill-gotten gains across borders and across oceans.

According to the Eizenstat Report:

In considering the actions of the neutrals, three phases can be identified:

- During the first phase, from the outbreak of war in 1939 until the battle of Stalingrad in early 1943, German military prowess was such that there was a legitimate fear of imminent invasion.

- In the second phase, the tide of battle shifted in the Allies' favor and culminated in victory. Beginning in mid-1943 with the Allied invasion of Italy, the D-Day invasion in June, 1944 and the diversion of German forces to halt the Soviet Army's advance, the Nazi occupation of Europe was rolled back and the threat to the neutrals greatly diminished, although there were still fears of other forms of reprisal. Commerce with Germany, however, continued. *German assets in neutral countries were not frozen, despite Allied requests and warnings. The neutrals continued to profit from their trading links with Germany and thus contributed to prolonging one of the bloodiest conflicts in history. During this period, the Allies suffered hundreds of thousands of casualties and millions of innocent civilians were killed.* (emphasis added)

- In the third phase, the immediate postwar period, the neutrals disputed the legality of the Allied request to control German assets; often denied they had any looted Nazi gold; defended their commercial interests; dragged out negotiations with the Allies; and eventually pressed their own claims for restitution against Germany. In contrast to the other wartime neutrals, Sweden was relatively forthcoming in terms of the extent and pace of its cooperation in transferring Nazi gold and other assets to the Allied powers. *Spain, Portugal, Switzerland, Turkey and others continued to resist cooperation even though the War was over.*[120] (emphasis added)

Safe Haven, Stay Behind, and Salzburg

One of the Allied operations designed to ferret out Nazi bank accounts and other sources of Nazi wealth was called Operation Safehaven. This was an OSS project run by Allen Dulles out of his Berne, Switzerland office. Ostensibly, the idea behind Safehaven was to deny the Nazis "safe haven" for their ill-gotten gains. It was designed to discover hidden sources of wealth and identify their provenance. The rationale behind Safehaven was to ensure that financial resources would not be available to enable a resurgence of the Third Reich, something that evidently worried Allied intelligence. This was connected to their concerns about the National Redoubt: an almost-mythical underground fortress where dedicated Nazis would hide and conduct a rear-guard action against the Allies. Declassified OSS and MI6 files show that details of this "Stay Behind" operation as it was known kept surfacing through informants and prisoners of war who were being interrogated about its existence.

There was already something in place known as the Werewolves. These were lone Nazi loyalists believed to have been left behind to conduct guerrilla operations against the Allies. While considered largely a myth perpetrated by Goebbels and other Nazi propagandists, there was still the danger that something like Werewolf could exist. The Ustashe had a similar program in place, a group known as the Krizari or "Crusaders" that actually *was* active in anti-Communist partisan activity in Yugoslavia after the war. If they (or the Werewolves) had access to millions of dollars in Nazi gold, then there was a very real possibility of a protracted guerrilla campaign in Europe. Hitler himself had personally authorized the evacuation of the Berlin Reichsbank

---

120 *U.S. and Allied Efforts To Recover and Restore Gold and Other Assets Stolen or Hidden by Germany During World War II, Preliminary Study*, Washington, DC: Department of Commerce, 1997, p. v–vi, emphasis added.

reserves to a secret location in the Alps in 1945 specifically in order to finance a Fourth Reich. These reserves were never fully recovered.[121]

The center of all of this clandestine activity was not Berlin or Hamburg, but lower Bavaria, the Tyrol, and Austria. This is where we find the Pöch couple at the war's end. It's also where the Ustashe had its headquarters at the same time; where Father Draganovic was active; and where so many Nazi war criminals made their way in the last days of the war and for months thereafter. It is this region of the disputed Tyrolean Alps—sometimes Italian, sometimes German—that was a hotbed of Nazi intrigue, Soviet espionage, and militant Catholic activism in 1945–1947. It deserves a closer look.

HITLER WAS A NATIVE OF AUSTRIA, not Germany. In fact, he came from a region to the north of the city of Salzburg. Salzburg figures prominently in our story, for it is where we first find the Pöch couple after the war.

The US Army intelligence unit known as the CIC had an office in Salzburg, and it was this office that gave the Pöch couple problems in 1945–1946, according to the diary found in Indonesia. Long before the CIC arrived in Salzburg, however, the region was famous for a variety of reasons.

Known to music lovers as the birthplace of Wolfgang Amadeus Mozart and the site of an annual music festival devoted to him and other classical composers, and as the setting for *The Sound of Music* (based on the real life story of a Salzburg nun), it nonetheless has other, less savory, associations. Austria had a large Nazi presence even before it was formally annexed to the Greater German Reich. Although the Nazis were banned in Austria in the days before the Anschluss, underground elements of the SS and the SD were active there and included such notorious figures as Ernst Kaltenbrunner and Artur Seyss-Inquart. Once the war was underway and Germany seemed unstoppable, the leaders of the Third Reich built country homes in the region. Hitler's fortress hideaway—the Eagle's Nest—is in Obersalzberg, not far from Salzburg itself in a region of lower Bavaria and close to the town known as Berchtesgaden. Göring had a home in the neighborhood,

---

121 Uki Goñi, *The Real Odessa*, p. 248

as did Martin Bormann. According to recently declassified OSS files, Salzburg was also believed to be the location of the headquarters of the Ustashi by 1944.[122] Even more arresting, Salzburg was also believed to be the center of the mysterious "Nazi Redoubt": a vast underground complex where the Nazis would regroup and continue to fight the war long after the formal surrender.

The Reich's Last Stand

As soldiers of the Reich ... it is our holy duty to exhaust every possibility. This is the only chance of success that remains. It is your duty and mine to take it.—*Adolf Hitler to Hanna Reitsch on mustering all remaining Luftwaffe aircraft to assist in the defence of Berlin.*[123]

A recent reliable report of an eyewitness gives evidence of the construction of an "inner fortress" position within the reduit area ...; the construction of fortifications is reported on a line running around the mountain massif to the SW of Salzburg ... This line of fortifications includes Berchtesgaden, but omits Salzburg and Hallein which lie to the NE and E. There is a slight puzzle involved in the recent reports of large quantities of material being unloaded to the east of this fortress position ... for storage in the endless caverns which lie to the SE of Salzburg ...[124]

In the last months of the war, great credence was given to French intelligence reports and other sources that claimed that the Nazis had

---

122 File GB-4773, classified "Secret", p. 4.

123 From the recently declassified interrogation of Hanna Reitsch dated 8 October 1945, from the Air Division, Headquarters US Forces in Austria, Salzburg, Air Interrogation Unit, Ref No AIU/IS/1, page 11, paragraphs 63–67. Reitsch's memory must have been faulty, for she states this conversation with Hitler took place at 1:30 am, the morning of April 30, 1945. However, according to all reports, she had already flown out of Berlin on April 28.

124 From a recently declassified OSS report dated 27 April 1945, GB-4773, entitled "Summary of Information on Reduit," paragraph 7.

created a vast underground fortress in order to continue the fight against the Allies. The region around Salzburg was riddled with salt mines and quarries, excellent hiding places, and the Mauthausen concentration camp itself had created underground complexes for the manufacture of parts for the Messerschmit aircraft as well as the V-2 rockets. If one were to create an underground city, one could think of worse places especially as so many tunnels, caves and mines had already been dug in the region.[125]

Estimates of the size of this mysterious fortress varied widely, from the ability to support 25,000 men for one year up to 60,000 men for a period of two years![126] It was believed that this fortress—called variously a Redoubt or a Reduit—would be the center "for directing the activities of the pro-Nazi and Fascist elements in all European countries, and particularly Germany ... The chief aim will be division of the Western Allies and liberated countries from Russia in the hope of reasserting Nazi doctrine and influence."[127]

This is, of course, exactly what happened. The Western Allies did, indeed, separate from the Soviet Union by 1947 when the Cold War began. At the same time, Germany began a slow recovery using former Nazis in positions of influence and power in industry, economics and politics. The activities of pro-Nazi elements throughout Europe continued long after the war's end, and these elements spread out from Europe to infect Latin America and the Middle East as well. Nazi doctrine and influence was reasserted in Argentina, Bolivia, Chile, Paraguay, Egypt and Syria as well as among the displaced persons in North America who owed their allegiance to any anti-Communist organization that promised them a return to their homelands once the Soviet Union was destroyed.

---

125 To be sure, a G-2 report dated 16 April 1945, File INF/2266, bore the subject line "Location of Caves in Germany" which included a map of caves in the Salzburg area. The same file included a list of caves in the area around Salzburg along with the statement: *This is the first of a series of Special Reports recording photographic evidence tending to confirm the enemy's preparation of the so-called "NATIONAL REDOUBT"*.

126 OSS Report FF-6273 dated 7 April 1945.

127 OSS Report GB-4773. Paragraph 2.

Historians dismiss the wild stories about the Nazi Redoubt as so much propaganda created by Goebbels and his department. There may be much truth to this assertion since, indeed, no physical Redoubt was ever discovered. However, the flight of Nazi personnel and capital from Europe to Latin America and elsewhere after the war via a network of safe houses, banks, political organizations and religious groups implies that at least a "virtual Redoubt" did, indeed, exist for the aims of that mission were largely accomplished.[128] And the center of this Redoubt was in the area around Salzburg in a circle that extended to the Austrian Tyrol ... exactly where the Ratline originated. It is where many Nazi war criminals fled as Berlin fell, including Hitler Youth leader, Artur Axmann, as well as Mengele, Rauff, Eichmann, and so many others. It is also where Hitler's favorite test pilot, the enigmatic and energetic Hanna Reitsch, flew when she left Berlin with the newly appointed head of the Luftwaffe, General von Greim.

Hanna Reitsch, the True Believer

> Mein Fuehrer, why do you stay? Why do you deprive Germany of your life? When the news was released that you would remain in Berlin to the last, the people were amazed with horror. 'The Fuehrer must live so that Germany can live,' the people said. Save yourself, Mein Fuehrer, that is the will of every German.[129]
> —Hanna Reitsch

---

128 Indeed, the flight of capital to Latin America was specifically linked to the Redoubt, in a Top Secret memo dated 6.7.45, file CSDIC/SC/15AG/SD 21, which states "... ample funds had already been planted in S AMERICA—mainly in the ARGENTINE—and would become available for financing agents in due course. In order to have "bankers" who could distribute this money, certain trustworthy key men had already been sent to live in SPAIN and SWITZERLAND." The source for this information was Olivier Mordrelle (1901–1985), a Breton Nationalist and Nazi collaborator who was captured in Bolzano in the Tyrol on May 24, 1945. His MI5 file was only declassified in the year 2011, as more information becomes available on the Ratline and its connection to information concerning the National Redoubt.

129 Hanna Reitsch interrogation, paragraph 22.

After the war, the celebrated Nazi test pilot, Hanna Reitsch, would wind up in Salzburg, as did her commander General Robert Ritter von Greim (who committed suicide shortly thereafter while in American custody in that city). Many assumed Reitsch had flown Hitler out of Berlin but it was Reitsch herself who dismissed the idea that Hitler had escaped; yet, at the same time, it was Reitsch who had destroyed valuable communications in the form of letters from Walter Hewel, Martin Bormann and even Eva Braun on her own volition, regardless of the historical or intelligence importance of the letters or the fact that they might have supported certain elements of her story of the last days in the Berlin bunker.

Hanna Reitsch (1912–1979) was Germany's most famous test pilot, having been awarded the Iron Cross with diamonds by Hitler himself, a medal she wore proudly to the end of her days. While there is no evidence that she was ever a member of the Nazi Party, she was certainly a true believer. She had flown into and out of beleaguered Berlin in the last days of the war when such a feat was thought impossible; but since her Führer had requested it, she had no thought but to obey. Like Otto Skorzeny, she was a daredevil and an expert pilot. Also like Skorzeny, she was a devoted Nazi.

Much has been made of her report of Hitler's last days. Trevor-Roper made substantial use of her "testimony" in his report, something that Reitsch herself has criticized heavily, claiming that she never said or did the things Trevor-Roper claims she said and did. The summary of her interrogation by her American captors has been declassified—all but one mysterious paragraph, number 87, which was redacted—and it is more a lens into the mind of Hanna Reitsch than it is a history of the last days of the war. She has since published a number of books about her experiences, but there are several elements of her story that resist logical analysis.

As mentioned, she has been often identified as one of Hitler's possible escape routes out of Berlin. She certainly had the skills to fly Hitler anywhere in Europe. But when she was questioned about the possibility that Hitler was still alive in the Tyrol and that she had flown him there:

… she appears deeply upset that such opinions are even entertained. She says only, "Hitler is dead! The man I saw in the shelter could not have lived. He had no reason to live and the tragedy was that he knew it well, knew it perhaps better than anyone else did."[130]

This is what is known as a "non-denial denial" among Watergate aficionados. She specifically does not deny that she flew him out of Berlin, only insists that Hitler is dead because he "had no reason to live."

According to her interrogation, she last saw Hitler on April 28 when he asked her and the newly promoted von Greim to organize the last-ditch aerial defense of Berlin as well as the arrest of Heinrich Himmler for treason.[131] It had been discovered that Himmler had attempted to contact the Allies in order to arrange surrender, an attempt that was rebuffed. Hitler had already fired Göring as head of the Luftwaffe since he had received a telegram from the corpulent Air Marshall saying that he considered himself the new leader of the German government absent any information that Hitler was still alive or at liberty. Hitler therefore saw himself as abandoned and betrayed by his closest comrades.

Reitsch flew out of Berlin with von Greim and a package of letters on April 28, escaping through a fierce Soviet anti-aircraft barrage and, after several stops to shore up resistance against the Russians and make contact with whatever was left of the Wehrmacht, eventually making it as far as Kitzbühel, about sixty kilometers south of Salzburg in the Austrian Tyrol. Von Greim had just been made head of the Luftwaffe. Göring—apparently a morphine addict, among other colorful traits—had remained in Berchtesgaden as Berlin fell, surrounded by the opulent furnishings he had stolen from public and private collections throughout Europe, refusing to believe that Germany was lost. He eventually committed suicide while a prisoner at Nuremberg.

Reitsch, however, read the letters she had been entrusted to carry and decided that she would destroy some and simply not deliver the

---

130   Hanna Reitsch interrogation, paragraph 51.
131   Hanna Reitsch interrogation, paragraphs 64–65.

others. A letter from Eva Braun to her sister was destroyed as Reitsch felt it was too melodramatic and self-serving. Letters from Walter Hewel to the Foreign Office and from Martin Bormann were also destroyed. We have only Reitsch's word as to the contents of all of these documents. Her assumption of the authority to dispose of these letters as she wished truly is astounding.

Reitsch and von Greim were taken to Salzburg by the American authorities and Reitsch spent eighteen months as a prisoner before being released. After a long and somewhat illustrious postwar career, she died—apparently a suicide—in 1979 and was buried in Salzburg, an unrepentant Nazi to the end.

An interesting aside to her interrogation by the American authorities relates directly to the theme of the Nazi Redoubt. According to Reitsch, the plan was still being discussed as late as April 15, 1945[132] but it soon became obvious that it was too late to put it into effect at that stage due to the deterioration of the military situation. In other words, according to Reitsch, the Nazi Redoubt actually did exist. It had been in preparation, and meetings were still being held in the bunker as to the state of its construction and organization as late as two weeks before the war's end. The implication is that the *inhabitants of the bunker* would not have been able to reach it due to the encirclement of Berlin by the Allies, but that it already had been in development for some time. This is in contradiction to other intelligence reports, which cast doubt on the whole idea of an "inner fortress" in the Salzburg region. Either Hanna Reitsch was lying about the Nazi Redoubt, or she was telling the truth. If she was lying, why was she lying and what else was she lying about? If she was telling the truth, then the Allies were mistaken in their assumption that the Redoubt was nothing more than a propaganda ploy concocted by Goebbels. According to Reitsch, the Redoubt was at least "partially completed" by April 15, 1945.

Thus, in Salzburg we have a confluence of personalities and plots. The Ustashi, whose most famous Ratline member was Father Draganovic, the creator of the monastery route; the mysterious Nazi

---

132   Hanna Reitsch interrogation, paragraph 85: "Why the 'Redoubt' was not Utilized."

Redoubt, a virtual fortress for the preservation of Nazis and Nazism after the war; the magnificent homes of the leaders of the Third Reich; the headquarters of the American forces in Austria; the CIC office responsible for the region; and the Pöch couple. In addition, there is one more aspect to the Salzburg region that requires mentioning for it bears directly on our case.

Ernst Schäfer and the Inner Asia Research Institute

One of the most peculiar departments of the SS was the Ahnenerbe, or "Ancestral Heritage" research division. It was a hothouse of racial theories, crank anthropologists and eccentric archaeologists, mystics, rune scholars, and developers of pseudo-scientific concepts concerning the nature of the cosmos, alternative energy sources, and the story of Atlantis. The SS-Ahnenerbe was the soul of Nazism, for within its ranks could be found every type of academic devoted to the core values of the Party. Scientific theories were made to fit the ideological mold of race science, or *Rassenkunde*. As history would eventually reveal, some of the worst atrocities of the Third Reich took place under the aegis of the SS-Ahnenerbe and its leader—Wolfram Sievers—would be executed for war crimes.

One of the strangest gaggle of academics within the organization was the group devoted to Tibetan research. Led by Ernst Schäfer, a small party of SS officers who were also anthropologists mounted a historic expedition to Tibet in 1938. Various reasons were given as the mission of the expedition, but surviving documentation—including film footage—shows that *Rassenkunde* was certainly one of its more important goals. Expedition member Bruno Beger, for instance, conducted anthropometric studies in Tibet, measuring the skulls of living Tibetans with calipers and recording the data. Schäfer himself collected all manner of flora and fauna to take back to Germany, and also made a detailed study of the religious rituals of the Tibetans. (He returned to Germany with a complete set of the *Kangschur*, the 108-volume sacred Tibetan scripture, as well as silent film footage of Tibetan rituals.)

The idea of conducting anthropometric research in the field while simultaneously recording the research on still and motion picture cameras owes a great deal to the pioneering efforts of Rudolf Pöch, Hella Pöch's first husband. Yet, at this time, there is no evidence that Schäfer and Pöch ever met although Schäfer would almost certainly have been familiar with her work, and the work of her late husband. The overall mission of the SS-Ahnenerbe was to discover evidence to prove Nazi race ideology through various means. One of its contributions to the Reich was the development of race tests that would identify people who were Jews as well as *Mischlinge*, or "half breeds": those with mixed Jewish ancestry. This was one of the research goals of the Pöch couple in the Netherlands, as well as of the SS-Ahnenerbe in general and of Ernst Schäfer in particular during an expedition to the Caucausus to ascertain whether or not the "Mountain Jews" [133] were Aryan or in reality descendants of Jews who were in diaspora from the time of the destruction of the First Temple.

Bruno Beger, the anthropologist who conducted surveys in Tibet with Schäfer, would later go on to participate in the selection of human prisoners from the camps for the creation of a skeleton museum. This macabre, mad-scientist endeavor was intended to demonstrate the anatomical differences between Aryans and Jews, and in order to be successful one had to have unblemished Jewish skeletal material at one's disposal. In order to accomplish this, Beger would select those prisoners he felt best represented stereotypical Jewish traits. These prisoners would then be executed in such a way as to ensure there was no damage to their crania or other skeletal structures. The bodies would then be macerated—a process requiring several weeks of "de-fleshing" the bones—and the resulting skeletons would then be prepared for display.

These activities were disrupted by the fast approach of Allied forces, and steps were taken to hastily remove whatever traces of this hideous process there were; however, the Nazis were not entirely successful in covering their tracks for many bodies remained, at least one with its concentration camp tattoo intact. Eventually a trail of documentation would lead straight back to the Ahnenerbe and to Bruno

---

133   For this story in greater detail, see Heather Pringle, *The Master Plan: Himmler's Scholars and the Holocaust*, New York: Hyperion, 2006, p. 251–253.

Beger, a man who had met the Panchen Lama of Tibet and who had spent months among the Tibetan Buddhists.

Beger was eventually indicted for these crimes, but the charges were never able to stick. He spent very little time in prison, and the rest of his life was a model of academic repose. He remained on good terms with the Tibetans, and there are extent photographs of Beger in audience with the current Dalai Lama. For awhile, he even published a brief account of his admiration for the Tibetan people that was carried on the official Tibetan Government-in-Exile website, until taken down at the insistence of those who knew very well who Beger was and what he had done during the war.

As the war progressed and it became obvious that the Allies would take huge chunks of Germany's empire—if not the whole thing—Himmler decided that the research of the SS-Ahnenerbe would have to take place in safer quarters. The main office of the organization was moved out of Berlin, and Ernst Schäfer's own operation moved to Mittersill, a town in the state of Salzburg that was once also the site of a sub-camp of the infamous Mauthausen concentration camp. It was there that Schäfer continued his research in relative peace and quiet, about two hours' drive from the home and office of Georg Anton Pöch in Salzburg.

Archaeology was one of the main interests of the SS-Ahnenerbe. Nazi archaeologists were sent to the far corners of the globe in an effort to discover traces of Aryan civilization. In the occupied territories, archaeologists working for the Ahnenerbe would simply seize those artifacts deemed valuable to this research and they would wind up either at Ahnenerbe headquarters or at Wewelsburg Castle, Himmler's sacred retreat. We know that the German Archaeological Institute was involved in some way with these activities but until more work is done at the Institute's archives in Rome we will not know the whole story.

Like his colleague Bruno Beger, Ernst Schäfer managed to escape any serious punishment for his role in the Ahnenerbe and lived to a ripe old age after more expeditions after the war in South America—principally Venezuela—before returning to Europe. Did the Pöch couple know Schäfer, especially after his move to Mittersill? Was Schäfer (or another member of the Ahnenerbe) their connection to the Deutsches Archaeologische Institut in Rome? Schäfer was successfully denazified long before he left for Venezuela in 1950. What was the status of the Pöchs?

WHILE THE EXPECTED WEREWOLF GUERRILLA WAR never materialized, and the exact location of the legendary National Redoubt never identified, the money stolen by the Nazis was used to help fugitives escape and also to prop up the Perónist regime in Argentina. Rather than finance a Nazi guerrilla war in Europe, Nazi gold helped finance fascist dictatorships throughout Latin America and the Middle East: regimes that utilized not only the stolen gold and other financial instruments but also the expertise of the Nazi criminals themselves.

We can take the case of Freddy Schwend as an example.

Friedrich "Freddy" Schwend (1906–1980) claimed the rank of SS-Sturmbannführer (although he was probably not a genuine SS officer and held the rank as a kind of cover) but his real job was as the manager of something called Operation Bernhard. Bernhard was the ambitious currency-forging project of the SS that managed to create beautifully-crafted British pound notes as well as other currencies. The original mission of Operation Bernhard was the destabilizing of the world's currencies as part of the overall war effort, but in the end it functioned as a kind of slush fund for secret operations, using the forged currencies rather than genuine money to pay off spies and bribe officials. The forged currencies were also used to buy much needed raw material for the war effort from neutral countries. Schwend conducted this operation from a villa in the Tyrol that was surrounded by SS men, and which oversaw transport of the forged currencies by the truckload and trainload to other countries in Europe. The forgers themselves were Jews: concentration camp prisoners chosen for their ability as printers and engravers.

By all accounts this was a very successful operation, and at the end of the war Schwend gave himself up to the CIC which "turned" him and used him as a double agent: first, in the location of stolen gold, currencies and artwork in a series of hiding places, mine shafts and safe houses throughout Austria and other parts of Europe, and then for counter-intelligence work under the code name "Major Klemp," and as code name "Flush" (for an operation created to "flush out" others like him in Italy). There is also evidence that Schwend was involved in

Dulles's Operation Sunrise, which ensured the peaceful surrender of SS and Wehrmacht forces in Italy.[134]

Schwend's network of wartime safe houses was then used for the Ratline. The same agents he had used to pass forged pounds sterling he now used to move SS men out of Europe. Operation Sunrise had presented the OSS with a considerable number of SS officers who had cooperated with them in the orderly surrender, and who now expected special treatment in return. Dulles himself was notoriously anti-Communist and relatively relaxed when it came to Nazism; like the Vatican and especially Pope Pius XII and his Secretary of State and future Pope Paul VI—Cardinal Pacelli—he saw the Nazis as a potential bulwark against the Russians.

An underground network of SS officers, working for the Allies rather than against them, would provide American intelligence with a ready-made spy network in Eastern Europe. This would eventually become the infamous Gehlen Organization, run by Reinhard Gehlen who had seduced his captors with promises of being able to penetrate Soviet intelligence and run operations behind Russian lines.

In the meantime, Schwend proved his worth over almost two years of work with the CIC and the OSS, and several of these files are still classified to this day. Eventually, however, Schwend would realize that Europe was getting too hot for him and he wound up using his own network to leave Europe and sail to South America. He used the false identity of a Croatian national, with International Red Cross documents courtesy of Father Draganovic, and fled with his wife to Peru in 1946. By the 1970s, however, Schwend found himself a wanted man again. The Italian government had demanded his extradition from Peru for the murder of a man who had been trying to steal a quantity of the forged notes Schwend had created: Schwend had shot him on the orders of SS strongman Ernst Kaltenbrunner.

Schwend was eventually released from custody and spent the remaining months of his life in Peru, where he died in 1980 ... taking many secrets with him to the grave. Reportedly, Schwend was deeply involved with Klaus Barbie and with Barbie's network of fascist murderers and arms dealers in South America and Europe who

---

134   See for instance Gerald Steinacher, *Nazis on the Run*, p. 168–169.

conducted assassinations as part of Operation Condor: the quasi-official agreement between the governments of Chile, Argentina, Bolivia, and Paraguay to seek out leftists and communist leaders and neutralize them "with extreme prejudice." Agents of Operation Condor were responsible for assassinations and assassination attempts in Italy and Spain as well as in South America, and in addition there were connections to the Italian Masonic lodge, Propaganda Due, or P2: the heavily-connected renegade Masonic association with members in the military, government, finance, media and the Church that was involved in assassinations and money laundering in Europe with a view towards resurrecting a Catholic, fascist dictatorship a la the Ustashe of Croatia.[135]

Schwend was not the only source of funds for the Ratline, of course. In addition to the gold and other valuables stolen by the Ustashe, there was a surging underground market in stolen art and artifacts from other parts of Europe. During the war, Hitler had decided to "repatriate" many of these artworks, while having others stored in hidden places in cities like Nuremberg where the famous Hapsburg Crown Jewels were taken from a museum in Vienna. But it is the strange story of the German Archaeological Institute that brings us back to Georg Anton Pöch.

In 1946, the Art Looting Investigation Unit (ALIU) of the OSS compiled a list of persons of interest who were implicated in the sack of public and private art collections that took place under the orders of the Third Reich. This list has generally not been consulted by those studying the ratlines as it is considered a separate issue entirely; however, the author's discovery of the Roman address of the German Archaeological Institute in the Pöch diary suggested a closer look at this list would bear fruit.

As it turns out, no fewer than ten individuals who were officials of the German Archaeological Institute or otherwise connected appear on the OSS list. To quote directly from the list, they are:

---

135 Interested readers should consult the author's own *Unholy Alliance*, New York: Continuum, 2002 for more information on this connection.

Crous, Dr Jan W. Librarian of the German Archaeological Institute in Rome (79 via Sardegna). In August 1942 confiscated goods of the Czechoslovakian Institute in Rome. In March 1944 went to Alt Aussee to arrange for storage in the salt mine of objects from Rome.

Curtius, Prof Ludwig. Director of German Archaeological Institute in Rome (79 via Sardegna). Reported to have assisted Prince Philipp von Hessen in his acquisitions for Germany.

Deichmann, Prof Dr Friedrich Wilhelm. Head of Christian Archaeology Section of the German Archaeological Institute in Rome.

Fuchs, Dr Siegfried. Deputy Director of German Archaeological Institute, Rome. Reported responsible for seizure of Czechoslovakian Archaeological Institute in 1942, and for transfer to Germany of the Archaeological Institute and the Herziana libraries. Assisted by Dr Hoppenstedt. Reported to be SS Gruppenfuehrer and to have remained in Rome attached to the SD.

Fuehrmann, Dr Hans. Chief, Photographic Section, German Archaeological Institute, Rome.

Fulnmann. Official of the German Archaeological Institute, Rome. Reported to have seized Czechoslovakian archives.

von Gerkan, Prof Arnim. Director, German Archaeological Institute, Rome.

Haas, Dr. (Rome). Member, German Embassy staff. Reported to have assisted members of the German Archaeological Institute in the transfer of works of art from northern repositories to Rome.

Kupers (possibly Kupper). Reported in charge of administration of the German Archaeological Institute in Rome; probably participated in the plan to transfer the German libraries from Rome.

Moellhausen. German Consul in Rome, reported to have worked with members of the German Archaeological Institute to protect Italian art treasures.

AS ONE CAN SEE, the above list includes two directors, a deputy director, and other officials of the Institute as well as a member of the German Embassy staff in Rome and the German Consul in Rome. This indicates that the Institute itself was involved deeply in the operation and that it was not merely one or two "bad apples" trying to make extra money or win points with the Reich. Indeed, as we see from the above OSS file Director Dr Siegfried Fuchs was himself believed to be an SS Obergruppenführer and was also a member of the SD (Sicherheitsdienst, or Secret Service) in Rome. (He was also summoned to join the Waffen-SS by 1943 when it appeared as if Rome were about to fall to the Allies who had landed in Sicily.) Fuchs had been insisting that the archives and artifacts at the Institute in Rome be evacuated; it seems his colleagues did not agree, but in the end (by December 21, 1943) the evacuation of the Institute's holdings had begun and the property of the German Archaeological Institute in Rome had been transferred to a salt mine at Bad Aussee,[136] about 100 kilometers southeast of Salzburg. (The area around Bad Aussee and its neighboring town, Alt Aussee, was where the Nazis had hidden a huge cache of stolen art in the salt mines, including priceless Michaelangelo and Vermeer works.) The Institute itself had strong links to the Ahnenerbe, and the two organizations had joined forces in order to compete with Alfred Rosenberg (1893–1946), one of the architects of the Reich's racial policies, who wanted his own archaeological and anthropological institute.[137]

This is a tantalizing lead, courtesy of the Pöch diary. It adds another dimension to what we already know of the Ratline, for in addition to the Ustashe, the SS, the CIC, the OSS, the Red Cross, and the Catholic Church we now have German academia in the form of the Archaeological Institute as another very possible link in the underground network of escaping fugitives, moreover fugitives with access to nearly unlimited funds in the form of priceless art objects and archaeological artifacts. If we remember the looting of the Bagh-

---

136   Bundesarchiv R 4901/14064. I am indebted to Heather Pringle for this material on Fuchs and the evacuation of the Institute's property to Austria.

137   This theme has been explored in depth by Klaus Junker, "Research under dictatorship: the German Archaeological Institute 1929–1945", in *Antiquities*, June 1998.

dad Museum at the time of the second Gulf War, and of how many Sumerian, Babylonian and Akkadian artifacts made their way into the international market at that time, we can imagine how easy it would have been in the days before computers and the Internet to hide, ship, and sell valuable paintings, sculptures, and ancient religious objects to interested parties who had no scruples about provenance in those unsettled and chaotic post-war days.

In addition to the men listed above, there were many SS officers and art specialists who were active in Austria and the Netherlands: the regions where Pöch and his wife were operating and, indeed, the Nazi thieves who were responsible for looting art from the Netherlands worked for Seyss-Inquart, the friend of the Pöch couple from their days in Austria and later as they attempted to work the Dutch camps over which Seyss-Inquart was the Reich's Commissioner. Amsterdam was a major European art center, and the Nazis lost no time in ransacking both the museums and the private collections in Jewish hands for precious objects to enhance the Reich's horde.

One of those in charge of seizing Jewish property in the Netherlands was SS officer Hans Fischböck, an aide to Adolf Eichmann and the Reich's finance minister in Holland under Seyss-Inquart. He was also a member of the *Freundeskreis Himmler*, along with Wolfram Sievers, Hjalmar Shacht, etc. and was thus a close confidant of the SS leader. After the war, it was the indispensable Father Draganovic who signed his fraudulent Red Cross passport application.[138] Fischböck assumed the name of Jakob Schramm and fled to Buenos Aires in 1951. This was the same year that the Pöch couple left Europe for the same destination. Fischböck arrived in Argentina in February, 1951, and the Pöch couple at the end of that year.

As noted in the previous chapter, the entry in the diary that mentions the address of the German Archaeological Institute reads:

Escape Organization. Mr. and Mrs. Oppenheim replacement. Krüger. Sardegna Roma 79A/1. Expenses for travel to South America.

---

138   Uki Goñi, *The Real Odessa*, p. 249

This directly implicates the Institute as the "Escape Organization" and would seem to link two names—Oppenheim and Kruger—directly with it. Unfortunately, we do not have the archives of the Institute at our disposal, something about which other historians have complained.[139] However, the names Oppenheim and Krüger do appear on the OSS list of "Red Flag" names associated with stolen art.

The name Oppenheim appears as "Oppenheim, Jean. Paris, rue du Fbg St Honore. Small dealer. Dealt only with Bornheim."[140] The name Krüger appears several times, in different versions:

> Krueger, Oberst. Commander of 71st Infantry Regiment and member of German Kunstschutz in Italy. Reported responsible for return of Oliveto deposit to Florence and connected with attempted theft of the Cranach Adam and Eve.
>
> Krueger, Wolfgang. Berlin, Nikolassee, an der Rehwiese 4 Koelpinsee, Insel Usedom, Pommern. Former director of Lepke auction house, Berlin who became an independent dealer. Active as buyer in Paris. Used Schenker Co as shipper.
>
> Kruger, Mme. Paris, 53 ave Foch. Sister-in-law of Petrides.[141] Reported to have hidden pictures he obtained from the Germans.

As you can see, the three Krügers represent Italy, Germany and France and none of them is linked directly to the Institute although all three could have used the services of the Institute to evaluate their

---

139 See, for instance, O. Dalley, C. Jansen, M. Linder, speakers, "History of the German Archaeological Institute in the 20th Century", Research Plan and Research Cluster of the German Archaeological Institute, from the Institute's website, last accessed September 8, 2011.

140 Not to be confused with Max von Oppenheim (1860–1946), a famous German archaeologist and contemporary of T.E. Lawrence. His last trip to Syria—in March, 1939—was financed by Herman Göring, but there is no indication that there was any connection between von Oppenheim and the German Archaeological Institute in Rome and not with the Ratline in any case.

141 "Petrides" was "one of the most active collaborationist dealers" who was born in Cyprus, but was a British subject and a naturalized Frenchman. He concealed some of his assets with Mme. Kruger.

thefts or to store them until they could be hidden in some other location. The first Krüger was a Wehrmacht officer, but he was also a member of the German Kunstschutz, or "Art Conservation" group in Italy. He would have been the most logical of the three Krügers to have been involved with the German Archaeological Institute during the war, and to have been involved in the underground networks after the war.

As we noted in Chapter Five, there was also a Krüger working for the mysterious Vianord travel agency in Buenos Aires, which arranged immigration documents for fleeing Nazis. While Krüger is a relatively common German name, to have come across it in two important locations—at the Institute whose address appears in the diary, and at the other end of the Ratline in Buenos Aires—suggests that we are on the right track with at least one of them. The one in Vianord is linked directly to SS officer Carlos Fuldner's leg of the Ratline. Both the Fuldner and the Draganovic links in the chain were operative in 1951, the year of the Pöch escape.

The more one investigates the scraps of information contained in the Pöch diary, the more one is lead to a stunning conclusion: the couple identified as Georg Anton and Hella Pöch were in the middle of a heretofore unknown and unacknowledged link in the escape system of Nazi war criminals, one that included not only former SS officers and their supporters in the Catholic Church and the intelligence communities of several nations—including the United States—but the governments of unaligned and "neutral" countries such as Argentina, Peru, Bolivia and Chile as well as the Arab nations of the Middle East. The threat of Soviet Communism was considered so dire and so immediate that roughly half the world signed a pact with the Devil in order to thwart it. The cabal of SS officers, Ustashe war criminals, Latin American fascists and Catholic prelates was convinced that a third world war was imminent, and that they would be in a perfect position to exploit that opportunity to create a new—Fourth—Reich. The Nazis had lost their country and their Third Reich, but in another sense they had won the war of ideas. They had convinced not only dictators like Perón of Argentina and Stroessner of Paraguay of their usefulness in this coming conflict, but could number seasoned American intelligence officials like Allen Dulles among the converted, as well as the generals running Operation Paperclip. It was due to this unholy alliance that a vast network of evil geniuses was allowed to expand throughout the world, poisoning every political system with which they came into contact with the venom of fear.

There is only one more link in this heavy chain of evidence, and that is the relationship between the fugitive Nazi networks and their collaborators in the Middle East. It is a link that will further validate the information represented by the Pöch diary, if in a most unsettling way.

CHAPTER SEVEN

GOD IS GREAT

Allahu Akbar! Allahu Akbar!—The first words of the daily call
to prayer

As the author writes these words, the Muslim call to prayer is rever-
berating out of a half-dozen loudspeakers on as many mosques.
Preparations are being made to travel to Surabaya, the site of the last
remaining synagogue in Indonesia as well as the Islamic cemetery
where Pöch is buried. The call to prayer tells us that God is great,
that there is no God but God, and that Mohammed is his prophet.
This happens five times a day, beginning in the early morning hours
when the sky is still dark and the air is still cool. Islam is the faith of
more than one billion of the world's population, and Indonesia has the
largest population of any Muslim nation with roughly two hundred
million of the faithful on more than 17,000 islands, with the majority
on Sumatra and Java.

One of the dirty secrets concerning the flight of Nazi war criminals out of Europe is the welcome they received by some of the governments of the Middle East who valued their expertise in military
and intelligence matters, as well as their ideological "purity" when it
came to anti-Semitism[142] and especially anti-Zionism, for the State of
Israel was created in 1948: only three years after the end of the war,
and with a population that was expanded considerably by Holocaust
survivors. Thus, the "human terrain" of Nazis and Jews had shifted
from the cities and ghettos of Europe to the cities and villages of the
Middle East. The Warsaw Ghetto was, in a sense, being recreated and
re-erected in Palestine, only this time with walls made of tanks and

---

142 The author would like to point out, unnecessarily perhaps, that the term
"anti-Semitic" is problematic for the word "Semite" can apply equally to Jews
and Arabs (although not to Iranians). However, in common usage the term "anti-
Semite" refers to bias and prejudice concerning Jews and is rarely, if ever, used to
describe anti-Arab sentiments.

cannons and with defenders who had already experienced the worst
that humanity could throw at them and who were prepared to resist
with brute force.

In the west, and particularly in post-9/11 America, this conflict
is seen through a monochromatic lens. There is only black and white,
us and them. This is further compounded by a general lack of knowledge concerning Middle Eastern history and the critical role that the
western powers played in the creation of the Arab states as we know
them today. It was this involvement by the west that led to the current
political and military situation and contributed to the rise and growth
of movements commonly referred to as Islamic fundamentalist. If they
are understood instead as anti-colonial movements they may be *better* understood. Perhaps. Although, now the time is long past when
anyone can afford to make these distinctions as life swiftly imitates
artifice and all the players succumb to their own stereotypes and begin
believing their own propaganda.

The author has often declared that we are still fighting World War
One. This is nowhere as obvious and as heart-breaking as in the Middle East. From the Balfour Declaration to the Sykes-Picot Agreement,
from the drawing of the boundaries of Iraq, Kuwait, Saudi Arabia,
Jordan and Syria to the British Mandate in Palestine ... the major
conflicts began with the first World War and the addled decisions
made by the victors in that conflict, already stunned by the hideous
excesses of the war and drunk on the fumes of blood and blinded by
the glitter of treasure. It was World War One that gave Europe Adolf
Hitler and the Nazi Party. World War Two would bequeath that legacy
to the Middle East.

Arab nationalists and Islamic fundamentalists—including the
groups associated with Al-Qaeda, Jemaah Islamiyyah and others—
often point to the Crusades as an example of western, Christian hostility against the Arab Middle East and against Islam in particular.
Normally, the historical precedent of Arab aggression towards Europe
beginning in the eighth century CE (and thus three hundred years
before the first Crusade) is often overlooked or ignored. The establishment of the Caliphate in what is now Spain and Portugal in the eighth
century would last for more than seven hundred years until the last
Islamic administration was expelled by King Ferdinand of Spain in

1492. Thus, the history of the Arab, Islamic Middle East and the history of Europe—western and eastern—is far more complex than jingoistic, shake-and-bake commentators and instant experts from either side would have us believe. It is a history of mutual hostility but also of cultural cross-fertilization. Islam gave the west much of ancient Greek science and philosophy, for instance. It gave the west algebra and alchemy: both words themselves borrowed from the original Arabic.

It is too easy to characterize Islam in terms of the Middle East alone. What is not normally considered is the fact that North Africa and the Levant are so close to Europe as to be neighbors, and that there is a long history of interactions between the two regions going back to before Solomon's Temple was built. There was Greek trade and cultural contacts in the Middle East long before Moses was born. Caesar's legions had traveled to Gaul and to Briton at the time of Jesus, and there is an old tradition of Joseph of Arimathea taking the child Jesus with him on a sales trip to what is now Cornwall in the British Isles. Whether true or not, the fact that such a tale could be believed is an indication of how deeply Europe and the Middle East were—and continue to be—involved with each other.

When it comes to Southeast Asia, however, the relationship changes considerably. The region was much too far away to be vulnerable to the type of military assault that typified the "missionary" activities of the Prophet and his descendants. Instead, the first contact many Asians had with Islam was in the form of trade.

While Muslim armies conquered much of India, having spread east from Babylon and Persia, by the time they reached China and Indochina their resources were spread very thin. It was far preferable to conquer by persuasion than force. And thus, gradually, areas like Sumatra and Java began to consider Islam as another belief system among the ones already in place, such as Hinduism and Buddhism as well as their indigenous religions. Islam became dominant in what is now Indonesia about the fifteenth century CE, at the time that the last Caliph on the throne of Grenada in Spain was being ousted by Ferdinand. Today, native Indonesian Islamic groups such as Jemaah Islamiyyah talk of establishing a Caliphate in the region that would extend from southern Thailand through all of Malaysia and Indonesia and including the southern Philippine island of Mindanao. For the

most part, however, this is a pipe dream of the fanatics for most of the
Islamic world in Southeast Asia has no interest in religious violence,
in establishing shariyah, or in creating a Muslim state. Indonesia, for
instance, is an example of a moderate, secular democracy that just
happens to be predominantly Muslim.

In 1945, however, the situation—both in the Middle East and in
Southeast Asia—was in danger of going another way altogether.

The development and growth of what is usually called Islamic
fundamentalism[143] in the west is believed to have begun with the writings of two important ideologues, the first being Muhamad ibn Abd-
al-Wahhab (1703–1792) and the second Sayyid Qutb (1906–1966).
Abd-al-Wahhab is usually identified with the movement that bears
his name, Wahhabism, which became the official sect of the rulers of
Saudi Arabia beginning in the nineteenth century and continuing to
the present day. Most Islamic scholars see Wahhabism as heretical for
it insists on a strict interpretation of the Qur'an and the Hadith that is
inconsistent with generations of Islamic thought and practice. However, due to the pre-eminence of the Saudi kingdom in the Islamic
world as the land of the two shrines of Mecca and Medina and to
the enormous financial contributions made by the Saudis to Islamic
communities all over the world, Wahhabism (sometimes characterized
as "petro-Islam") and its intolerant ideology have become familiar to
Muslims everywhere, if not actually embraced.

Often confused with Wahhabism is the movement most identified
with the Egyptian thinker Sayyid Qutb. Although not the founder of
the Muslim Brotherhood, Qutb was this radical group's most prominent and outspoken member, a writer with a keen sense of the differences between western and Islamic thought and practice. A visitor to

---

143 The author is aware of the inadequacy of this term. There is a tendency to
equate fundamentalism with fanaticism or even terrorism; however, most Christian
fundamentalists (who consider themselves fundamentalists) would strongly deny
that they are fanatics or terrorists, and with reason. Thus, the linkage between
Islamic "fundamentalism" and terrorism is contrived and counter-productive, even
as it serves as a kind of journalistic shorthand. Some authors have suggested the
use of "scripturalist" to replace "fundamentalist", but this author finds that term
awkward and equally misleading in this case.

the United States in the 1940s, he was appalled by what he considered the crass materialism and loose morals of the American population. He criticized jazz as so much "noise", looked in dismay upon the "indecent" awareness of the American woman of her physical beauty and natural powers of seduction, and the "bestiality" of the "Negro."

One may say that both Abd-al-Wahhab and Qutb perceived that the Islamic world had lost its dominance in the world and even within its own territories. The Ottoman Empire had conquered much of the Middle East and North Africa and the caliphates had all but disappeared from the face of the earth. In Wahhab's time, the enemy was the Turkish state; in Qutb's time, it was the secular Egyptian state and its collusion with western countries and its relationship with western ideas. If Islam was not the dominant ideology in the Arab world, then it was the fault of Muslims who had become degenerate, complacent, and spiritually polluted by foreign ideas and customs. In a sense, both Wahhab and Qutb were Islamic Jeremiahs, pointing to the decay of their civilization and assigning the blame to the lack of piety and faith among their own people. This is not a new phenomenon, and it has been repeated in many countries over many centuries, with Christian fundamentalist preacher Pat Robertson blaming Hurricane Katrina on God's wrath against homosexuals in New Orleans, and the earthquake in Haiti on voodoo practitioners and their "satanic pacts," as only two of many recent examples.

But before there was a Sayyid Qutb—executed by the Egyptian government in 1966 for treason—there was a Grand Mufti of Jerusalem, Haj Amin al-Husseini (1897?–1974).

Having begun his career working for the British during the first World War, al-Husseini became embroiled in the Arab nationalist cause during a riot in 1920 in Jerusalem against the Balfour Declaration: the statement by a British statesman guaranteeing a Jewish homeland in what was then known as Palestine. Once the Turks had been driven out of Arabia by the combined British and Arab armies, the Arab leaders found themselves at the mercy of agreements and treaties that had been negotiated between the European allies with virtually no Arab representation or input and certainly no agreement by the Arabs themselves. The Balfour Declaration was one; the Sykes-Picot agreement was another.

Signed in secret in 1916, this agreement between the British and the French governments—with Tsarist Russia as a minor partner—carved up the Ottoman Empire between the two European powers. This was in addition to promises made by the British government to the Arab leaders that they would have independence once the Ottoman Turks were defeated. There were, in fact, so many conflicting promises made that it is impossible to separate them and qualify their respective legal standings. In one case, the Arabs were promised the land of Palestine and what is now Syria and Jordan[144]; in another, the Balfour Declaration, the Zionists were assured of their right to a homeland in Palestine so long as the rights of the non-Jewish population were protected. These two, both issued by the British government, are obviously mutually-exclusive. With the addition of the secret Sykes-Picot agreement, the chaotic status of present-day Palestine and Israel was assured.

It was within this heavily-charged atmosphere that Arab nationalism was born. It had begun with the revolt of the Arab tribes against the Turks during the First World War and extended to their rejection of the European treaties and agreements that decided their boundaries, their independence (or lack of it), and their political futures. It was the last gasp of European colonialism in the Middle East: an attempt to create "independent" colonies that were nonetheless subservient to European influence. The British and the French were in the position of king-makers, with the rulers of the newly-created nations of Iraq, Syria, Jordan, Saudi Arabia, etc. as mere puppets of foreign powers, ruling at the pleasure of European politicians. This was nowhere more obvious than in the "British Mandate" of Palestine: the land promised by the British to European Jews as their homeland.

That there was anger directed towards the Europeans—and by extension, to the west in general—due to this perceived betrayal of the Arab revolt is beyond doubt. That this anger turned violent almost immediately was predictable. And the most tangible target of this violence was the proposed Jewish state in Palestine. In this way,

---

144 A letter dated October 24, 1915 (only declassified in 1964) by Sir Henry McMahon of the British Foreign Office to Sherif Hussein of the Arab revolt, guaranteeing that Palestine was within the boundaries of the independent Arab state that was being promised in return for the Sherif's assistance against the Turks.

Arab nationalism and anti-Zionism became closely identified in the minds of many people including the Arabs themselves. As the notorious forgery known as the *Protocols of the Learned Elders of Zion* came to be published in many languages at the end of World War One, this "proof" of an international conspiracy of Jews, bankers and Freemasons to control the world ironically found its best evidence in the Balfour Declaration and the British Mandate in Palestine. It was the same *Protocols* that would convince Hitler and other Nazis of a worldwide Jewish conspiracy. As Hitler came out of the trenches of World War One to find Germany decimated, "betrayed" by the bankers and the oligarchs, Haj Amin al-Husseini came out of the same war to find the Arab revolt similarly betrayed, and the lands of the Arabs similarly decimated, and by the same Allied governments of England and France.

It was probably inevitable then that these two men would meet. It would be 1941, and by that time Hitler had become the leader of the Greater German Reich, and al-Husseini would be the Grand Mufti of Jerusalem. They would join common cause against the Allies and most particularly against the Jews. This would eventually result in the establishment of another link in the Ratline, the Middle Eastern segment that saw the flight of SS and other Nazi specialists to Egypt, Syria, and Iraq where they would help prop up dictatorial regimes in the region by training the secret police in torture and interrogation techniques and in developing weapons of mass destruction such as ballistic missles and chemical and biological agents.

The relationship was curious, since the Nazis were true "anti-Semites": that is, to the Nazi purists, both Arabs and Jews were members of an inferior race, the Semites, and were slated for destruction. Iranians might possibly be spared, since they were not Semitic peoples and were, by definition, "Aryan". But, as in the case of the Croats who were most assuredly Slavs and not much higher than Semites in the opinion of the Nazi leadership, there was a pragmatic argument to be made in their favor. By enlisting the Arab world in the struggle against the British and the other Allies, Germany could be assured of a warm welcome in the region once they had been successful in crossing the Suez Canal and would not have to worry about subduing the local populations who would, presumably, welcome them with open arms.

Indeed, the Grand Mufti of Jerusalem raised an army to support the Nazi war effort. Called the SS-Handschar Division, it was composed entirely of Muslims—mainly, but not exclusively, Bosnian Muslims—who were violently opposed both to Communism and the Jews, and who conducted operations in Yugoslavia against the partisans and the Communists. Thus, the circle became complete: from a shared hatred of the Allies to a shared hatred of the Jews, to raising military forces to combat both the Jews and the Communists, both the Nazis and the Arab nationalists under al-Husseini saw their fortunes rise dramatically and then fall just as precipitously. With the end of the war, al-Husseini fled from Berlin and made his way to Egypt along his own Ratline.

He had a lot of company.

According to declassified CIA files[145], there were a number of high-ranking Nazi officers who made it to the Middle East and greater glory in various capacities, including the intelligence services. Among these were the following:

Franz Rademacher (1906–1973)—From 1937 to 1940, Rademacher served as a diplomat for the German Foreign Office in Montevideo, Uruguay until recalled by Ribbentrop to take charge of the Jewish question. It was Rademacher who came up with the Madagascar Plan, which was a proposed project to deport all of Europe's Jews to the island of Madagascar ... a plan which never materialized. Instead, he was responsible for the executions of Serbian Jews as well as the deportation of Jews from France and the Low Countries to concentration camps in Poland. After the war, he was arrested for war crimes against the Serbian Jews but escaped to Syria in 1952. At the time of the creation of the CIA document in 1958 that mentions his name, he was living in Damascus as a businessman. He eventually returned to Germany and died there in 1973.

Paul Leverkühn (1893–1960)—a lifelong diplomat, spy, and banker, Leverkühn was also a devoted Nazi who joined the Party

---

145   See the recently (2000, 2005) declassified CIA file EGMA-32934, dated March 19, 1958 regarding "UPSWING Near Eastern Connections". UPSWING was the code name given by the CIA to the West German intelligence service, the BND, which at the time was being run by former Nazi intelligence officer Reinhard Gehlen.

before the war began and who held various important posts in Germany during both World Wars. He had an extensive background running Abwehr operations in Turkey, and according to the CIA report referenced above he also ran a spy network after the war "based on Lebanon and extending into the Middle East." Leverkühn, for the benefit of those with a conspiratorial frame of mind, was also in attendance at the very first Bilderberger meeting in 1954, as president of the European Union.[146] It should be pointed out that this meeting took place four years *before* the CIA report was written claiming that Leverkühn was running agents in the Middle East.

Johannes von Leers (1902–1965)—A nasty piece of work, von Leers was a rabid and unrepentant Nazi starting with his involvement in the Freikorps of post-World War One Germany and extending to his membership in the Nazi Party beginning in 1929. He was a propagandist who worked for Goebbels, and who eventually found himself working for Perón in Argentina before finally getting a job in Egypt with the Nasser regime. He had a proficiency in five languages, and could speak and write both Hebrew and Japanese fluently. His seminal tract—"Judaism and Islam as Opposites"—provided the theoretical framework for a union between the Nazis and their Muslim counterparts in anti-Semitism:

> As a religion, Islam indeed performed an eternal service to the world: it prevented the threatened conquest of Arabia by the Jews and vanquished the horrible teaching of Jehovah by a pure religion, which at that time opened the way to a higher culture for numerous peoples ...[147]

He fled Germany for Italy and in 1950 went to Argentina where he worked for the pro-Nazi newspaper *Der Weg*. After a few years in

---

146 It should be noted that the first Bilderberger meeting was organized by Prince Bernhard of the Netherlands who (as we have seen) has been accused of harboring Nazi sympathies. Incidentally, his brother was actually an officer with the Wehrmacht during the war.

147 "Judentum und Islam als Gegensätze", *Die Judenfrage*, Vol. 6, No. 24 (15 December 1942), p. 278, quoted and paraphrased by Jeffrey Herf, *The Jewish Enemy*, p.181.

Argentina, he went instead to Egypt circa 1954. A close associate of the Grand Mufti, al-Husseini, von Leers eventually converted to Islam and took the name Omar Amin. According to the CIA report, he worked as a translator and language instructor for the Egyptian Information Department. He died in Cairo—successfully fighting extradition for war crimes—in 1965.

ONE OF THE MAJOR WAR CRIMINALS to have made the Middle East a link in his own escape was SS-Standartenführer Walter Rauff. We encountered Rauff earlier as the inventor of the mobile gas vans that were used to exterminate thousands of Jews in Poland and elsewhere during the war. Although Rauff eventually wound up in Chile, where he died peacefully after having successfully fought every extradition attempt, his first port of call after the war was Syria.

Rauff already had experience in the Arab world. During the war, he made a trip to Nazi-occupied Tunisia where he oversaw the liquidation of more than 2,000 of that country's Jewish population. He then flew to Egypt to negotiate the annihilation of Cairo's Jewish population as well as Palestine's Jewish community—known as the Yishuv—with Field Marshall Erwin Rommel who opposed the project. The plan was to take effect once the Nazis had seized the Suez Canal and occupied Palestine, and seems to have been the result of a deal reached between the Mufti al-Husseini and Hitler. It is important to point out that—just as we saw with regard to the Gestapo in Java—the Nazis were intent on exterminating the Jews wherever in the world they could be found. This extended to the Jews of North Africa and Palestine as well as to the Jews of Southeast Asia. Holocaust deniers who claim that the concentration camps were not intended to kill Jews and that the Jews who died there were victims of illness, etc. have yet to respond to the mountain of documentation detailing the earnest efforts of SS commanders to exterminate the Jews of other countries and even of other *continents*. They have also not responded to the fact of Rauff's mobile gas vans and the only possible purpose they served: mass murder.

In the last years of the war, Rauff was stationed in Northern Italy where he was in charge of Gestapo and SD operations in Turin, Genoa and Milan. He managed to escape the Rimini prisoner of war camp in

December of 1946, and wound up in Damascus working for Captain Akram Tabara (alias Dr John Homsi) of the Syrian intelligence service. He worked in that capacity in Syria during the 1948 Arab-Israeli war, and in 1949 he was hired as an "advisor" to newly-elected Syrian President Husni Za'im, but lost his job when a coup against Za'im succeeded a few months later.

Oddly, newly-declassified CIA documents show another side of Rauff (and of the Ratline). It seems that while Rauff was employed by the Syrians he was also working for British intelligence. He was sending copies of sensitive Syrian intel reports and organization charts to MI6 at the same time he was spying on Jews for the Syrians. To make matters even more complicated, Rauff was also employed by a mysterious agent known as Ted Cross (alias David Magen) who was an officer of Israeli intelligence! Cross wanted to use Rauff to penetrate Egyptian intelligence circles, essentially following the CIA's use of former Nazis to spy on the Soviets. That Rauff did work for Cross and thus for the Israelis at the same time he was working for the Syrians and the British, seems beyond doubt, and is partly based on a 1993 interview[148] with a branch director for the Israeli Foreign Ministry's Political Department, Shalhevet Freier, who admitted that he did, indeed, hire Walter Rauff to spy on Syrian military and intelligence operations.

When Rauff had to leave Syria in a hurry after the coup that ousted Za'im, he wound up first in Lebanon and then in Italy where he was sheltered by the Church, specifically Bishop Hudal according to CIA reports[149] and by the Archbishop of Milan Ildefonso Schuster,[150] and by the Israelis who helped him get the necessary travel documents for South America as well.

This was not the only instance of a known war criminal under protection of both American intelligence and the Israelis, however.

---

148 The interview was conducted by journalist Shlomo Nakdimon and published in *Yedioth Ahronoth.* See also Shraga Elam and Dennis Whitehead, "In the service of the Jewish state," in *Haaretz,* March 31, 2007.

149 See the CIA Name File for Walter Rauff, released by the Interagency Working Group (IWG), Record Group 263, located in RC Box #42, RC Location 230/902/64/7 at the National Archives, Washington DC.

150 Gerald Steinacher, *Nazis on the Run*, p. 193.

In 1982, at a time when all hell was about to break loose concerning Klaus Barbie and the Ratline, a seventy-two-year old man died of natural causes in a hospital in Sacramento, California. He had just surrendered his US citizenship the year before, over revelations of his role in the Holocaust. He appeared to be a businessman with excellent credentials in Europe and Latin America. He was a friend of American politicians and business tycoons, and one of the companies he worked for—Trans-International Computer Investment Corporation—was said to have done work for the Pentagon.

But Baron Otto von Bolschwing had a past. He had been an SS officer, and was the man who encouraged a young Adolf Eichmann to become an expert in the "Jewish problem." He had enriched himself with money and other valuables confiscated from the Jews, according to systems he himself had developed.

He joined the Nazi Party in 1932 and almost immediately became an intelligence operative for the Third Reich. He served as a spy in Jerusalem until 1939, posing as a businessman and cultivating excellent contacts among both Arabs and Jews. One of those contacts was Fieval Polkes, a commander of the Haganah: the Jewish defense organization in the British Mandate of Palestine. Von Bolschwing arranged meetings between Eichmann and Polkes, as it was believed that there were some common issues. The Nazis wanted the Jews out of Europe, and the Jews wanted the British out of Palestine. Polkes then agreed to provide the SS with intelligence on the British situation in Palestine in return for money as well as cooperation in encouraging as many young Jewish men and women as possible to emigrate to Palestine.[151]

Von Bolschwing was busy with other matters as well, such as his involvement with the Romanian Iron Guard: the pro-Nazi, anti-Semitic paramilitary organization that was responsible for its own atrocities during the war. But it was the post-war period that was kindest to the Baron, for he almost immediately—in the spring of 1945— began working for the CIC in Salzburg. As the Cold War intensified, former SS-Hauptsturmführer von Bolschwing found himself working

---

151 For more details on the relationship between Von Bolschwing and Eichmann, see Christopher Simpson, *Blowback: America's Recruitment of Nazis and Its Effects on the Cold War*, New York: Weidenfeld & Nicolson, 1988, p. 252–260

first for the Gehlen Organization and then directly for the CIA, and it was the CIA that helped him emigrate to the United States in 1954 by disguising his Nazi past and his membership in the SS. Once in the US, he became involved in various business enterprises—including one with the Trans-International Computer Investment Corporation, which ended in a financial scandal in 1971.

There is no question about von Bolschwing's role in developing the mechanisms by which the Jews lost first their property and then their lives. He was a dedicated anti-Semite and a committed Nazi; but he was cultivated and protected by American intelligence as one of its soldiers in the fight against Soviet Communism. Even his role as go-between for Adolf Eichmann and the Haganah raises many more questions than answers, but it is an educational and cautionary tale.

This is a revealing example of how realpolitik created the Ratline. If even the *Israelis* could knowingly and willingly employ a mass murderer like Walter Rauff who was responsible for the extermination of upwards of two hundred thousand Jews or more, or negotiate with a von Bolschwing or an Eichmann, then there can be no wondering or surprise at the role of American and British intelligence—among others—in collaborating in the escape of men like Barbie, Mengele, Priebke, Eichmann, Stangl and so many, many others. If even *Israel* could sign a secret pact with a devil like Walter Rauff, should anyone be surprised if one of the Allied governments (having proved themselves to be hardly Jewish sympathizers or supporters) had arranged the escape of, say, Martin Bormann, equally as secretly, on pragmatic—if not entirely cynical—grounds?

Or concealed—or even enabled—the escape of Adolf Hitler?

IN ADDITION TO RAUFF IN SYRIA, there were many other Nazis—some scientists, some SS-men with specialties in interrogation and torture—who wound up in Egypt. There were some eighty of these specialists working for the Egyptian Ministry of War in the late 1940s, busy developing the Egyptian war machine in order to prepare for the conflict with Israel.[152] In some cases, these were rocket scientists

---

152   Ibid., p. 263.

busy developing modifications of the V-2, designed to be used against Israel.[153]

The flight of Nazis to the Middle East should be seen in the context of the times. Israel had been officially created on May 14, 1948 and immediately war was declared on the new nation by all of its Arab neighbors. In 1948, the Ratline was still very much in operation and Nazis were still escaping to South America and elsewhere from safe houses—sometimes called "rat houses"—in Austria and Italy. The war with Israel provided excellent opportunities for Nazi military and intelligence specialists who could combine their hatred of Jews with their training of an enthusiastic population equally determined to destroy their common enemy. It was less of an escape from justice than it was a lateral move; a simple relocation from Europe to North Africa and the Middle East, but with the same basic job description. For these men in particular, the war had not ended in April or May of 1945 but had simply moved a few miles south and, if anything, had become more focused. The anti-Semitic project of the Nazi Party was still in full swing; had the Arab nations been successful in their destruction of the State of Israel, the surviving SS officers would have counted themselves redeemed. While Hitler's grand plan called for *lebensraum* and the ensuing subjugation of Eastern as well as Western Europe to the forces of the Third Reich, the Final Solution was still an important (if irrational and mystically-grounded) goal. The Arab nations could not get Germany's territories back or restore the Reich; indeed, they had no interest in doing so. But they could carry on the most cherished goal of the Nazis and most especially of the SS: the utter annihilation of the race they deemed to be humanity's greatest enemy.

While the governments of Latin America were more interested in incorporating the Nazis into their anti-Communist programs, the Arab nations saw the Nazis in a different light. The Nazis and the Catholic Church cooperated because their common, post-war enemy was the Soviet Union and her satellites; the Nazis and the Arabs cooperated because they were ideologically similar on a much deeper level.

---

153 This point is made in the Frederick Forsyth novel (and later movie) *The Odessa File*, and is based on documented evidence.

Communism knows no race or national boundary; it is an international movement of class against class, of workers against the bosses regardless of ethnicity or national origin. It is purely political, economic, materialistic and atheistic. Anti-Semitism, however, is based on the irrational, the unscientific, the mystical. It is a war of race against race. Of blood against blood. The Nazis extended that conflict to other races: the Slavs, the Africans, the Asians, the Native American populations. All were inferior to the Aryan, represented by the Greater German Reich as well as by Scandinavia and, to a certain extent, Great Britain. Nazism is not international, it is not materialistic in the same way that Communism and Capitalism are materialistic. And it is definitely not atheistic.

For all these reasons and more, the Nazis could make common cause with the Arabs who were largely Muslim and who had at least a theoretical basis for anti-Semitism. Citing a few inflammatory verses from the Qur'an concerning the Jews, a new generation of Wahhabis and their fellow travelers—inspired by the Grand Mufti himself, al-Husseini—could see themselves fighting alongside the most famous anti-Semites in the world, men motivated by the same mystical impulses as they were; men who identified their movement with something larger, more transcendent, than the dictatorship of the proletariat or a workers' paradise. The Nazis were believers, and while their belief system did not match those of their Muslim collaborators, there were similarities.

The Muslims believe in submission to God; the word "Islam" means "submission." The Nazis believed in the Führer Principle: complete obedience to the Führer and to his representatives. The Nazis never placed the rights of the individual above that of the community, and certainly not above that of the Führer, God's representative on earth. Both the Muslims and the Nazis yearned for the past: the Muslims, for the glories of the Caliphates that had ruled the Middle East, India and even parts of Europe for centuries; the Nazis, for a glorious past in the distant mists of ancient history, when Teutons fought the armies of the Caesar and even further back, when the pagan gods were still worshipped with fire and sword. The Nazis saw the Jews as both an ancient enemy and a current one; so did the Arabs, and for almost the same reasons. To both, the Jews were an alien race bent on world domination. To the Nazis, the Jews represented the faith of a demonic god who masqueraded as the Creator of the universe. More than this, their very blood was a poison. It was not simply a matter of a belief system that was wrong or hateful in some way: it was the very existence of Jewish blood, of Jewish genetics, that threatened the spiritual as well as the physical life of the world. A Jew could conceivably convert to Islam and be spared; but a Jew could not convert to Aryanism and be spared by the Reich.

So men like Walter Rauff and SS-Haupsturmführer Alois Brunner (1912–1996?) could find sanctuary in the Middle East. Brunner had been in charge of mass deportations of Jews in various European countries as the personal emissary of Adolf Eichmann. After the war, Brunner claimed that he worked for awhile for the US military (possibly with the Gehlen Organization, the espionage facility created by the CIA out of former Nazis to spy on the Soviet Union) and then fled first to Rome, using the same Catholic Church connections as his colleagues, and then to Egypt where he worked as an arms dealer and finally to Syria where he found employment with the regime as an interrogation (i.e., torture) expert. Brunner was so confident in his status that he gave interviews to magazines and newspapers from his home in Damascus as late as 1985[154] and 1987[155]. The fact that the various Syrian regimes from 1954 to the present—including the Assad regimes—would protect him for so long is an indication that he had proved his usefulness in some way that permitted him to outlast the various political storms that beset that country over the last fifty years. This was either due to his particular expertise in various military and intelligence areas, his connections with the worldwide Nazi network, or possibly also to an infusion of Nazi gold to bribe his way into security. Unfortunately, the German government has destroyed its files on Alois Brunner and unless something surfaces from the current political turmoil in Syria (or from US intelligence files, particularly those of Allen Dulles and the OSS) we may never know the truth.

---

154 To the German magazine *Bunte*, where he complained that he wished he had killed more Jews. See also "In Syria, a Long-Hunted Nazi Talks," in the *New York Times*, November 29, 1985.

155 To the *Chicago Sun Times*, where he insisted he would "do it all again."

The *entire* history of Nazi-Arab collusion is too long and complex to go into detail here. We have seen the basic elements, however, and understand that there was a natural alliance between the Nazis and the Arab nationalists both during and for many years after the war. This alliance is still nurtured. Hitler's autobiography and political manifesto, *Mein Kampf,* is always in Arabic translation and easily available everywhere in the Arab world, as is the *Protocols of the Learned Elders of Zion* (a notorious hoax which is nonetheless accepted as fact by many readers). There are close connections between neo-Nazi movements in Europe—particularly in Austria—and terrorist groups such as Al-Qaeda. While these groups could conceivably turn on each other eventually, for now the immediate threat is the existence of the state of Israel and the perceived "global Jewish conspiracy." This is a theme that has been picked up as far away from the battlegrounds of World War Two as present-day Southeast Asia

WHEN THE ASIAN ECONOMIC CRISIS occurred in 1997—the crash of Asian currencies that contributed to the fall of Indonesia's dictator Soeharto in 1998 during the Reformasi movement—Malaysia's then Prime Minister, Mahathir Muhammad, blamed it on George Soros and a cabal of international Jewish bankers considered to be partners in a conspiracy to destroy the developing economies of Southeast Asia. That a national leader and Muslim statesman in 1997 could make such a claim demonstrates that the theory of "a global Jewish conspiracy" is still very much with us, regardless of how often that theory is exploded by reference to the facts. Later, Indonesia's Soeharto would make the same claim when asked about his fall from power in 1998.

This is a charge that sits well with the more radical Muslims of Southeast Asia who, like their Arab counterparts, seek a scapegoat to blame for their lack of power and economic parity with the west. However, Malaysia could hardly be considered an economic backwater and young Malaysian Muslims have opportunities and access to power and resources that far exceed those of their co-religionists in the Arab world. Indeed, Mahathir had called for Malaysia to become a completely developed nation by the year 2020, putting it on par with its neighbor, Singapore. He had invested billions of dollars in major infrastructure projects, such as the new Kuala Lumpur International Airport, the Kuala Lumpur City Center (with the tallest buildings in the world at that time), and the Cyberjaya and Putrajaya projects which promised a complete high-speed fiber-optic network in the capital city. Malaysia was hardly a "third world" country in 1997, yet Mahathir felt justified in blaming the crash of his country's currency on the Jews. Indonesia, while not as economically advanced as Malaysia at the time was still in a relative position of strength when the crisis began with a large trade surplus. Unfortunately this led to over-borrowing by Indonesian corporations in US dollars and as the Indonesian currency slid the debt position of these corporations rose considerably, leaving Indonesia to suffer as the rupiah lost more than 80% of its value (compared with the Malaysian ringgit which lost 39% of its value). This put Soeharto's thirty-year regime in danger. People took to the streets in revolt against the rising prices, the corruption and impotent yet dictatorial powers of their government. The International Monetary Fund made humiliating demands on Indonesia in return for aid in propping up the economy, and this (among many other issues) inspired the Reform movement that toppled Soeharto and ushered in an era of democracy, pluralism, and free elections. Yet, Soeharto could still blame an international Jewish conspiracy for his country's problems.

We have seen that there is a precedent for this reaction in Southeast Asia. The existence of a Nazi Party in Indonesia and the collusion of rebel leaders like future Indonesian president Sukarno with the Japanese invaders and their German partners would seem to indicate that there was already a degree of anti-Semitism in that country. This would be a mistake, however. The Nazi Party recruited its members from among the European expatriate community and not from the local Indonesians themselves. Sukarno is acknowledged to have cooperated with the Japanese for purely pragmatic reasons: they would help him ensure that the Dutch would finally lose their Indonesian colony after 350 years of dominance in the region. Sukarno made several speeches during the war that praised Japan and the Axis powers, but there is no evidence to show that he harbored genuine pro-Nazi or anti-Semitic sentiments.

In recent years, however, attempts have been made to show parallels between Sukarno and Hitler. Both were dictators; both had delivered their respective countries from oppressive circumstances and both had challenged the European powers of Great Britain and the Netherlands, as well as of the United States. Both were skillful orators who understood the power of the spoken word and the theatrical gesture. Both saw the Japanese as their allies. And neither man was afraid to stand up to the entire world in order to raise his country's profile on the global stage.

In 1945, with the surrender of the Japanese forces in the region, the opportunity came for Sukarno to force the hand of the Dutch. The Japanese had promised Indonesia its independence, and declared it on their way out of the country. Sukarno raised his forces to begin the struggle against the Dutch who were coming back to reclaim their "territory." Thus would begin years of armed struggle until finally Indonesia was recognized by the world as an independent country.

During that immediate post-war period, however, Sukarno had problems not only with the Dutch but with violent political parties in Sumatra and Java that had a different agenda. While Sukarno saw Indonesia as a secular state—and was accused of flirting with Communism as well—there were those in his country who wanted to create an Islamic government. This tension between secular and sacred agendas continues to this day and there will always be those in Indonesia who desire the creation of a *khalifa* or Caliphate in the region. In some cases—such as the Jemaah Islamiyyah organization of fundamentalist firebrand Abu Bakr Ba'ashir—this Islamic struggle takes on pronounced anti-Semitic contours.

As in the Arab world, *Mein Kampf* is available in Indonesia in local translation as well as a number of conspiracy-oriented books that emphasize the idea of a global Jewish conspiracy. Many of these books would be familiar to anyone who had read similar conspiracy literature in the United States, or in the Middle East. Henry Ford's *International Jew* is also readily available (usually paired with an Indonesian language translation of *The Protocols of the Learned Elders of Zion*), and the prestige associated with the name of Ford lends additional credibility to the famous American inventor's anti-Semitic ravings.

But in 1954, the year the mysterious Georg Anton Pöch and his equally enigmatic wife Hella arrived in Indonesia, the country was still in the grip of sectarian struggles, political intrigues, violent confrontations, and the constantly looming threat of either a Communist or an Islamicist takeover. Of one thing the couple could be sure, however: there were virtually no Jews at all in Indonesia. More than Argentina—which had a sizeable Jewish population—or any other country in the western hemisphere, for a Nazi war criminal in 1954, Indonesia could be considered one of the safest places on earth.

CHAPTER EIGHT

FLIGHT

Argentina is still the place to look for—I don't discount a
monastery in Tibet.[156]

For more than two decades after the end of World War Two, persistent rumors that Hitler was still alive and had escaped Germany were taken seriously by the world's intelligence services. Declassified documents reveal that there was no consensus among the Allies as to the fate of the century's most infamous dictator, even after Hugh Trevor-Roper's report and insistence that the Führer died an ignominious death in Berlin.[157] Stalin consistently declared his belief that Hitler was still alive, and possibly being harbored by the Allies to use as some kind of weapon against the Soviet Union. Historians usually take Stalin's statements to be a propaganda move, an attempt to discredit the capitalists in the eyes of the world or to make their intelligence services waste valuable time and resources on a wild goose chase; but as we have seen there is no forensic evidence at all to prove that Hitler died in the bunker and the Nazi prisoners in Russia gave so many conflicting stories about the "last days" of Hitler that it was impossible to take any one of them seriously. Thus, it is entirely possible that Stalin was sincere in his belief that Hitler survived or could have survived. He was sincere enough to have convinced General (and later U.S. President) Eisenhower of the possibility.[158]

---

156 FBI BUfile 65-53615-4, letter dated October 28, 1945 from unidentified source.

157 The fact that the Allies took seriously reports of Hitler sightings in South America is an indication as to the degree of skepticism with which they greeted the Trevor-Roper analysis.

158 See, for instance, the article by Henry Wales, "Hitler's Fate Still Mystery to Army Says Ike's Aid," n.p., September 9, 1945 and contained within the declassified FBI file on Hitler.

Stalin suggested that Hitler had either wound up in Spain or in Argentina, or possibly had gone to Argentina from Spain. As we have seen, so many Nazis were using that particular escape route as to make Stalin's theory entirely plausible on its face. That Stalin would have known about—or suspected—the Ratline established by Carlos Fuldner in Spain, or had somehow divined that the Nazis would make use of their U-boat facilities, the Etappendienst, for this purpose indicates that at least Soviet intelligence was onto the Nazi escape plans.

Stalin also suggested that the Allies had Hitler in their possession and that they were waiting to use him to rally Germany against the Soviet Union. Again, as we have seen, the Allies most assuredly *did* have numerous Nazis on their payroll or kept "on ice" in Europe, the Middle East and Latin America so as to make that theory equally plausible. The fact that the American FBI, the CIC, the OSS and eventually the CIA would all take these rumors and scenarios seriously indicates that no one was especially secure in the Trevor-Roper fiction.[159] Of course, there was no *corpus delecti* and that contributed to everyone's unease about the fate of Hitler. This is especially so due to the inescapable fact that the entire Goebbels family was found with relative ease in the craters outside the Berlin bunker. Why, then, did the bodies of Adolf Hitler and Eva Braun escape discovery?

A review of declassified FBI files on Hitler's escape reveal some extremely detailed reports of Führer sightings in Latin America, from Colombia to Argentina. Some are rather convincing, while others seem fanciful. We should remember that sightings of Elvis Presley are also plentiful, and that people report the oddest things to the authorities ... and to the tabloid press. However, a look at some of these

---

159   See as evidence an undated radiogram contained in the declassified FBI file on Hitler, page 343, from the FBI to the US Embassy in Buenos Aires, which reads "Bureau intensely interested in all rumors concerning whereabouts of Hitler, particularly rumors he and Eva Braun may be in Argentina. Advise daily by radiogram for the present results of all investigation based on rumors and leads on whereabouts Hitler." This indicates a very high level of interest by Hoover in the possibility of a Hitler escape. This was followed by a flurry of reports to Hoover on the famous landing of German U-Boat U-530 in Argentina and rumors that several persons were off-loaded by the submarine before it was surrendered to the authorities.

sightings will prove educational, particularly as American intelligence agents as well as the mainstream media at the time took some of them seriously.

THE RUMOR THAT HITLER HAD NOT DIED in the bunker began with a remark made by Stalin on May 26, 1945 in a meeting with Averell Harriman, Russian language interpreter Charles Bohlen and U.S. presidential advisor Harry Hopkins at the Kremlin. During this meeting, Stalin stated that he believed Hitler was still alive and had escaped Berlin entirely and was living "somewhere in the West." The official CIA version of this story[160] claims that it was the beginning of a Soviet disinformation campaign, but the CIA has no proof of this.

At the Potsdam Conference—attended by Churchill, Stalin and Truman on July 18, 1945—Stalin once again made the statement that Hitler was still alive and probably in Spain or Argentina. This insistence by Stalin on Hitler's fate was being made at the same time that SMERSH was busy burying and digging up what they believed was Hitler's corpse no less than four times, and during which Soviet intelligence had numerous Nazis in custody whom they were subjecting to merciless torture and "enhanced interrogation" techniques to determine Hitler's whereabouts.

As part of the FBI file on Hitler, there are numerous newspaper clippings (most sadly undated and without further publication data) which demonstrate the depth of public skepticism concerning reports of Hitler's death in the bunker. They often contain interesting information on matters tangential to Hitler's fate and are worth considering here.

One such article, entitled "Hitler Mystery Deepens as Other Nazi Leaders Make Pleas to Live" by John F. Sembower dates from a time before the Nuremberg trials had begun in November, 1945. It contains the prophetic sentence:

---

160   Benjamin Fischer, CIA History Staff, "Hitler, Stalin and 'Operation Myth'", n.d., n.p. Benjamin B. Fischer—for decades a respected intelligence analyst with CIA—was dismissed from CIA in connection with the Aldrich Ames affair under circumstances that are still unclear.

... the chances are that for years to come there will be persons all over the world who will report that they saw him alive after the fall of Berlin, that he got away and lived out his natural life.

Concerning the burning of Hitler's body, Sembower goes on to write:

> Many of the world's greatest criminologists are on the hunt. They doubt the story of Hitler's chauffeur who contends that he burned the bodies of Hitler and his mistress Eva Braun, with a can of gasoline in a shallow trench outside the chancellery. ... Ninety-two charred and broken bodies were removed from a mass grave near Hitler's bunker ... They were subjected to much worse destruction than burning with gasoline, yet the remains were sufficiently identifiable to convince experts that none were those of Hitler and Eva Braun.

Speculating as to how Hitler may have escaped, Sembower quotes an un-named "Japanese navy staff officer" who:

> ... told details of a plan to evacuate Hitler and Eva Braun to Japan after the fall of Germany, and that a large Japanese submarine embarked on the enterprise.
>
> Nothing further was heard of the submarine, according to the Jap. [sic] At the same time, some of the huge German U-boats are still unaccounted for.

> ... That there may have been considerable submarine traffic between Germany and Japan was indicated by the interception last July of a Nazi U-boat Japan-bound with a $5,000,000 cache of mercury and other valuables sorely needed by the Japs for a last-ditch stand.[161]

---

161   John F. Sembower, "Hitler Mystery Deepens as Other Nazi Leaders Make Pleas to Live," n.d., n.p., but published before November, 1945. Accessed in the declassified FBI file on Adolf Hitler.

Thus, we have all the elements here that we have been researching since the book began. We have rumors of Hitler's disappearance and survival elsewhere in the world; the lack of credibility afforded stories of the cremation of Hitler's body; and the connection with U-boat traffic to Japan. In fact, Sembower also mentions the rumor "... to the effect that the Russians have Bormann in secret custody, and that they know the manner of Hitler's death, perhaps even possessing his corpse."[162]

Thus, John Sembower presents in mid-1945 the entire range of the theories as to Hitler's disappearance that have persisted—as he predicted—to this day. He even goes on to state that the US Army is "carefully checking the approximately three thousand Germans gathered in the remote mountain district of Ashinoyou [sic], whose tall peaks resemble those of Hitler's beloved Bavaria." Ashinoyu is in Japan, south of Tokyo and to the west of Yokohama, and if this story is true then the U.S. military was still looking for Hitler months after April 30, 1945 and, in fact, after August 28, 1945, which is the day the American occupation began. There was thus an impression that Hitler could have escaped—not to Argentina—but as far away as Japan. This was considered credible enough to enlist U.S. Army intelligence personnel in occupied Japan on a search through the local German population.

If this was credible then how much more so is Hitler's possible escape to an even more likely and much safer Asian locale?

Item: October 27, 1945. Otto Abetz, the Third Reich's ambassador to the Vichy government of Occupied France, told an interviewer for the French newspaper, *France-Soir,* that Adolf Hitler "is certainly not dead."

Item: October 17, 1955. Ten years after the above article appeared. A CIA report[163] marked "Secret" and not declassified until after the Nazi War Crimes Disclosure Act was signed into law by President Bill Clinton, begins:

---

162 Sembower, op. cit.
163 Dispatch No. [A]—472, dated 17 October 1955 to Chief, WH from an unnamed author at CIA, Reference [A] -2592, 3 October 1955.

With reference to the information submitted by Station
[CIA/LA] concerning the alleged report that Adolf HITLER
is still alive, the files of the [CIA/LA] contain similar information received from the same source, who resides in [redacted].

The memorandum goes on to give information received from a
February, 1954 memo detailing a conversation between a CIA agent
and one Phillip Citroen (a co-owner of the *Maracaibo Times* newspaper of Venezuela) that he met someone who resembled Hitler in
Tunja, Colombia (a region known to be heavily populated by former Nazis, according to the source). What is interesting in the present
context is the fact, noted in the CIA report, that Phillip Citroen "is
reported to be employed with a Dutch steamship company." He and
his brother Francois Citroen went into partnership with one Alexander van Dobben "the Dutch Consul in Maracaibo" to establish the
Maracaibo Times. Parts of this file are still classified to this day, marked
"Access Restricted" with no explanation given.

Another report—dated fifteen days *earlier*—gives additional information concerning Phillip Citroen. Evidently, Citroen was a "former
German SS trooper" who claimed to an unidentified friend that Hitler
was still alive and that he, Citroen, visited him about once a month
in Tunja, Colombia while Citroen was employed by the Royal Dutch
Shipping Company. Citroen went on to tell his friend that Hitler had
left Colombia "around January 1955" for Argentina.

More strikingly, a photograph was attached to this file showing
Citroen sitting next to a man who very closely resembles Hitler. The
legend on the back of the photo states "Adolf Schüttelmayer, Colum-
bia, Tunja, America del Sur 1954". It is to be noted immediately that
there is a misspelling of the word "Colombia" which may be due
to a foreigner's error, but if Citroen was traveling regularly between
Colombia and Venezuela it is unlikely that he would have made this
simple mistake. The handwriting, however, is unmistakably that of a
European or someone trained in European penmanship.

The cover page to this report—signed off by a number of unidentified CIA employees—bears a handwritten notation on the lower
right hand corner: "Have fun."

To which someone added the note: "May not be so funny."

An SS-man with Dutch connections in South America. A CIA report that is still redacted and pages of which are still restricted. A report to the CIA dated February, 1954 (which we still have not seen) on Hitler's presence in Colombia. His subsequent disappearance from that country at the same time that Georg Anton Pöch arrives in Jakarta, Indonesia, the former Dutch colony.

No, indeed. This "may not be so funny" at all.

On November 4, 1955, CIA employee J.C. King wrote:

> ... it is felt that enormous efforts could be expended on this matter with remote possibilities of establishing anything concrete. Therefore, we suggest that this matter be dropped.[164]

And so it was.

THE FEDERAL BUREAU OF INVESTIGATION, however, continued following up Hitler sightings for decades after the CIA seemed to have lost interest. The Bureau was nominally in charge of espionage and intelligence matters in Latin America, at least until the creation of the CIA in 1947 when a turf war began between Hoover and CIA over who would control intelligence gathering in the western hemisphere. As we know, the CIA eventually won, but that did not stop Hoover or the FBI from keeping files on Hitler sightings in South America and elsewhere for decades longer.

One of the earliest sightings was reported to Hoover on November 13, 1945 and reflects an OSS report that was dated a month earlier and which wound up on Hoover's desk. The FBI report is in the form of a letter to a member of the US Embassy in Buenos Aires, Argentina (whose name is still redacted, even after 65 years) and is entitled "Hitler Hideout in Argentina." The information it contains is solid where the pro-Nazi sentiments of a certain area of Argentina are concerned, and is very revealing of the type of environment that the Nazis could expect to find there.

---

164 Memo dated November 4, 1955 from J.C. King to an unidentified CIA employee, Dispatch No. [A]-1105.

IT CONCERNS A MRS. EICHORN who at the time ran a spa in the town of La Falda, Argentina. Eichorn claimed that she heavily supported— financially—the Nazi Party and in particular the propaganda efforts of Goebbels. She further claimed that she had made the necessary preparations to host the Führer should he be so kind as to come to Argentina. She claimed that when she and her family used to visit Germany, that they stayed with Hitler.[165]

At first glance, this may appear to be the ravings of a dotty old lady in some remote South American village. However, news reports of the time reported that La Falda, Argentina in particular was a major center of pro-Nazi sentiment and pro-Nazi activity before, during and after the war. According to an article by the respected journalist Johannes Steel,[166] and included in the FBI dossier on Hitler, the Argentine chief of the German Labor Front "is now believed to be in Calamuchita in Cordoba province. This town and La Falda are considered important centers of clandestine Nazi cells."

He goes on to write that "[German Labor Front chief] Schroeder is reported to have arrived in Argentina with full instructions to prepare hiding places for other Nazis in that country. The vast territories of Entre Rios, Chaco and Misiones are said to be ideal for harboring sought-for Nazis and to be, actually, the headquarters of clandestine Nazi organizations." He writes that one of the financiers of this operation is none other than Admiral Karl Dönitz, along with Nazi Finance Minister Count Lutz Schwerin von Krosigk and the notorious Robert Ley, head of the German Labor Front and Schroeder's boss, who committed suicide rather than face the Nuremberg tribunals.

More recent research has revealed that the "spa" mentioned in the FBI/OSS report was in reality a famous hotel and resort that had been visited—among others—by Albert Einstein in 1925. Known as the Eden Hotel, it had been in operation since 1897 and was bought by Walter and Ida Eichorn in 1912. The Eichorns were members of the Nazi Party and did, in fact, raise considerable funds for the Party over the years. According to one source, the amount raised was in excess

---

165   FBI BUFile 65-53615-48.
166   Johannes Steel, "The Nazis Are Winning in the Argentine," *Facts* magazine, n.d. but sometime in 1945. Included in BUFile 65-53615-52, p. 30–35

of thirty million Reichsmarks in 1944. There is documentation to prove that Hitler was personally acquainted with the Eichorn couple, including letters to and from the Führer praising their devotion to the Party. Indeed, Hitler himself received the Eichorns at the Reichs Chancellery on May 15, 1935, at which time it is believed that the couple offered their resort to the Führer as a sanctuary whenever he needed it. This offer of a refuge to the leader of the Third Reich is what finally appeared in the OSS report mentioned above and gave Hoover enough cause for concern that he forwarded the information to an embassy official in Buenos Aires.

The town of La Falda grew up around the famous resort, which was decorated in a European style and surrounded by Bavarian-style chalets that catered to a growing German population and which had a room especially reserved for Hitler. The hotel had its own movie theater, a dining room that could seat 250, and a radio tower for communicating directly with Germany.

There is a persistent rumor that Hitler himself visited the Eden Hotel after the war and there are two photographs at the hotel that seem to show a blurred image of the Führer. Former employees of the hotel insist that they saw and in some cases served Hitler there after the war. The rumors were so persistent that Ernesto Guevara Lynch—the father of Che Guevara—used to spy on the Eichorns during the war. As if to prove these rumors had some foundation, more than one thousand Germans in the area around La Falda filed for Argentine citizenship in the final months of the war: that is, before April 1945.

After the war, the Japanese ambassador would be interned at the Eden Hotel for months, along with his entire diplomatic corps. Ownership of the hotel was murky at the time, since it had been appropriated by the Argentine government as "enemy property" once Argentina formally and rather cynically declared war on Germany in the weeks before the end of the war. One does not know what happened to the Eichorns, but the legacy of their spa and resort lingered. Adolf Eichmann was known to have visited La Falda and its famous hotel during his exile; his son Adolfo would marry the daughter of a former gardener of the hotel, a man named Pummer. In addition, Erich Müller—a former sailor with the famous German battleship *Graf Spee* that was scuttled in the waters off Montevideo, Uruguay after the Battle of River Plate in December,1939—married a former maid of the Eden Hotel.[167] Thus, it can be shown that this hotel, situated 450 miles northwest of Buenos Aires in an area surrounded by hills and lakes, was a major nerve center for the Nazis for decades spanning the pre-war, war and post-war years. We are thus presented with a well-documented scenario: trustworthy and fanatic Nazis in Argentina managing a large resort in a remote area of the country which was made available to Adolf Hitler should he need to escape. It was an area populated heavily by Germans who were pro-Nazi, and was frequented by Nazis—including Adolf Eichmann—for decades. It was run by Nazis who had come to the attention of not only the OSS but also of the FBI. Put that together with the well-reported appearance of Nazi U-boats along Argentina's coast in the months after the war's end, and you have a scenario that is not only possible but also probable. Hitler knew he had a bolthole already prepared for him in pro-Nazi Argentina, a country accessible by U-boat and which had a large population of admirers prepared to hide him and to repel all outsiders. What is more, he knew the owners of the property personally; they had been major contributors to the Party, and had been decorated by the Führer himself for that reason.

In addition, and perhaps apocryphally, there is a tantalizing reference in Michael Bar-Zohar's book *The Avengers* concerning a remark made by Admiral Karl Dönitz. It is to be remembered that Hitler trusted Dönitz to the end, making him his successor as leader of the German government after his own disappearance from the scene. The reference reads as follows:

> In 1943 Admiral Doenitz had declared: 'The German U-boat fleet is proud to have made an earthly paradise, an impregnable fortress for the Fuhrer, somewhere in the world.' He did not say in what part of the world it existed, but fairly obviously it was in South America.[168]

---

167   Much of this information can be found in a book by local historian Carlos Panozzo, *El Hotel Edén de La Falda*, n.d., n.p., and in a blogspot devoted to the hotel, http://hoteledensandro.blogspot.com/2009/03/hotel-eden-fotos-del-pasado-y-presente.html.

168   Michael Bar-Zohar, *The Avengers*, p. 99. The author has been unable to verify

THE AUTHOR WOULD LIKE TO POINT OUT the curious symmetry between Dönitz's remark concerning an earthly "paradise" and the name of the Eichorn hotel, *Eden*.

Oddly, a man known variously as Mattern Friedrich and Willibald Mattern has written a book concerning UFOs as Nazi secret weapons. He is said to be a German living in Chile, and has written that Admiral Dönitz told a graduating class of naval cadets in 1944 that "The German Navy knows all hiding places for the Navy to take the Fuhrer to, should the need arise."[169] The author has no way of knowing if the Admiral actually said this, but it is worth mentioning in light of the other evidence.

As the anonymous wag noted on the CIA file, "May not be so funny."

ANOTHER LENGTHY FILE[170] contains a detailed description of events in and around two south Brazilian towns: Rio Grande and Casino. Rio Grande was settled by German immigrants in the mid-nineteenth century as part of Brazil's efforts to populate the area to keep it from being encroached upon by neighboring countries. Later, Italian immigrants followed to bolster the population and to begin wine production. Casino is about fifteen miles from Rio Grande and close to the Uruguayan border, and that is where most of the action in the BUFile takes place.

---

the accuracy of this statement, and in communication with Mr Bar-Zohar learned that the source material for this book was lost over time and that he has no recollection of where the quotation came from. Since Bar-Zohar is a respected historian of the war, this episode is cited here for its possible relevance and importance to our case.

169 Willibald Mattern, *UFOs: Unbekanntes Flugobjekt? Letzte Geheimwaffe des Dritten Reiches*, Toronto: Samisdat Publishers, 1974. It is to be noted that Ernst Zündel—the owner of Samisdat—was a German national and Holocaust denier who was arrested and convicted in Germany in 2007 for incitement of Holocaust denial, which is a crime in Germany. More than a Holocaust denier, this 72-year old man is a fervent Nazi who published such works as *The Hitler We Loved and Why*.

170 12 page Memorandum dated June 5, 1947 from SAC Los Angeles to FBI Director J. Edgar Hoover, "Subject: Adolf Hitler and Eva Braun, Information Concerning [redacted]."

The report is sober, cautious, and painstaking in its meticulous account of what appeared to have been a Hitler sighting in that country. The report was written by the SAC (Special Agent in Charge) of Los Angeles, addressed to Hoover, and is dated June 5, 1947 and still is heavily redacted (sixty-five years after the events in question!). The SAC is recounting a meeting he had with someone whose credibility he seems to vouch for, and who claims to have met both Hitler and Eva Braun in the Grande Hotel de Casino in March of 1947. There was supporting documentation in the form of passports, visas, etc. which proved that the informant had indeed been to the countries in question on the dates mentioned.

The hotel had its own radio antenna, which was remarkable in that it was installed parallel to the ground rather than in a tower, and was fenced off. The owner of the hotel, according to the file, also had an interest in a manufacturing plant in the area that made woolen products.[171]

The informant claimed he had worked for the French Underground during the war and recognized immediately one of the patrons of the hotel, a German officer by the name of Weissman who was involved in the Propaganda Department. He then recognized at the same table a woman he thought resembled Eva Braun, and finally a man he was certain was Adolf Hitler.

His description of Hitler is interesting:

> "This man was described as having the same general build and age of HITLER, was clean-shaven, and had a very short German crew haircut. This man was rather emaciated ... "

The report goes on to describe a few evenings in which the Hitler/ Braun couple was observed closely, as well as a young seventeen-year-old woman who was the niece of the "Eva Braun" figure who was observed giving the "Heil Hitler" salute one day. The informant sub-

---

171   This is reminiscent of another German operation, that of the Lahusen Company based in southern Argentina, which was also involved in the wool trade but served as a front for Nazi activity in the region. See the article by Johannes Steel, cited above.

sequently learned from the niece that they were from Chile; however, they did not speak Spanish but only German the entire time, which made the informant doubt the Chile story. When the informant discussed the possibility of doing a travel piece about the picturesque hotel and the surrounding towns, the hotel owner became hostile immediately and the informant then discovered that there were no more rooms available to him and he had to leave the area. Upon his return to Rio de Janeiro he narrowly avoided what seemed to be two murder attempts.

The FBI then interviewed the informant and several others who were his colleagues. They were checked out, and everything seemed above-board. One interesting fact emerged, and that is that the informant—after the fall of Paris—had somehow and for an unexplained (or possibly redacted) reason, visited Tibet.

Tibet comes up again in our story, which is why the author points this out. Tibet is one of the countries mentioned in the Pöch diary along with the names and places of other contacts around the world. It also appears in what seems to be an incoherent letter to Hoover about Hitler's possible whereabouts, as quoted at the beginning of this chapter. It is jarring to find this country in this context, to say the least, and we will have more to say about it as we go forward in our investigation.

The Bureau evidently felt that it was possible that the informant was a Communist or perhaps a Russian spy. They based this on the fact that he was a member of the French Resistance during the war, and while there were Socialists and Communists who belonged to the Resistance it was by no means a given that a partisan was automatically a Communist.

On August 6, 1947, Hoover received a reply from an unidentified agent in Rio de Janeiro, Brazil, who confirmed that Casino and Rio Grande had large German populations and that "it could be expected that a Nazi refugee would seek asylum or assistance in the Casino area because of the existence of the predominantly German element."

Then, a large part of the memorandum is heavily redacted. Following the redaction there is a list of correspondence between two important individuals on this matter: Frederick D. Hunt, the American Consul in the island nation of Martinique, and US Ambassador to

Brazil William Pawley. Unfortunately, copies of this correspondence are not included in the declassified FBI files, but there is enough known—particularly about Pawley—that can lead us to some interesting conclusions.

IN CONTEXT, THE POLITICAL ATMOSPHERE at the time was poisonous when it came to pursuing Nazis in South America. There was a much-publicized struggle going on between two US government representatives over the fact of pro-Nazi sentiments in Argentina. On one side was US Ambassador to Argentina, Spruille Braden, who was insisting that Argentina live up to its promise to stamp out Nazism in that country; on the other side was William Pawley, a co-founder of the Flying Tigers and a man later deeply involved in the Bay of Pigs invasion, who was an enemy of Braden and who tried to have him destroyed.

Running Interference

William Douglas Pawley (1896–1977) was an American businessman whose father was based in Cuba where young Pawley went to school. In 1927, Pawley began working for the Curtiss-Wright Corporation that manufactured aircraft. A year later would find Pawley back in Cuba as president of the Nacional Cubana Aviación de Curtiss, the local Curtiss-Wright affiliate. This relationship with Cuba would continue his entire life.

The Curtiss-Wright company was sold to Pan American Airways in 1932, and after that Pawley would go to China where he built aircraft manufacturing facilities for the Chinese Nationalist leader, Chiang Kai-Shek. Pawley was also friendly with Claire Chennault, the man most closely identified with what would become the Flying Tigers.

Pawley wound up selling 100 P-40 fighter planes to the Flying Tigers. This was not patriotism at work, but profit. The P-40s were considered obsolete by the Royal Air Force, among others, but Pawley—using his connections with his old company—managed to arrange a sale to China and the Tigers. They would be used in the war against the Japanese in a project that had the blessing of American

President Franklin D. Roosevelt. Pawley even went so far as to get Walt Disney to design the Flying Tigers logo.

The Flying Tigers was a romantic and effective air force composed largely of American volunteers. It was created in 1941, long before the United States officially entered World War Two. It was essentially a secret war against the Japanese begun eight months before the attack on Pearl Harbor. It would prefigure groups like the CIA airline Air America of the 1960s.

After the war, Pawley went on to a number of other airline companies around the world before eventually becoming President Harry S. Truman's ambassador to Peru, and in 1948 became ambassador to Brazil. At this time he began a smear campaign against Spruille Braden, insisting that he was a Communist stooge because of his strong stand against the presence of Nazis in Argentina. Braden was himself a Republican and a conservative, but Pawley could be considered a proto-neocon. Pawley began running interference for Perón and other Latin American dictators—such as Batista in Cuba—while ignoring the Ratline and the steady stream of war criminals that flooded the continent. His political stand was unabashedly anti-Communist and he typified the mentality of certain American politicians who—like those in the Vatican—saw Communism as a greater threat than Nazism and who had no moral scruples about giving covert assistance to war criminals.

This would become clear with Pawley's later involvement in the CIA's Bay of Pigs operation and other covert action adventures around the globe. In January, 1977 he was found dead of a gunshot wound which was characterized by his family as the result of a debilitating case of shingles which caused Pawley considerable pain; however, to observers it seemed curious that Pawley would have killed himself at the time of the House Select Committee on Assassinations investigations which might have revealed Pawley's involvement in the Bay of Pigs as well as his close association with Allen Dulles and Ted Shackley of the CIA and most especially of the infamous JMWAVE station in Miami (the largest CIA station in the world at the time).

Spruille Braden, Pawley's nemesis in the Republican Party, was an open opponent of fascism and this, to Pawley, smacked of a socialist mindset. He did what he could to get Braden out of Latin America since he was fouling the pond for everyone by insisting that the Argentine government live up to its commitment to find and deport Nazi war criminals ... something Argentina was not about to do. A New York *Times* story dated February 20, 1961[172] shows that Braden had been successful in keeping Pawley out of the Argentine ambassadorship; while Braden admitted that he blocked Pawley's ambassadorship to Argentina, he did not elaborate on his reasons why. Pawley, however, as late as 1961 was still trying to smear Braden over events that took place almost fifteen years earlier. He gave secret testimony to Congress asserting that Braden had been dismissed by President Truman due to Pawley's revelations concerning Braden's alleged Communist sympathies, a charge that Braden (and Truman) denied. In fact, Braden was awarded the Medal of Freedom, America's highest civilian honor.

To Pawley, Braden was jousting at windmills in Argentina: he was looking for non-existent Nazis and creating a firestorm of animosity where Pawley needed it least. Pawley supported Batista and Perón unequivocally and wanted to insure that Latin America remained free of Communist influence. In order to do that, he needed the Nazis in place. Thus it transpired that an American ambassador ran interference for the Ratline and aided in the escape and sanctuary of hundreds of war criminals. As the CIA was also involved to some extent in this operation, and as Pawley's relationship with Dulles was secure, it can come as no surprise that Braden's voice was shouted down and Argentina could conduct its business as usual.

Frederick D. Hunt, a correspondent with Pawley in the memoranda mentioned above, was a Foreign Service officer who was based in Shanghai in 1941[173] and who presumably had dealings with Pawley since those early days in China with the Flying Tigers. Hunt's name appears sporadically—but quietly—in a number of suggestive places, and his wife was a member of the AAFSW (American Association of Foreign Service Wives), an association that was invited to a lunch

---

172 "Ex-Envoy Scores Spruille Braden," New York *Times*, February 20, 1961, Associated Press.
173 See Benis M. Frank, "Oral History Report: Bleasdale and Taxis Interviews", *Fortitudine: Newsletter of the Marine Corps Historical Program*, Volume XV, Winter 1985–1986, Number 3, p. 16

at the Nixon White House in 1973.[174] What he was doing in Martinique in 1947 is anyone's guess. However, it seemed it was Hunt who provided Pawley with all the ammunition he needed to shoot down this story. According to Hunt, the Martinique authorities were suspicious of the informant and stated that he and an accomplice had been indicted for passing a bad check in France in 1946 and were wanted by the French authorities. The Martinique governor could not arrest them until the evidence had arrived from Paris, thus allowing the two men sufficient time to get off the island. It seems—according to the story as outlined in a memo dated August 29, 1947 from the SAC Los Angeles to Hoover—that the two men had arrived in Martinique intending to shoot a historical documentary on and about the island. The story of the bad check was enough to discredit the detailed testimony of the informants.

The upshot of this correspondence is that a potentially vital piece of information from a known French resistance fighter concerning the escape of Adolf Hitler was devalued and then ignored completely because of a rumor concerning a bad check in Paris in 1946. This occurred even though the information concerning the German community of Casino and Rio Grande was verified by a redacted memorandum from Rio de Janeiro to Hoover. Once again, Pawley had run interference for the Ratline. The flight of war criminals—to Latin America and to Asia, both areas of the world with which Pawley and his colleagues were intimately familiar—was assured. Pawley allowed no information concerning Nazis in Latin America to be entertained seriously. He ridiculed Braden—who was himself a staunch anti-Communist—for suggesting otherwise; he ran interference on the Casino story; he openly and aggressively supported right-wing dictatorships in Asia and Latin America. This is a case of morality taking a back seat to ideology, and of the ends justifying the means. It is a position that runs neatly parallel to the Nazis' own methodology. Braden—whatever his faults might have been as a lobbyist for United Fruit and a supporter of the Somoza regime in Nicaragua as well—was responsible for the overthrow of Arbenz in Guatemala, among many other

---

174 See President Richard Nixon's Daily Diary, Appendix "D", AAFSW White House Tea, March 13, 1973, p. 8

charges that could be made against him. He was an anti-Communist who nevertheless wanted Nazi war criminals identified and brought to justice. To Pawley (and to so many like him), this was an absurd position to take, a political oxymoron.

Ironically, Braden died of heart disease in January,1978: almost exactly a year to the day after Pawley's own suicide.

As we can see, this article and the others contained within the FBI files consist of detailed information not otherwise available to the general reader but which was current at the time: the immediate post-war period. Uki Goñi's definitive text on the Argentine end of the Ratline—*The Real Odessa*—does not mention the Dönitz and Schwerin von Krosigk connection, and does not describe La Falda, Casino or the other Nazi enclaves mentioned in the Steel article or the BUFiles. The subject is too vast, rather than too narrow, and the documentation (when available, when not shredded by the authorities: in this case, the Argentine or US governments) is damning. A complete study of the ratlines would have to be encyclopedic and run to many thousands of pages. All we can do here is to point to wherever the facts as we know them will lead us in our particular quest.

What is important to realize is that the networks were global, were well-financed from a variety of sources, and included covert assistance from the International Red Cross, the Vatican, European *and* Latin American *and* Middle Eastern *and* Asian governments, Allied military intelligence, and their later incarnations as the CIA, the BND, etc. The world went from a hot war to a cold war, and in that change of temperature decisions were made that were morally bankrupt, regardless of concerns for national security. It was as if there existed no one person, no one group, that could defend the United States and the West in general from the perceived Soviet menace than the most hateful, most iconic butchers of the twentieth century. It was this failure of nerve more than anything else, this loss of faith in our own institutions and their capability of defending us, that led US and Allied intelligence services—and the Roman Catholic Church, an institution dedicated to the highest forms of morality—into this heinous contract. Like the grimoires of Dark Age sorcerers, each page of the FBI files, the OSS and CIA files, the CIC files, and the files of MI6, contain signatures of the demons with whom pacts were made in the naïve belief that they could be controlled by men whose capacity for evil action was actually far less than that of the demons they evoked to visible appearance. The men of the intelligence services were not sorcerers: they were sorcerers' apprentices, and like Mephistopheles in Goethe's *Faust*, the demons soon came to take over and demand the payment of their collective souls.

THE FBI FILES GO ON TO RECORD every rumor, every piece of gossip, every lead in the search for Adolf Hitler. The story of a Hitler sighting in Colombia—that was reported heavily in the Colombian press—is exhaustively recorded, translated, and analyzed. Now Hitler is seen washing dishes in Miami; now he is on a railroad car in St Louis. These leads are professionally followed-up, even though the agents in charge know in their hearts that the information is bogus. But Hoover, like Stalin, suspects the worst: that somehow, Hitler has escaped. There is far too much smoke to doubt there's fire.

U-boats in Argentina and Japan. Sightings in Colombia and Argentina and Brazil. Mysterious operatives coming out of the woodwork and relaying information to American agents before disappearing again. And the background to all of this is the very real operation taking place under everyone's nose: the escape of men like Mengele and Eichmann and Rauff. Considering what we now know of the Ratline, and about the mistaken nature of the Russian forensic evidence, it is about time to go back over all these cold leads and begin to re-evaluate them. We know that the Eden Hotel in La Falda, Argentina was offered to Hitler by serious Nazi Party supporters who knew Hitler personally. We know that regions like Casino in Brazil were hotbeds of Nazi intrigue before and after the war. We know that American politicians in authority took great pains to cover up this information. Knowing what we know now, it is time to take another look at the disappearance of Adolf Hitler and his possible escape to the one country in the world where he would have been the most secure from Allied and Israeli capture, and where the German Navy and the Nazi Party had a documented presence: a Muslim nation on the other side of the world.

CHAPTER NINE

THE MYSTERY DEEPENS

On January 19, 1970 an elderly European man died suddenly of a heart attack in Surabaya, Indonesia. Less than three months later, in April of 1970, a Soviet intelligence squad rushed to an unmarked grave at a secret police station in Magdeburg, East Germany, dug up a body and cremated it, throwing its ashes into a tributary of the Elbe river. This was on the orders of KGB chief—and future Soviet premier—Yuri Andropov himself.

This juxtaposition of these two seemingly unrelated events in space and time is deliberate, for in each case the dead man was believed to have been Adolf Hitler.

Did the death of the mysterious European man in Indonesia in January trigger the response of the KGB in East Germany in April? The author would like to suggest that it did. Imagine for a moment this scenario: the real Adolf Hitler dies in relative obscurity in a far-away land. Word reaches the KGB, and an embarrassed intelligence chief orders that "their" Hitler corpse be dug up and destroyed in order to avoid one day having to tell the world that they buried the wrong guy. Then, twenty years later, the man who ordered this bizarre exhumation comes forward—this time as the Soviet premier—and tells the world that they had Hitler's body all along, confident that no one will be able to prove otherwise since they cremated the body (again) and scattered its ashes into the river. He is certain that the body in the Indonesian cemetery has completely disintegrated by this time in the tropical grave and that there would be no way to prove its identity.

This scenario is not as far-fetched as it may seem, for if one were to visit the gravesite of the Indonesian "Hitler" today one will notice a stunning anomaly about its headstone.

Georg Anton Pöch is buried in a Muslim cemetery in the district of Ngagel Rejo in Surabaya, not far from the hospital where he died.

The plot is in a far corner of the cemetery, and the gravesite is designed in the Muslim fashion. It consists of a flat slab of stone with a shallow depression on its surface where flower petals are strewn. On top of the slab are two markers—one at either end of the rectangular stone—upon one of which is usually inscribed the name and dates (birth and death) of the deceased. In the case of Pöch, his name and date do not appear on the marker, but on the stone slab itself. This is not so unusual, for some of the other gravesites show the same method. What is jarring, however, is the fact that the stonecutter never carved the date of birth or the date of death of Dr. Pöch. In fact, the date of his death was literally pencilled in more recently by someone using what appears to have been a Magic Marker. This is not only most unusual, it makes no sense at all. One could understand that there might have been confusion over Pöch's birthdate; he was a foreigner and it is possible (though not likely) that no one had the information at the time . . . but did the stonecutter creating Pöch's tombstone not know when he *died?*

In addition, the lower part of the plaque shows a mysterious legend: *CC.258.* No other grave markers that the author could see during his visit to the cemetery bore anything similar. It is believed by some that this is a grid location for the gravesite. If so, why does the Pöch stone have it prominently displayed whereas no other tombstone in the cemetery does?

No birth date. No death date. A mysterious legend, in more ways than one.

Who is *really* buried in Pöch's tomb?

ONE POSSIBLE REASON FOR THE LACK OF A BIRTH DATE, of course, is confusion over who really died. Should they use the birth date for Pöch (which would be November 1, 1895) or the birth date for . . . someone else? It seems no one wanted to commit themselves to writing it "in stone," not even at the time of the man's death. The inscription was deferred to a later date, a date that never came. It was only sometime in the last few years that the death date was written with what appears to have been a felt-tipped pen, for there are photographs of the gravestone taken as late as 2007 that do not show the date at all. It seems there was no controversy over the date of death; the only controversy that remained—and remains to this day—is the date of birth. Since Pöch's date of birth is well known from official Indonesian documents, there seems to be no reason to delay inscribing that date on his tombstone.

Unless someone in power knows that the tomb is not that of the Salzburg medical officer at all, but of someone else entirely.

The Sosro Affair

As we have seen, Dr. Sosro Husodo met Georg Anton Pöch on Sumbawa in October and November of 1960. It would be another twenty-one years before Sosro would think of him again. This time, his memories were triggered by an article in the Indonesian magazine *Zaman*, in their January 15, 1980 issue, which was brought to him by a family member in 1981. The article was by Heinz Linge, as we have seen one of the SS guards at the Bunker who claimed to have known about Hitler's suicide, and was entitled "True Story: the Last Days of a Dictator." It had been translated into Bahasa Indonesia, and Linge's description of Hitler's physical state—including the tremors, the dragging of the left foot, etc.—immediately brought to mind the old German doctor Sosro had met in Sumbawa Besar.

Sosro began reading anything he could find about Hitler, and the more he read the more he became convinced that the old man on Sumbawa was the former Nazi dictator. Then, in October 1983, an article in the Indonesian magazine *Intisari* contained the story of Klaus Barbie, the Nazi murderer who was discovered living in Bolivia, and of how he escaped to Latin America. It was the first time most people heard of the name Draganovic, and of the Ratline.

According to Sosro, this is when all the pieces began to come together. It started to seem likely that Hitler could have escaped using the same Ratline as Barbie. He began to make some calls.

The first call he made was to Sumbawa Besar. He was eventually informed that the German doctor had left Sumbawa to go to Surabaya with a patient, and then died himself in that city in January of 1970. Further calls revealed that Pöch had remarried, this time to a Sundanese woman named Sulaesih, who had herself, returned to her home town of Bandung.

Sosro eventually tracked down Sulaesih, and she showed him the Pöch diary, with its references to Draganovic and the addresses of the monastery route safe houses in Rome and Genoa, as well as the unidentified address in Rome that turned out to be that of the German Archaeological Institute.

Dr. Sosro Husodo then wrote his own article on Pöch, setting out the evidence that this strange German doctor could have been Adolf Hitler. In the article—published in the magazine *Pikiran Rakyat* in 1983—he referred to Sulaesih only as "S", in an effort to protect her identity. After all, who would want to be known as the widow of Adolf Hitler?

He found that some of the diary contents were written in shorthand, and he went to some effort to have it translated in Germany. But his attempts to have historians acknowledge the possibility that the man buried in Surabaya was actually Hitler were met with ridicule. One of the typical objections was made by a researcher, Dr. Asvi Warman Adam, of the Indonesian Institute of Sciences, who expressed doubt that any Nazis at all had escaped to Indonesia.

Of course it was counter-intuitive, since "everyone knew" that the Nazis had gone to Argentina. (Actually, the Pöch diary does refer to Argentina as their destination.) But the objection was a valid one, and the insistence by Dr. Sosro that at least one "Nazi" did make it as far as Indonesia seemed bizarre when this author first heard of it. It was only after considerable effort and investigation did this part of the story begin to make sense. Regardless of who Pöch really was—the Chief Medical Officer of the Salzburg Gau, or the leader of the Third Reich—he was definitely a Nazi who made it to Indonesia.

One of the problems faced by this author in evaluating the Sosro narrative is the fact that all of the action seems to take place in 1983 when the world was learning of Klaus Barbie and the Ratline for the first time. It could be argued that Sosro had conflated the news current that year with his memories of Pöch in 1960. It could also be argued that his reference to Frank G. Spisak was motivated by the same conflation, since the story of the multiple murderer with a Hitler complex made the headlines (at least, in the United States) the same year.

However, as the author began to deconstruct and reconsruct the Sosro account it became clear that the Pöch diary was genuine. It contained references to people and places that Sosro could not have known about in the pre-Internet days of 1983 and, indeed, could hardly have been discovered even now. Pöch was an unknown name to most people, but it has been demonstrated that he did exist and that his wife did exist and that both lived in Salzburg in 1945. The Pöch diary, therefore, is genuine and should be taken seriously. Whether or not convicted killer Frank Spisak ever lived in Sumbawa as a child, or whether or not Pöch was Hitler, are different matters entirely. Yet, what this Indonesian doctor from Project Hope and his own research has done is open the door to a segment of history that was heretofore either unknown or ignored. The contents of the Pöch diary sent this author on a search that revealed a great deal about the role of Nazi anthropologists in the Holocaust, the involvement of the German Archaeological Institute in the Ratline, the existence of Nazi U-boats in Southeast Asia, and the creation of the Nazi Party in Indonesia by Walter Hewel ... none of which is common knowledge to the public at large and most of which will be new even to historians of the war. It also invokes the very real mystery of what happened not only to Georg Anton Pöch, but to his rather more celebrated wife, Hella.

The Pöch couple

If it was really Georg Anton Pöch who arrived in Indonesia in January of 1954, then it is unusual that we have no further information about his famous wife, Hella (or Helena) Pöch, neé Schürer von Waldheim. After all, it was Hella Pöch who held important positions in Viennese anthropological circles and institutes. It was Hella Pöch who married the man considered to be the father of modern ethnology, Rudolf Pöch. It was Hella Pöch who conducted anthropometric and other experiments on prisoners of war in the camps. And it would have been Hella Pöch who had the interest to travel to Indonesia since her previous husband , Rudolf, had done important work there, albeit forty years earlier. Yet, we know very little about Hella Pöch's life in Indonesia with Georg Anton.

In fact, we know nothing.

Attempts to obtain information from European institutes and

universities concerning Hella Pöch have proved strangely fruitless. We are told that she died in 1976, and presumably in Europe ... but there is no more information than that. We have no idea what she was doing from 1945 to 1976, a span of thirty years, or where she was doing it. Did she hide from the Allies once the Netherlands and Germany fell? Did she claim ownership over Rudolf Pöch's estate? What happened to her research notes, artifacts, and field work?

Did she really go into hiding, travel along the Ratline from Austria to Italy to South America and then to Indonesia? Why? Was she really wanted by the Allies?

Aside from the snippets we have of her husband's diary, she might have dropped off the face of the earth in 1945. This, for a celebrated anthropologist with her pedigree, is incredible. Many of her colleagues survived the 1940s and thrived afterwards, even those who demonstrably had committed crimes during the war. It would have galled someone like Hella Pöch to see lesser lights reinstalled in their previous posts, even honored for their contributions to science, while she languished in some remote backwater, ignored and forgotten after such a brilliant career.

In short, she would have done this only if she (or her husband) had committed crimes that were so heinous that there would have been no mercy shown to either of them.

But ... there is no indication that the Allies even knew who she was. She appears on no wanted list that the author has been able to find. She appears and then disappears just as mysteriously as her second husband, Georg Anton Pöch.

There is one possible explanation. Hella Pöch was not Hella Pöch at all, but someone who assumed her identity in order to flee along the Ratline. Someone for whom the world was searching. Someone with a terrible secret.

Heinrich Himmler himself, the head of the SS and one of the most wanted men in Europe after the war, shaved off his mustache and stole the identity of a real German police officer in order to avoid capture. This is what the Nazis (and particularly the SS) were doing. Aside from the forged papers and assumed names, in the immediate aftermath of the war many of the hunted simply took the identities of real persons as their own. In Himmler's case, the choice of a police officer was not a wise one: the Allies were on the alert for policemen and had orders to arrest them on sight.

But no one would have arrested an anthropologist on sight. Not unless they were already on a list.

There are no photographs of Hella Pöch among the effects left behind by her husband, and yet Georg Anton was said to be an avid photographer. And, one day a few years after their arrival on the island of Sumbawa, she disappears again. No questions. No answers. No trace.

Her husband then converts to Islam and takes a young Sundanese bride. Photographs of the couple show a man who fits an earlier description:

> This man was described as having the same general build and age of HITLER, was clean-shaven, and had a very short German crew haircut. This man was rather emaciated ...

WE RECALL THIS DESCRIPTION from the previous chapter, contained in a June, 1947 report to FBI director Hoover about a couple seen in Casino, Brazil. It fits existing photographs of Georg Anton Pöch rather well, except for the fact that Pöch eventually sported a Hitleresque "Charlie Chaplin" mustache. But in Indonesia he appeared, indeed, rather emaciated with a very short German crew cut.

It is important at this time to draw the reader's attention to photographs of Pöch and to do a simple comparison with known photographs of Hitler when he was rather more emaciated-looking than later photos and newsreels show him to have been later in life. Special attention should be paid to the ears and the jawline of both the young Hitler and the older Pöch. In terms of anthropometrics—ironically, the field pioneered by Rudolf Pöch and championed by Hella Pöch herself—these are important determinants of identity and difficult to mask with cosmetic surgery.

The photo on the left is of Adolf Hitler as a young soldier in the trenches of World War One. The photo on the right is of Georg Anton Pöch, taken in Sumbawa Besar in 1965. In this photograph he

Adolf Hitler at left. Georg Anton Pöch on the right.

is wearing glasses, which distorts the image somewhat, but the ears and jawline seem virtually identical.

So, what do we know about Georg Anton Pöch? How can details about his life in Indonesia help us to determine who he really was, and what he was really doing there? For that, we have to consult two sources. One is the doctor who visited Pöch from the hospital ship Hope. The other is the collection of Pöch documents that have only appeared in one place: a small pamphlet written by an Indonesian prince who took a special interest in the story. Yet, neither of these sources helps us to understand who *Hella* Pöch was, or what she was doing there. If Hella Pöch was not really Hella Pöch, then it is entirely possible—no, probable—that Georg Anton Pöch was not who he claimed to be either.

The Documents

The first document at our disposal is a copy of Georg Anton Pöch's Indonesian entry permit, dated January 6, 1954. In this document, Pöch is described as of German nationality, but his passport was issued in Rome and bears the date September 28, 1951, with passport number 2624/51. We can assume that this number system indicates passport number 2624 that was issued in 1951. His place of birth is listed as Przemysl, November 1, 1895. His place of arrival is Jakarta.

There are a number of problems with this document. In the first place, Georg Anton Pöch was an Austrian and not a German. Przemysl was—at the time he was born—part of the Austro-Hungarian Empire, even though today it is part of Poland. Thus, he could have been Austrian or even, today, of Polish nationality but not German. This is reinforced by his namesake, Rudolf Pöch, who was Austrian and by his wife, Hella Pöch who was also Austrian. We thus have an embarrassment of Pöchs, none of whom could be considered German nationals in 1951, although they might have been considered citizens of the "Greater German Reich" (which included Austria) in 1945. (There is another possibility, of course, and that is that Pöch was a Nazi Party member and thus automatically a citizen of the German Reich, a state that was demolished anyway in 1945.)

But what passport did he really have? The Indonesian immigration official wrote the word "Djerman" which was the Indonesian spelling current at the time. "Djerman" could mean "Germany" the country as well as "German" the nationality. Did Pöch have a German passport?

West Germany did not become an independent state, the Bundesrepublik Deutschland, until 1949, when it was considered to encompass both West and East Germany (even though East Germany at that time was under Soviet control and did not recognize West German claims to the territory). Under the *Grundgesetz* or "Basic Law" Constitution of 1949, the boundaries of "Germany" were established as those that existed in 1937, i.e., before the Anschluss that annexed Austria to the Greater German Reich. If the Pöchs were living in Salzburg, and were native Austrians, there does not seem to be any way in which they could have claimed "German" citizenship in 1951, unless they had been members of the Nazi Party or the SS in which they would be German citizens under the laws of the Reich, a technicality that helped some Nazis escape extradition to the countries where they had committed war crimes. In addition, Austria was still occupied by the Allies as late as 1955 when the occupation officially ended. Therefore, their legal status was confused, to say the least.

Did West Germany issue only 2624 passports in the first nine months of 1951? And why did Pöch have to go to Rome to get it? The obvious answer, of course, is that the passport he held was not a German passport (which did not use that numbering system anyway) but one issued by the International Committee of the Red Cross (ICRC), which thoughtfully made Pöch a German rather than an Austrian citizen. We know from Pöch's diary that Draganovic was involved, which means a Vatican identity document was used to generate the Red Cross passport.

The problem with this scenario is that the numbering system used by the ICRC was not the same as the system used in the Pöch passport number. The ICRC numbers did not end in a slash with the two-digit year following it. That system was used for visas by many countries, such as the Argentine immigration documents issued by Draganovic. What is further problematic, however, is that by 1950—the year before the Pöch passport was created—the number system for the Argentine visas had already reached 397954/50: that was the Argentine immigration number for Klaus Barbie, who got his paperwork started in Salzburg around the same time as the Pöch couple. For comparison purposes, the immigration number for Josef Mengele (as "Helmut Gregor") was 211713/48. So the "passport number" 2624/51 remains something of a mystery, unless it was not a passport number but an *Indonesian* immigration number, created especially for clients of Monsignor Draganovic.

Draganovic caused thousands of Argentine immigration documents to be issued and they rarely contained the real identities of the persons holding them. That would have been counter-productive, to say the least. We can be relatively sure that if Draganovic had a hand in the generation of these travel documents, then Pöch's nationality was not German, and his name was possibly not even Pöch! Otherwise . . . why go through Draganovic at all?

As we have seen, the names of Georg Anton Pöch and Hella Pöch do not appear on any lists of war criminals that the author has been able to locate so their names would have been safe to use for those whose real names were somewhat more notorious. The necessity of going through the Vatican Ratline is questionable unless the two individuals in question were not the Pöchs at all. As an example Barbie, who left less than a year before the Pöch couple, used the name Klaus Altmann. Adolf Eichmann (Argentine immigration number 231489/48) used Ricardo Klement. Hans Fischböck (Argentine immigration number 238136/48) used Jacob Schramm.

There is no documentary evidence to show that the famous Viennese anthropologist Hella Pöch was in Indonesia in 1954. All of the available documents are on Georg Anton Pöch. That there was someone with him—a European woman—in Sumbawa seems certain, based on the testimony of Dr. Sosro Husodo as well as on that of Pöch's second wife, Sulaesih. We just don't know for sure who she was.

Pöch's immigration form does not contain any information on a wife, but that is not unusual. Hella Pöch would have filled out her own immigration form but this is not available, if it ever existed. It would have gone a long way to identifying her, but we have no way of finding such paperwork. Instead, all the paper we have is on Georg Anton and we will have to make do with that until more details come to light.

Pöch's occupation is not noted on his immigration form. It is much later that documents surface showing he is known as "Dr. Med. G.A. Pöch." The real G.A. Pöch *was* a doctor or, at least, a researcher with a degree in medicine[175] if not an actual surgeon or general practitioner. According to Dr Sosro's account, Pöch had little knowledge of practical medicine and, indeed, his medical degrees or diplomas have not surfaced. Several pre-war peer-reviewed articles by Pöch have

---

175   As mentioned in Chapter Five, one of his articles that has survived is "A Diptheria Immunization Campaign in Austria," co-authored with Charles N. Leach, and published in the *American Journal of Public Health*, Feb. 1935, p. 113–118. At that time, Pöch is listed as "Georg Pöch, Director, Local Health Department, Eisenstadt, Austria," whereas Charles Leach is listed as representing the International Health Division of The Rockefeller Foundation. Another article, also co-authored with Leach, appears in the *Journal of Immunology*, November 1935, p. 367–369 and is entitled "Schick Reactions and Serum Antitoxin Titrations on Children Injected with Diptheria Formol Toxoid". These articles were published in the mid-1930s, before the Anschluss when Austria was annexed to Germany in 1938, yet research by Brigitte Fuchs has shown that the Pöch couple were already completely "Nazified" as early as 1926, and Hella Pöch had published articles on Jewish "inferiority" as early as 1934. (See the Brigitte Fuchs article on Hella Pöch, cited below.)

appeared, and they bear the stamp of a man who was more involved in research than the actual practice of medicine. A recent source, *Zur Geschichte der NS-Euthanasie in Wien: Von der Zwangssterilisation zur Ermordung* (On the History of Nazi Euthanasia in Vienna: from Coerced Sterilization to Murder), which was published in Vienna in 2002, long after the Pöch story originally broke in the mid-1980s, only mentions Pöch twice, in passing[176] but mentions Pöch as the "medical officer" of the Salzburg Gauleiter. This is important, as the Pöch diary begins in Salzburg after the war.

Brigitte Fuchs[177] gives a brief biographical sketch of Hella Pöch, in which her involvement in the studies of Jewish prisoners in the Dutch camps is mentioned, as well as the fact that her project was interrupted due to the deportation of her research "subjects" to the concentration and death camps in Poland. Again, Pöch (this time Hella) is mentioned as having gone to Sumbawa in Indonesia "where she continued her biological research", only to return to Vienna "some years" later, which is presumably where she died in 1976.

One shudders to think what type of biological research she conducted on the island of Sumbawa, but there is no further information available. There is also no precise date of her return to Europe. However, in 1957 an article under her name appeared in the German anthropology journal *Anthropologischer Anzeiger* entitled "Uber die *athiopide* und die gondide Rasse und ihre Verbreitung, ("On the Athiopide and the Gondide Race and their Distribution)" which was a

---

176 Eberhard Gabriel, Wolfgang Neugebauer, *Zur Geschichte der NS-Euthanasie in Wien: Von der Zwangssterilisation zur Ermordung*, Böhlau Verlag, Vienna, 2002, p. 268, footnote ("Georg Pöch fled with his wife, the Anthropologist and Race-Consultant Hella Poch, to Indonesia") and p. 286 ("Whether [Heinrich Wolfer] fled to Indonesia as did the medical officer of the Salzburg Gauleiter, Georg Pöch, is unclear.") Heinrich Wolfer was an Austrian psychiatrist attached to the State Hospital in Salzburg; responsible for forced sterilizations and euthanasia as part of the notorious T4 program. It is believed he died during the battle for Berlin on May 2, 1945, but as shown by this citation, there were lingering doubts. The use of the word "fled" (*flüchtete*) is suggestive, for it implies that the couple were wanted fugitives and this is simply not apparent from available documentation. In any case, they did not "flee" until 1951, fully 6 years after the war's end.

177 Brigitte Fuchs, "Hella Pöch," in Ilse Erika Korotin, *Wissenschafterinnen in und aus Österreich: Leben-Werk-Wirken*, Böhlau Verlag, Vienna, 2002, p. 587–589.

study of African language groups in the region of the Sudan and what is now the Central African Republic. This obviously had nothing to do with Indonesia, and one wonders how she was able to write this article when she had—presumably—not been to the Sudanese region since before the war. One wonders when the article was actually written and if, indeed, she wrote it. Further, is it possible that the notations in the Pöch diary mentioning Africa are relevant to this question? If so, then there are other tantalizing hints that the peripatetic Pöch couple might have gone even farther afield before landing in Indonesia in 1954.

Salzburg in Austria, just a few kilometers to the northeast of Berchtesgaden, Hitler's retreat, and down river from Branau-am-Inn, where Hitler was born, was the base of operations for Georg Anton Pöch. As the medical officer he was nominally in charge of the euthanasia programs for the Salzburg Gau. (A "Gau" is a region within a country, and a "Gauleiter" is the Gau "leader" or administrative head, similar to a governor; these were medieval terms that the Nazis revived during the war and were positions held by Nazi Party members and were typically SS or military roles.)

As medical officer in Salzburg, Pöch's boss was Gustav Adolf Scheel (1907–1979). Scheel was himself a medical doctor as well as Gauleiter of Salzburg. A fanatic and devoted Nazi since long before Anschluss, Scheel had been involved with the underground Nazi movement in Austria, joining the Nazi Party in 1930 and bringing with him other doctors and academics who would eventually wind up committing unspeakable atrocities in Eastern Europe. An SS-Brigadeführer, he became Gauleiter of Salzburg in 1941 and remained in that position until the end of the war. Scheel was himself arrested and interned several times after the war until his "denazification" was complete, after which he eventually wound up working in hospitals as a doctor again as early as 1948. However, he was arrested again—this time by the British—in 1953 for his involvement in the Naumann Circle. This was an ODESSA-like organization, a secret group of former SS officers that was believed to be plotting a resurgence of the Third Reich.

The Naumann Circle was run by a devoted Nazi—Dr Werner Naumann, who for several days in May of 1945 had been Goebbels's successor as Reich Minister of Propaganda, and who was one of the last people to leave the Berlin bunker in 1945—who felt that only the

Nazis could stand up to the Soviet threat in Eastern Europe. His contacts included numerous members of the Ratline, from Skorzeny and Rudel to members of the Perón network. That the Naumann Circle was being financed and supported by influential Nazis and former SS-men seems beyond doubt, but when Naumann was arrested most observers felt that the British were over-reacting. In hindsight, that does not seem to have been the case. The Naumann Circle—had it survived—would have been another link in the Ratline, but its primary purpose was not to help Nazis flee Europe but to enable them to stay behind and reconstitute the Third Reich.

Scheel (like Naumann) was eventually cleared of these charges, and he spent the remainder of his life running a medical clinic in Hamburg. All of this once again begs the question: why did Pöch and his wife feel the absolute need to leave Europe, when so many of their colleagues—most much more notorious and guilty of greater crimes than they, men like Gustav Scheel—had not? Even more compelling: did Georg Anton Pöch's documented connection to Scheel provide him with access to the element of the Ratline operated by Skorzeny and Rudel in the Middle East and South America? Since Scheel was involved with the Naumann Circle, a pro-Nazi, anti-Communist cabal of former Reich dignitaries and officials, was something of the sort expected of Pöch as well?

CIC Austria

The immediate post-war period was, as we have already noted, a confusing and chaotic mess of Communists, anti-Communists, fascists, Nazis, and Allied military and intelligence agendas and personalities. This was especially true of Austria, and of Salzburg itself, until the Allied occupation of Austria ended in 1955.

Like Germany, Austria had been divided into four zones by the Allies: the Russian, British, French and American zones, with Vienna as a kind of Berlin, occupied by all four. Salzburg was squarely in the American zone. That did not mean that the Russians, for instance, stayed out of the American zone. There were spies from all the Allied services working in all the zones. If one remembers the film *The Third Man* one has a good idea of the atmosphere in Austria in those days.

The headquarters of 430th CIC (Counter Intelligence Corps) was in Vienna, but the center of the American zone was in Salzburg, the city where the Pöch couple lived and where Georg Anton Pöch had been medical officer during the war. In 1946, the head of CIC in Vienna—Lt. Col. James Milano—had created the military version of the Ratline in order to spirit out of Austria those Allied agents who had been operating behind enemy lines and who were in danger of being rolled up by the Soviets. He and his colleague—Paul Lyon—were in the process of developing the false papers and covert transport systems that would enable their agents to leave Austria for safer destinations, out of reach of Soviet spies. At the same time, there was pressure to locate and identify Nazi war criminals. Initially, there seemed to be no interest by American military intelligence in recruiting SS officers or other criminals. That, of course, would change.

One of the most notorious Nazis believed to have escaped via Salzburg to Latin America was Martin Bormann.

Paul Manning, the journalist who bravely covered this story in the 1970s, cited several instances of persons who claimed to have specific knowledge concerning Bormann's escape.[178] One of these was no less a personage than Roman Catholic Bishop Johannes Neuhausler of Munich who claimed—in 1972—that Bormann had escaped to Spain. Neuhausler (who had been a prisoner at Dachau) made this claim based on Church documentation. Even more arresting was Nazi "expert" Hugh Trevor-Roper's own admission (in 1973) that Bormann might have escaped.[179]

It is important to point out that the only real evidence of the Bormann "death" in Berlin of 1945 was, once again, dental records and these were, once again, identified from memory by the dentist who had identified the Hitler and Eva Braun dental work.[180]

The theory of Bormann's escape is predicated on the idea that the Reichsleiter had control over vast sums of Nazi assets that had been transferred from the Reich to banks and corporations abroad. The Allies were nervous about this activity at least a year before the end

---

178 Paul Manning, *Martin Bormann: Nazi in Exile*, Seacaucus NJ: Lyle Stuart, 1981, p. 15–16.
179 Paul Manning, p. 16.
180 Paul Manning, p. 16.

of the war, as revealed by declassified American and British intelligence records which indicate that money had been transferred for safekeeping to Switzerland, Spain and Argentina (among other locales) in 1944 and 1945.

From 1945–1947, the emphasis was on Nazi hunting. The CIC was deeply involved in the search for war criminals and as such was often stepping on the toes of British, French and Soviet intelligence operations taking place at the same time and same place, sometimes involving the same wanted men. Beginning in 1947, however, there was a dramatic shift in focus away from Nazi war criminals and towards defeating—or at least containing—the perceived Soviet threat. Suddenly, Nazis who were highest on the most-wanted list found themselves enlisted in the fight against Communism.

There was an active Communist Party in Austria, being supported by the Soviet presence there.[181] There was also a battle over the South Tyrol, which the Allies were intent on delivering to Italy regardless of its large ethnic German population. The reason behind this policy was the danger of Italy becoming Communist; American and British intelligence officers felt that moving a large German (and pro-Nazi, anti-Communist) population from Austria to Italy would help keep that country from voting for the Communist Party.

Also during this time there were numerous representatives from various South American countries combing through the prison camps and the displaced person camps looking for skilled workers. Countries like Colombia, Peru, Bolivia and Brazil were in the market for electricians, plumbers, carpenters and other tradespeople who would become useful immigrants and help develop their own economies. Many of these persons had no identification papers or passports and were considered "undocumented." In order for them to leave Europe and immigrate to South America they would need some form of offi-

---

181 The extent of this support only became revealed when documents from the Moscow archives became available after the fall of the Soviet Union. They detail a deep relationship between the Austrian Communist Party and Russia, and the very real danger of a split of Austria into a "west" and an "east", after the model of West Germany and East Germany. The Austrian Communists were only able to win four seats in the parliamentary elections of 1945, and this brought increased pressure to bear on the Austrian Communists from the Soviet Union ... to no avail.

cial government identification. Some of this documentation would be provided on humanitarian grounds by the ICRC, with very little in the way of supporting paperwork, thus opening the door for the unscrupulous and the desperate to create a veritable document mill of identification papers, visas and passports. It would become easy for those who had every reason to escape Allied justice to make use of the same mechanisms to effect their disappearance.

One of the CIC agents at the center of the storm was William Gowen. Only in his twenties at the time, Gowen found himself stationed in Austria and trying to keep tabs not only on the Nazis but also on Allied interests where the Nazis were concerned. This was no easy task.

Part of the problem arose from the fact that there were competing agendas, even within the same government. Allen Dulles of the OSS had his agenda, as did his associate James Jesus Angleton (who would become counter-intelligence chief for the newly-formed CIA). The military had its agenda, largely (but not entirely), determined by the civilians in Washington, DC.[182] Add to that the Vatican's own anti-Communist "crusade," as well as the Ustashe network—the Krizari or "Crusaders"—fighting behind Communist lines in Tito's Yugoslavia, and perhaps a dozen other networks, organizations, and spy operations and one truly needed a scorecard to keep up.

Gowen saw first-hand how the mission changed from one designed to ferret out and arrest Nazis to one designed to ferret out and recruit Nazis. Gowen inherited Father Draganovic—variously known as the "Golden Priest" or the "Good Father" from Milano and Lyon, with all the trouble involved in trying to control a fascist sympathizer within an American intelligence operation. But Draganovic was eminently useful, for he was a master at running the Ratline: providing the right paperwork, with the impeccable Vatican identification papers, so that the ICRC could issue the passports and groups like Vianord prepare the requisite visas for Argentina and other South American locations.

---

182   The infamous Operation Paperclip was a US Army program being run counter to specific instructions from President Truman not to hire Nazi war criminals, and was thus a military operation run without civilian control or oversight.

So what if Draganovic slipped a few of his own people down the line every once in awhile?

By 1947, however, as the mission changed from prosecuting Nazis to recruiting them, agents like Gowen found themselves on dangerous moral ground. Gowen resented his role to coddle the war criminals, and made his feelings known in a series of memos that have become declassified in recent years.[183] But the die was cast: the reason Klaus Barbie lasted so long in Europe after the war, only fleeing to Argentina in late 1950 or early 1951, was because he was working for American intelligence all that time.

Could this be the reason the Pöch couple lasted as long as they did before taking the same route out of Europe? So far, a search of relevant intelligence files does not result in their names appearing anywhere, but the author has to rely upon *declassified* files. Considering, however, that most of the high-value Nazi targets had left Europe years before with only those remaining who had some relationship with Allied intelligence, it seems possible that the Pöch couple was similarly involved. CIC was evidently aware of the couple—according to the Pöch diary—as early as 1946, yet did not arrest either of them. According to the same diary it was a "Jew" who told them that the local Communist newspaper would publish a story about them, exposing their role in the war, whatever that may have been. This is given as the reason for their sudden departure from Salzburg and their wandering around Europe trying to get papers to leave. If they left Salzburg in 1946 or 1947, then they would have had to use the Ratline to lay low. They would have made for the Tyrol as the most logical choice. The insistence of Dr. Sosro Husodo that they went to Yugoslavia is problematic but not impossible, as we have seen.

They could have gone to Graz, as it was in the British zone of occupation at the time that would have put them within striking dis-

---

183   In San Francisco in 1999 William Gowen appeared as a prosecution witness against the Vatican Bank, the Franciscan Order, the Croation Liberation Movement (the Ustashe) and several other defendants in a lawsuit seeking restitution and the declassification of CIA and other government documents concerning the Ratline. In his testimony, Gowen linked the Church and specifically Cardinal Montini (later to become Pope Paul VI) in the protection of Nazi war criminals as well as in the theft and laundering of Jewish property.

tance of Maribor, in Slovenia (part of Yugoslavia at the time). Maribor was the site of a POW camp during the war, and might have been the "Camp Macorr" Pöch refers to in his diary, for the Nazis did regard Maribor (and Slovenia in general) as being German and established a German government in the city after the Nazi invasion of June 22, 1941.

Regardless, the "denazification" of Austria's Nazis had been completed by 1948 so that the Pöch couple should have been out of trouble by then. There should have been no earthly need for them to escape after 1948 unless they had other motivations.

Or unless they were not whom they claimed to be.

Other motivations

Ernst Schäfer of the SS-Ahnenerbe had survived the war and, in 1950, went to Venezuela to conduct ornithological research.[184] His colleague from the Tibet expedition, Bruno Beger, similarly survived the war and wound up going on expeditions to the Middle East in 1954, 1958 and 1959, along with other colleagues from the Ahnenerbe. While reports of the hideous experiments on human subjects conducted under the auspices of the Ahnenerbe rendered many of their members unemployable, at least at home, some did manage to eke out an existence and even to thrive. There was still work to be done, after all.

As is evident from Beger's attitude towards the end of his life[185] he never abandoned his racist beliefs or accepted any responsibility for the crimes he committed. None of the true believers—the real Nazis, the committed SS men, the diehard Party members, the race scientists—ever abandoned the faith. And a faith it was.

A declassified OSS memo marked "Secret" and dated 19 January 1945 bore the subject line "The Nazi Underground in Bavaria and Austria." Its source was French intelligence and concerned the organi-

---

184   This information is contained in Heather Pringle's *The Master Plan: Himmler's Scholars and the Holocaust*, New York: Hyperion, 2006, p. 307 et supra. Pringle's book is the definitive study of the Ahnenerbe in English and is highly recommended.

185   Pringle, *The Master Plan*, p.319–325

zation of the Nazi movement after the war, with specific reference to the Tyrol and to Salzburg.

Paragraph 5, however, is quite revealing in another way. It reads:

> However, the Nazi underground is based on a sect of a religious and politico-military nature. This movement is conceived as a politico-religious community of men, fighting to protect the intellectual heritage of National Socialism, which must be carefully nurtured until the establishment of a democratic form of government in Germany will allow them to intervene and take action.

Paragraph 6 expands the idea:

> In view of the evolution of the situation in Germany, the underground is conceived as a meeting ground for opposition groups with [radical?] tendencies. The disciples and priests of this movement will have learned, under great pressure, to take up the work from the beginning, or any point whatsoever.

This characterization of National Socialism as a "sect of a religious and politico-military nature" is a theme this author has developed in his earlier work on the Nazi phenomenon.[186] One has the image of a kind of satanic order of knights, meeting in torch-lit caverns and salt mines, taking the oath of loyalty to the Führer. Considering how many of these rituals actually did take place, especially within the SS, the scenario is not that far-fetched.

It is important to understand this idea because it is what motivated men like Rauff, Barbie, Skorzeny and Rudel—among many others— to continue their work after the war. While Rauff and Barbie were military and SS men whose job description included mass murder—and who continued to be involved in military, assassination and espionage activities after the war—others, like Schäfer and Beger, continued the research they had been doing before the war's end. The dreams of the SS-Ahnenerbe were not dead; their devotees simply—in the words of

---

186   Levenda, *Unholy Alliance*, New York: Continuum, 2002.

the OSS memo cited above—"will have learned, under great pressure, to take up the work from the beginning, or any point whatsoever." They would have wanted to prove themselves to the scientific community at large; they would have wanted to vindicate the principles of Rassenkunde through their expeditions, their research reports, their whole attitude towards science, anthropology and archaeology.

If the couple that arrived in Jakarta in 1954 were in reality the Pöchs, then they would have picked up where they left off in 1945. Georg Anton Pöch would have sought another medical administration position, and his wife Hella would have tried to continue her fieldwork in race science. If Georg Pöch had been involved in the euthanasia program in Salzburg, which is likely considering his position with the Salzburg Gau, then he must have been tempted to apply some of these same principles in Indonesia, at least insofar as he would have been able to do so without arousing suspicion. Hella Pöch would have found a rich field for anthropometric, ethnographic and other biological anthropology research. Indeed, as we have seen, Brigitte Füchs claimed that Hella had continued her "biological research" in Indonesia.

Indonesia was not Europe, and Sumbawa was far from the center of things. The temptation to engage in ethnographic research must have been great, considering the wealth of "material" at her disposal. Yet, there is no evidence that Hella Pöch engaged in any of that: no evidence in Indonesia, and none in her European circles. If there is any evidence at all, it is buried somewhere in a museum or institute in Vienna courtesy of her former colleagues.

What if the travels of the Pöch couple were not so much to escape as to continue their work elsewhere, outside of Europe? They remained in Europe for six years after the end of the war; did they, like Barbie and so many others in the same circumstances, work for Allied intelligence in some capacity? Was that sighting of "Hitler" in Slovenia really a sighting of Georg A. Pöch, undercover in some mysterious mission for CIC or MI6? And, when they were no longer of service, did they use the Ratline to disappear into South America first, and then to Indonesia? A man and wife team of mad scientists, a euthanasia doctor and a race specialist, collecting specimens for a new collection of skulls and bodies in some more forgiving part of the world?

And, perhaps just as importantly, did the arrival of that American hospital ship, the SS Hope, throw a monkey wrench into the system? Did the Pöch couple suddenly realize that their little sanctuary, comfortably far from the old European theater of war, now was compromised?

The Ratline: Asian Division

One of the countries mentioned as represented in the Pöch diary is Tibet. The appearance of that name may seem outlandish in this context, but there is a reason for it.

As we have seen, Tibet was a valuable destination for the members of the SS-Ahnenerbe. It had political and military value as well as cultural and "racial." India was divided in its allegiances at the time, for it was under British occupation and Indian nationalists like Subhas Chandra Bose were openly pro-Nazi and admirers of Hitler whom they viewed as a liberator and as an "avatar." Hitler's symbol, after all, was the swastika: an ancient Indian sign of auspiciousness.

Tibet was in a similar situation. China had claimed sovreignty over Tibet, and the Tibetan government wanted assurances from any foreign power that their autonomy would be protected. It was a difficult situation for Nazi Germany, for most of its military leaders tended to support China against Japan, and would have supported Chinese claims to Tibet as well. However, after a power struggle in Berlin, Nazi Germany came down on the side of Japan against China. That meant that the Nazis and the Tibetans might be natural allies. Ernst Schäfer and his SS-Tibet Expedition had already formed contacts with the government of the Dalai Lama in 1938, and brought back stories of magic and mysticism that titillated their boss, Heinrich Himmler.

As the war progressed, however, there was less and less focus on Tibet. The war was a lot closer to home. But as the war in the Pacific ended in August of 1945, there was a fresh problem to be solved: that of the Chinese Communist revolution, led by Mao Zedong.

The political situation in Europe—the tug of war between the Americans, British and French on one hand and the Soviet Union on the other—was now mirrored in Asia. The goal of American intelligence was to do what it could to stop Soviet advances in Europe; their goal in Asia was to stop the spread of Chinese-flavored Communism in the Pacific.

Allen Dulles, now of the CIA, understood that it would be politically expedient to support the regime of the Dalai Lama but only if it could be done covertly. The United States was a staunch supporter of the Guomindang regime on Taiwan that opposed Mao, but both Mao and Chiang Kai-Shek of the Republic of China (Taiwan) claimed Tibet as Chinese territory. Dulles decided that what he needed was a properly-equipped and trained Tibetan militia. And to do that he needed guns.

China had been flooded with German weapons for decades. Finding ammunition and spare parts for German guns would be no problem; finding the same for guns manufactured in the United States or Great Britain would be problematic. So Dulles asked a young CIA agent to scour Western Europe for caches of German weapons that could be sent to the Tibetan resistance movement.

At the same time, there was a major problem of communication. The CIA had very few people who knew the country and the people and no one who was current on the political situation in Lhasa, the capital of Tibet. In short, Dulles knew of no one he could trust to carry messages back to the Dalai Lama. He would have to painstakingly develop new assets inside Tibet.

By 1953, Dulles had become the director of the CIA and began to promote the Tibetan resistance movement energetically. Thousands of Tibetans were trained in Nepal and given crash courses in espionage, sabotage and cryptography as well as in the use of modern weapons. What eventually happened, of course, was that Tibet was lost to the Chinese government and the Dalai Lama escaped from the country, aided by the CIA.

Between 1945 and 1953, when Dulles took complete charge of the Tibetan campaign, the history of the conflict is a little sketchy. Would the CIA have wanted to use Germans who had experience in Tibet, and moreover who had personal connections to the Dalai Lama? It would seem logical to have hired Schäfer and Beger, for example, as CIA agents in Tibet but there is no evidence for this at all. Yet, the CIA had no qualms about using Nazis in important espionage positions in Eastern Europe to fight the Communists there. Why not in Asia? Skorzeny was already running agents in Egypt; Alois Brunner was in Syria. So many others were half a world away in Latin America. It makes perfect sense—in the context of the times, in the context of CIA and fears of a worldwide Communist threat—to hire Nazis to assist in the anti-Chinese Communist Tibetan resistance movement.

And wouldn't an anthropologist like Hella Pöch be a logical choice, if members of the Ahnenerbe were too notorious to employ in such a sensitive mission?

THE READER MAY FORGIVE some of this speculation. After all, we are fresh out of documents where this moment in history is concerned. Ernst Schäfer, the fellow race scientist whose headquarters was in the Salzburg area in 1945, burned his files and records when he knew the end was near. And he was not alone. So many documents were destroyed in that period, which may explain why we know so little about the Pöchs. We are left collecting and connecting dots where we can. If the man and woman who showed up in Jakarta and later in Sumbawa really were the Pöchs, then we have to ask a lot of very uncomfortable questions. We have begun to realize that the Ratline was much more extensive, much more nuanced, and perhaps even better funded than we had been led to believe until now. We have to realize that the Pöchs were most likely war criminals of a very serious nature, with a record every bit as heinous as that of a Mengele or a Rauff or a Barbie. Remember that *neither Ernst Schäfer nor Bruno Beger needed the Ratline to get out of Europe.* These were men with damning histories and sickening lists of sins to their names. They were race scientists, like the Pöchs, and members of the Ahnenerbe whose leader was executed at Nuremberg. They were SS officers, and close to Heinrich Himmler. But they fared much better after the war than the Pöchs. They lived out their lives in Germany, and died peacefully there in the last few years.

On the other hand, *the Pöchs needed the Ratline.* Even six years after the war's end. They needed the monastery route. They needed Father Draganovic. And they left Europe soon after Barbie's own escape, and from the same city in Austria. They either had sinister motivations for doing so, or they were not who they claimed to be.

Other identities

As mentioned earlier, Dr. Sosro claimed that Pöch lived in Sumbawa with a woman named "Gerda" and a small child of 7 years old named "Frank G. Spivak." This has to be a mistake, some conflation of details that Sosro read in the press at about the same time he was reading about Klaus Barbie and Heinz Linge. As mentioned in Chapter Five, Sosro's Frank G. Spivak would have been about the same age as the real Frank G. Spivak, a convicted serial killer and neo-Nazi. Did Sosro read an account of this killer's rampage in an Indonesian magazine in 1983 when he was apprehended, and then conflate this story with that of some other small boy he saw in Sumbawa Besar at the home of the "German doctor"? None of the author's efforts to identify where the American killer Frank Spivak spent his childhood has yielded a period in Indonesia. The author cannot locate a copy of an Indonesian magazine or newspaper of the time that carried the Spivak story, but the Indonesian press is a raucous industry and there is every possibility that the story was carried in any one of hundreds of newspapers and other media that the author has been unable to source.

The Spivak story nearly thrust a monkey wrench into the investigation, for it seemed too contrived and invented, a detail created to cause a tabloid sensation ("Neo-Nazi serial killer lived with Hitler in Indonesia!"), except that there is no further mention of this boy in any context. Sosro never writes a word about the adult Spivak as a Hitler-loving serial killer. He never banks on this information, but only mentions it in passing. If he did not see a boy with that name—that very specific name with the middle initial—then why did he mention it and then ignore it?

And who was "Gerda"?

To make matters more interesting, one of Eva Braun's sisters was named Margarethe, or "Gretl" for short. It's possible the Indonesian doctor confused the two names, but since he got Frank Spivak's name correct one has to give him the benefit of the doubt.

However, "Gerda" is a common German diminutive form of the name *Gertrud* or, in English, Gertrude. Martin Bormann's wife was named Gerda, but she died in 1946. Eva Braun's closest friend was her cousin, Gertraud Weisker, who spent time with Eva at the Berghoff in the waning months of the war. In 1960, she would have been 37 years old. "Gertraud" is another German variant of the name Gertrude, and it is not beyond the realm of possibility that "Gerda" refers to Eva's cousin and best friend.

Another—albeit remote—possibility is that Gertuud Seyss-Inquart is intended. The wife of convicted and executed war criminal Artur Seyss-Inquart, the friend and patron of the Pöch couple, Gertruud escaped from the Netherlands as it was falling to the Allies and was never heard from again. The last anyone knew, she was on her way to Salzburg when she disappeared. Again, Salzburg comes up in this story in unexpected ways.

At this point, the mystery of Gerda and Frank Spivak must remain unsolved.

As Sosro continued his investigation, he came into possession of Sulaesih's recollections as well as of the Pöch documents. He managed to find Sulaesih and to question her about her life with the doctor, and of how she came to find herself in Sumbawa Besar.

According to the account published in *Hitler Mati di Indonesia*, Sulaesih left Bandung for Sumbawa in search of a job. While there, she met and married the nephew of the Sultan of Sumbawa. A year into their marriage, her husband developed a mysterious disease which is not otherwise described or identified in the account. She took him to the hospital in Sumbawa, where the Chief Medical Officer was Dr. Georg Anton Pöch.

It is fascinating to learn that Pöch managed to obtain the same title in Sumbawa as he had in Salzburg. As Chief Medical Officer, it is entirely possible that he was more of an administrator than a practitioner of medicine; however, the medical situation in Sumbawa was considerably less advanced than what he had been used to in Austria and it is likely that he would have been pressed into service as a regular doctor.

There is no indication anywhere that he was a surgeon or in any way participated in operations. There is, however, anecdotal evidence that he diagnosed illness and prescribed drugs as mentioned in Sosro's account. His wife is conspicuous by her absence in this narrative, and one wonders how she spent her time while her husband was busy dispensing pharmaceuticals.

Sulaesih's husband's condition did not improve. Thus, after several years of this chronic illness it was decided that Sulaesih should divorce her husband and seek another.

Around this time—in 1964—Pöch's wife left Indonesia, presumably forever. The reason given in the Sosro account is that she found the climate uncomfortable. However, she did manage to live there for ten years before leaving, which makes the climate excuse rather less than compelling.

The date is suggestive, however.

Eva Braun's immediate family enjoyed tremendous longevity, from her mother to her two sisters, all of whom survived the war for decades. Her father, however, died in 1964: the same year that "Mrs Pöch" left Indonesia for Europe.

This may be pure coincidence—like the KGB digging up "Hitler's" body less than three months after "Pöch's" death in Surabaya?—or it may suggest that Eva needed to return home for her father's funeral or had been alerted to the fact that he was ill and near death. Whatever the reason, Georg Anton Pöch, the "German doctor", was suddenly alone in Sumbawa.

According to Sulaesih, she knew the doctor's wife and was told by her to "take care of my husband." Sulaesih took this to mean she should marry him, even though he was thirty years her senior. The reasoning seems rather slim. A more appropriate explanation may be that Pöch needed a caretaker, someone to look after him and essentially function as a kind of maid, cook and nurse all rolled into one. Another scenario may be that Sulaesih was already having an affair with Pöch, and that there was pressure in the local community to formalize their relationship.

In any event, by 1965 the two had married but not before Pöch converted to Islam, taking the name Abdul Kohar, i.e., "servant of the Conqueror". There are several photos of Pöch and Sulaesih at their wedding, showing a rather expressionless and taciturn Pöch sitting or standing next to a much younger Sulaesih with a sweet—if somewhat bewildered—smile. There is not very much information on their married life, except for the fact that Pöch would often refer to himself as Hitler in her presence alone and tell his wife not to mention it to anyone. He also told her to avoid political discussions and political activities of any kind with any of their friends or colleagues.

According to a friend of Sulaesih, a Mrs. Omik Koswara, quoted in *Hitler Mati di Indonesia,* Pöch kept himself apart from social events and public gatherings whenever possible. Her friend Sulaesih had very little to tell her of her life with Pöch and, in fact, it would be Sulaesih who often would show up alone when the couple was invited anywhere.

There is another strange anecdote in Sosro's account that bears repeating here. Sosro states that Sulaesih told him that in 1964 or 1965 Pöch went to Bali to meet with Konrad Adenauer, one of the more famous and controversial Chancellors of West Germany. She was impressed with Pöch's ability to meet heads of state, and of the respect they showed him. This would have immediately been a cause for concern in vetting Sosro's story, because how would it have been possible for Adolf Hitler to meet Konrad Adenauer on friendly terms, as if they were old friends and World War Two had never happened? Although Adenauer has been roundly criticized for placing former Nazis in positions of influence in his government and for supporting their reinstatement in German industry, no one has suggested that the Chancellor was a Nazi himself. Fortunately, this story is a complete fabrication for Konrad Adenauer was not Chancellor in 1964 or 1965, having left that post in 1963.

And he never went to Bali. The author has this last fact directly from the Indonesian branch of the Konrad-Adenauer-Stiftung in Jakarta, from which it is also possible to view Adenauer's appointment book and schedule for the years after he left office. It would appear that the German statesman had never set foot on Bali in his life.

Thus, was Pöch merely lying about Adenauer to impress Sulaesih? Did Sulaesih invent this story, or simply get the name wrong?

Or had Pöch been meeting with someone else on Bali?

1965 was the famous "Year of Living Dangerously" in Indonesia. There was a military coup against the government of Sukarno—believed to have been instigated by western fears of Sukarno's connections to the Communist Party of Indonesia (PKI) and a brutal crackdown by the armed forces took place everywhere in the country, including Bali, beginning in October of that year. The massacres that took place in Bali would have made traveling there—and meeting German statesmen there—highly dangerous and rather unlikely as well. These were volatile times in Indonesia, yet there is nothing in the Sosro or Sulaesih narratives that refers to these events.

This, unfortunately, is understandable. Few Indonesians will freely discuss what transpired in those days. It is a very sensitive, very painful subject. It was a time when Indonesians brutally attacked and killed other Indonesians; when the army committed what can only be described as atrocities against its citizens; and when resistance groups were quickly and effectively suppressed. One talks about that period of history at one's peril.

What that means, however, is that there are glaring holes in the accounts of those days. If Pöch indeed had gone to Bali at this time and met with foreigners there, they most likely would have been anti-communists of some type. Pöch had been a ranking member of the Nazi establishment in Salzburg; his wife was a celebrated race scholar. They had both attempted to coerce the government of Reich Commissioner Seyss-Inquart to allow them to measure Jews in the concentration camps. If Pöch had met with anyone on Bali in 1965, it very likely would have been with other Nazis or their fellow travelers, not official German statesmen.

The threat of a Chinese Communist takeover in Indonesia would have worried Pöch considerably. If he had any political influence at all he would have put it to the use of anti-Communist, "anti-Bolshevik" forces. If the reason he and his wife spent so long in Salzburg after the war was because they were cooperating with Allied intelligence (as was Barbie), then it is also possible that the same intelligence organs made use of Pöch's connections in Indonesia to provide information on the political situation there. It is widely understood that the CIA had been involved in the coup that toppled Sukarno. Did Langley reach out to an old friend, an anti-communist crusader like Pöch, in the weeks and months leading up to the coup?

If this sounds a little surreal, remember that it is Sosro's account, and Sulaesih's, that introduces the story that Pöch made a trip to Bali that year and met with German officials. In the context of 1965, the scenario as presented here is the most probable.

It also should be remembered that Hjalmar Schacht—Germany's former finance minister and a person of tremendous political and financial influence—made trips to Indonesia beginning in the mid-1950s. There have been rumors that Skorzeny—who was married to Schacht's niece—also made visits there. Skorzeny's activities in the post-war years were almost entirely devoted to supporting former Nazis and to propping up anti-communist regimes wherever they could be found, from the Middle East to Latin America to Europe. Skorzeny would have seen in Sukarno a kindred spirit ... at least, until the Indonesian dictator began making advances to Communist regimes and flirting with Socialism at which point Skorzeny would have felt betrayed and would have thrown his weight behind any faction able to stop Sukarno before Indonesia was handed over to China as a satellite. This was successfully accomplished in 1966 when General Suharto took over the government and deposed Sukarno, becoming in the process a dictator for the next thirty years.

Was there a connection between Pöch's alleged visit to Bali in 1965 and the massacre of suspected Communists there the same year? Clearly more research has to be done, but it is doubtful that any answers will be forthcoming due to the purging of official records of that era and the reluctance of anyone to come forward and give evidence against the military or the government. What is known is that there was a significant Nazi presence in Indonesia from about 1927 to the end of the war, and that members of the Dutch SS were sent to Indonesia in the post-war period to suppress the independence movement, even establishing two concentration camps there in the process. Pöch arrived in Indonesia in 1954 and there is every possibility that he made contact with existing members of the Nazi underground at that time. After all, he was traveling along the Ratline and no one who used that route arrived in a foreign country without some sort of local welcoming network. It is highly unlikely that he would have gone to Indonesia without being assured that he would be accepted, (and not immediately arrested), by the government and assisted by local sympathizers or fellow war criminals. This network would have enabled him to get the job on Sumbawa as a "medical officer," even though it is probable he was not carrying the appropriate medical credentials (if he had, they have not shown up so far). The other Nazis—those in

Latin America and the Middle East—all had support services waiting
for them: temporary lodging, jobs, political connections and protection. Either the government of Indonesia offered this to Pöch, or there
was an existing clandestine network of supporters who did. In other
words, the Ratline: Asian Division.

Thus, while we are forced to take the story of Konrad Adenauer
with a grain of salt, there is every likelihood that Pöch did go to Bali
in 1965 and did make contact with "German" officials of some type.
While the Sosro/Sulaesih account seems contradictory and contrived
in places, a look beneath the surface of what they claim reveals deeper
levels of connection, particularly if one understands the political context of the times. The Sosro and Sulaesih stories must be read as a
kind of coded text, like the Pöch diary itself, which *was* encoded and
intended for the "right" sort of audience.

In 1966, Georg Anton Pöch renounced his German citizenship
(if he ever had it) as attested by a certificate from the West German
embassy in Jakarta that is reproduced in *Hitler Mati di Indonesia*. It
gives Pöch's name and birthdate and birthplace in Prezmysl (which
was not German territory when Pöch was born there, nor was it German territory when the Third Reich was in charge). This adds to the
confusion, of course.

In 1967, he is awarded Indonesian citizenship, and this document
is also reproduced in *Hitler Mati di Indonesia*. It states that Pöch was
born in Prezmysl, *Austria*.

There is not much more to the tale of Sulaesih and her "German"
husband. All we know at this point is that they left for Surabaya in
January of 1970 to accompany a patient to a hospital there. Around
midnight, Pöch himself suffered a heart attack. According to Sulaesih,
he knew the end was near. By eight pm that evening, he was dead.
According again to Sulaesih, he died with the words "Allahu akbar"
on his lips. Muslim custom demands that the body be buried within
twenty-four hours. It is assumed this is what happened. Sulaesih then
distributed all of her husband's books and other belongings to friends
and colleagues, and then retired for the rest of her life to Bandung.
All she kept was his diary, a few photos and some other (Indonesian)
documents. There was nothing left of his European paperwork at all.
Georg Anton Pöch, if he truly was Georg Anton Pöch, never again

saw his homeland. Never again set foot in Austria or Germany. He died as a Muslim convert on Indonesian soil, with the phrase "God is great" on his lips.

His tombstone was carved with his European name and nothing else. There was a space for his date of birth, and another for his date of death, but the stonecutter never filled in either. They remained blank for decades, until the story about the mysterious German doctor made the news in 1983 with Sosro's published article that the old man had in reality been the leader of the Third Reich ... and then the story died again, until a few years ago when tests of a human skull in the FSB (former KGB) archives in Moscow revealed that there was no forensic evidence to prove that Adolf Hitler had died in the bunker. At that point, someone decided to pencil in the date of Pöch's death in 1970.

But the date of birth still remains, to this day, suspiciously blank.

CHAPTER TEN

THE DISAPPEARANCE OF ADOLF HITLER

> The idea of going to Berlin seems to be coming off, that is,
> I won't believe it until I am really in the Reich Chancellery.
> Let's hope it all turns out well.
> —Eva Braun, diary entry dated February 15, 1935

It is appropriate to begin this last chapter with a quote from Eva Braun, for it is Eva who most likely is the key to this whole mystery. As everyone searched for Hitler—alive or dead—in the last days of the war, no one was really looking for Eva Braun. In the first place, her very existence had been a state secret until the fall of Berlin. In the second place, those who knew of her considered her an unimportant, empty-headed girl. While this characterization has been challenged of late[187], it was the operative image at the time. Who cared about Eva Braun?

But if she did survive the war ... if she did escape Berlin as historians such as Hugh Thomas have suggested ... then she holds the answer to one of the twentieth century's most enduring puzzles. For where Eva was, there was Hitler. Or, at the very least, knowledge of his survival and his whereabouts. Yet, she could have shown up in Berlin in a red dress and dancing shoes, and no one would have known whom she was.

HELLA PÖCH'S LIFE IN INDONESIA was also a cypher. Her husband got all the attention, all the glory. No one seemed to know very much about her. She has left no trace at all of her existence in Sumbawa. This is totally unlike the historic Hella Pöch who was a whirlwind of activity for decades and who held important positions within the anthropological community ... but that description is very like the real Eva Braun. So when Hella disappeared from the scene entirely, no one

---

187   See Heike B. Goertemaker, *Eva Braun: Life With Hitler*, New York: Knopf, 2011.

seems to have missed her or gone looking for information about her. All the focus was on her husband, Georg Anton Pöch.

The author has spent considerable time, money and effort in the search for the real Hella Pöch. All he has to show for his trouble is her history up until 1945 and even then it is spotty. We don't know how it was possible for her to marry two men named Pöch, for instance. Recourse to old phone books and address registries from Austria produce very few people with that patronymic. One wonders if Rudolf Pöch and Georg Anton Pöch were related, but there is no proof of this relationship that the author has been able to find. It seems likely that Rudolf and Georg would have been siblings or cousins, but there is little biographical information on Rudolf and virtually nothing on Georg.

Then there was Sulaesih, the second "Mrs. Pöch."

The author's attempts to locate and question Sulaesih were constantly frustrated. She still lives in Bandung, but she is housed in a very expensive and fortified estate. How she is able to afford this lifestyle is anyone's guess. There are what appear to be military personnel involved. She cannot answer questions about her life with the "German doctor" without other, plainclothes persons present who monitor the conversation. On this subject, the author is unable to say more.

The same is true of Dr. Sosro Husodo. He also lives in Bandung, in a house that is difficult to find and set back from the street, with a kind of superintendent who runs interference for him and who claims no one by that name lives there. It is Dr. Sosro who still has—it is believed—the original documents concerning Pöch's life that he received from Sulaesih, but these may now be in the possession of the Solonese prince who wrote the book, *Hitler Mati di Indonesia,* which contains blurry copies of some of these. All efforts by the author to contact the prince have been similarly frustrated. A curtain has dropped down over this story: an impenetrable fabric of disinformation, misdirection, and suppressed documents. At least one group of investigators has blamed this on the Indonesian government itself[188], but at present there is no absolute proof of this.

---

188 Tim Investigasi Solomongrup, *Melacak Garis Keturunan Hitler di Indonesia,* Yogyakarta: Solomongrup, 2011

What we do have are bits and pieces of the story and tantalizing clues, against the background of the inescapable fact that everything we have been told about the death of Adolf Hitler and Eva Braun has been a lie. First it was Operation Nursery. Then it was Operation Myth. Nursery and Myth: children, and the fairy tales told to them.

The intelligence agencies of the world knew of the existence of the Ratline, even before the end of the war. Memos detailing the efforts of the Nazis to expatriate gold and currency were rife. Operation Safehaven was designed to thwart those attempts, but as we have seen it failed miserably. Money and personnel were being moved abroad with swiftness and precision. Fairy tales were invented to discredit Hitler in the eyes of his followers and many of these same fairy tales became the operative narrative after the war.

Neutral countries like Spain and Argentina were central to the efforts to save Nazis and their gold. SS officers were sent to these countries to ensure that these channels remained secure. And once the money was safely abroad, the personnel followed.

There is no doubt about the escape of men like Mengele, Eichmann, Rauff, Roschmann, Priebke, Pavelic, Barbie, and so many other war criminals. Their escape routes have now become a matter of public record. The files have been declassified. Most of these men have escaped justice as well. Eichmann was snatched in a well-publicized raid in Argentina; Barbie was extradited to France. For the most part, however, the war criminals thrived in their new identities, in their host countries. How could they not? They were supported in their efforts by the Catholic Church, the International Red Cross, American intelligence, British intelligence, and the governments of so many countries it has become impossible to keep it all straight. The program to rescue and hide these vicious murderers—the Ratline—was practically universal. And these men did not go quietly into the night; on the contrary, they became very active politically and militarily, in Latin America and the Middle East in particular. For them, the war—the real war, the war of ideas, of ideology, of race—was not over. It never ended.

The Allies applauded themselves on the success of the Nuremberg trials, and why not? So many of those responsible for heinous crimes were arrested, tried, convicted and either imprisoned or executed. But it was only a relative handful of those responsible who faced the well-publicized Judgement at Nuremberg; the biggest culprits never stood trial.

Himmler escaped by taking poison before he could face justice. Bormann was never found. Mengele lived out his days in South America.

And Hitler disappeared.

WE CAN ONLY SAY WITH ANY DEGREE of certainty that Hitler "disappeared." We know that all the evidence we were told existed to prove his suicide in the Berlin bunker on April 30, 1945 was either nonexistent or fabricated. The same is true of Eva Braun. Both of these individuals disappeared. Their bodies did not turn up in Berlin as was claimed by the Russians. The skull they possess is not Hitler's (or Eva's) skull. The bodies they burned in 1970 were not those of Hitler and Braun.

We are thus left with the inescapable conclusion that both Hitler and Braun disappeared at the end of the war. We would like to believe otherwise. It would be a lot easier to accept the conventional wisdom and "believe" that the two died in Berlin in April of 1945. But, as we have shown, this story is the result of something called—rather cynically—Operation Nursery.

So, if Hitler and Eva Braun did not die in the bunker as has been claimed, then what happened to them?

HITLER'S FAVORITE COMMANDO—and one of the more prominent administrators of the Ratline—Otto Skorzeny laid out one scenario, mapping how Hitler could have escaped the bunker. The idea that a small private plane could have picked him up and spirited him away to Denmark or Spain was a rumor that had astonishing longevity in the weeks and months after the war. Hanna Reitsch was specifically asked about this during her interrogation by American army intelligence, and she dodged the issue by insisting that Hitler was dead. How dead could he have been for someone like Reitsch, who was an unrepentant Nazi to the end of her days, a true believer who it is believed took cyanide herself in 1979?

Whatever the actual method of escape from Berlin, there had to be a destination. Hitler knew that the Allies were aware of Berchtesgaden and the estates in Lower Bavaria where he and his colleagues had their homes. The Allies were also aware of the possibility that the National Redoubt was a reality, somewhere in the area between the Tyrol and Salzburg. These would have been dangerous places to use as sanctuary. But it is claimed that Hitler was deathly afraid of the Soviets, and suspected that his body would be mutilated and dragged through the streets by the triumphant Russians. He also knew that nothing of the sort would happen if he were to be captured by the Americans or the British. If he had to choose, he would have made for the American or British sectors, to the west, and avoided the east like the proverbial plague.

An alternative route would be via plane to Spain. So much gold had been moved through Spain and to prop up Franco, and so many preparations had been made in Spain to hide Nazi war criminals on their way to Argentina, that Hitler could have been assured of a warm welcome there by members of the German underground. Admiral Dönitz, who was supremely loyal to Hitler and who became the head of the government after Hitler's disappearance, boasted of the German Navy's ability to hide Hitler in an overseas sanctuary. Dönitz, of course, had served with the U-boat fleet in Spain, as we have seen.

Spain didn't lose much in the war. Spain once had colonies in North Africa and the Philippines. While she lost the Philippines to the United States after the Spanish-American War, her influence in Asia was still very strong. There is every indication that Spain expected to benefit from Japan's defeat of American forces in the Philippines, and the pro-Nazi Falangist groups in that country were very active in providing a fifth column to support the Japanese invasion in 1941.

When Japan's defeat was certain, Spain still had not declared war on either Germany or Japan. Franco remained in charge of the government for decades after the war, thus ensuring some continuity of the Ratline and of the "virtual Redoubt". The relationship between Franco and Juan Perón of Argentina was strong; an indication of this relationship is the fact that Evita Perón's body was taken to Spain and hidden there for years after her death. Meetings were held in Spain as late as the 1970s to arrange assassinations of anti-fascist political leaders in Europe and Latin America, all with the blessing of the Franco regime.

Thus, while it can be argued that World War Two began in Spain with the Civil War and the presence of German and Russian troops battling each other in that country, it could also be said that World War Two continued there long after the end of formal hostilities in 1945. Stalin believed that Hitler had escaped to Spain and from there to Argentina; it is a theory that should be revisited now, in light of all the recent evidence demonstrating the weakness of the official version of events. While it may be inconceivable to an American—for instance—that anyone would have protected Adolf Hitler, it is important to realize that there existed in many countries around the world a great deal of sympathy for the Nazi leader and his ideology. With the Cold War, many otherwise intelligent and thoughtful military and political leaders decided that the greatest threat to world peace was "bolshevism": the Communist bloc in Europe and in Asia, as well as in Latin America. The world became polarized between Communists and anti-Communists, and Nazis were definitely anti-Communists.

The nuanced position that Nazis were as much a threat to western democracy as Communism was voiced by very few. Spruille Braden was one of these, and his campaign to rid Latin America of Nazi influence has been well-documented, if little appreciated. A committed anti-Communist and conservative Republican, he nevertheless understood that Nazis were also the enemy, not a position that was easy for the more single-minded of his colleagues to appreciate. Braden was the exception, however, and not the rule.

When mass murderers were protected by America and other governments . . . , when the Catholic Church was demonstrably involved in the protection of these same murderers . . . and when even the Israeli government decided to use some of these men in espionage activities against their Arab neighbors and to drop their Nazi-hunting activities in order to cultivate trade and military agreements around the world . . . why should any of us be shocked to learn that Hitler may have, indeed, escaped and done so with the cooperation, collaboration and complicity of one or more of the world's governments?

The Scenario

Hitler and Eva Braun escaped Berlin sometime during April 30, 1945. Other bodies were burned in the Reich Chancellery garden and left there for the Russians to find. Dentures were placed in the bodies to provide identification, and the facial features of the two corpses were burned enough so that absolute visual identification would be impossible. The bodies were not burned completely beyond recognition, however. There had to be enough left of them to convince the Russians they had the real bodies.

In the case of Eva Braun, a cyanide capsule was broken in the mouth of an anonymous female corpse that had shrapnel wounds. There was no trace of cyanide in the body's internal organs.

The Goebbels family *did* commit suicide. That was an important element of the ruse. Goebbels was a true believer and a fanatic; he knew that his death and the deaths of his wife and children would further reinforce the idea that Hitler also had committed suicide. The dead dogs were a nice touch. There was no way Hitler could have escaped with Blondi anyway.

Hitler had not been seen in public since the July 1944 assassination attempt. No one had any recent photographs of him at the time. In addition, there were known Hitler doubles in Berlin. The plot to create misdirection—after the manner of a stage magician—was in place as early as 1944, if not earlier.

With the simple expedient of shaving off his famous moustache and covering his head with a hat or a blanket, Hitler easily could have escaped Berlin and Germany itself as an old man in a wheelchair. His nurse could as easily have been Eva Braun. If they had not managed to get a plane out of Berlin to either Spain or Denmark, as has been alleged, then they were able to go via the surface roads to another location. A painstaking journey, but who would have questioned a sick old man in Berlin in April of 1945?

He could not have traveled so easily without some form of documentation, however. Neither could Eva Braun.

Enter the Pöchs.

At some point in the last days of the war it was decided that a husband-and-wife scenario would play out best. Those looking for

Hitler would not be looking for a married couple, for no one knew that Hitler and Eva were married or that Eva even existed. But they needed verifiable documentation, real papers but with false identities. Like Himmler using the identity of a real German policeman, Hitler and Eva used the papers of a real married couple. They had to be Austrian—Hitler's German might have given him away—and they had to be the right age. There also should be some physical resemblance.

With Georg Anton Pöch they had all of this. With Eva there was a problem, but only in her age. She was thirty-three at the time of the fall of Berlin. Hella Pöch was forty-seven. But by 1951, when the Pöchs left Europe, Eva would have been thirty-nine and Hella fifty-two. That thirteen-year difference in their ages could have been compensated for with the judicious application of makeup or surgery.

At some point between April of 1945 and September of 1951, the transition was complete. Adolf Hitler and Eva Braun had become Georg Anton and Hella Pöch. The author contends that the identities would not have been used until it was certain that the Allies had no interest in the Pöchs (which may be related to the stories of CIC interest in the Pöchs in 1945 and 1946 and their eventual disinterest after that time). When the dust had settled, the newly minted "Pöchs" would have to leave Salzburg. After all, Georg Anton Pöch had been the medical officer of the Salzburg Gau. He would have been recognized. So the odyssey began: first to Graz in the British sector, then to Slovenia, and eventually to Rome and Genoa. The Pöch diary may very well be genuine; or it may be something German intelligence had mocked up to provide what the intelligence people refer to as "litter": paper artifacts that help reinforce a false identity.

Hitler and Braun then make it to South America. The Hitler sighting in Colombia is suggestive; so is the sighting in Brazil. Hitler could not have stayed long in either place, for there were so many Germans already emigrating to these countries that it would only be a matter of time before he was identified and the authorities alerted: by a survivor of the death camps, perhaps, or by a low-level Nazi who wanted to be a hero to the Allies. As we have seen, the Israelis snatched Eichmann out of Argentina in 1960. While Latin America may have been far from Europe, there were still too many possible ways to get identified and caught.

Thus, we can account for the missing years 1951–1953. Eventually, a deal was struck with the Sukarno regime to accept a German refugee couple. The passport number is troublesome, as it does not match any of the known passports used at the time by members of the Ratline. However, it is entirely possible that it represents an Indonesian immigration permit, something special worked out by Draganovic with perhaps a gold transfer to sweeten the deal. The Indonesian government would not have known whom they were letting into the country. They would have been under the impression that it was a Nazi, but not someone very important.

Pöch's old job title was "Chief Medical Officer" and the job he eventually gets in Sumbawa is the same. An article is planted in an anthropological journal in 1957, purporting to be by Hella Pöch, to reinforce the idea that she was still alive and working. But she becomes a non-entity, fading into the background until 1964 when news of the sickness or death of Eva Braun's father reaches her and she decides she has had enough of the tropical, third world lifestyle and returns quietly to Europe.

Georg Anton Pöch, in order to further reinforce his stolen identity, converts to Islam, takes a Muslim name, and marries an Indonesian woman who more or less serves as his assistant and nurse. The transformation is complete. Adolf Hitler completely disappears.

As for the real Pöchs?

Buried somewhere in the "National Redoubt" would be the author's guess, a bullet hole in the back of each cranium. Another two martyrs for the Reich.

ALL THIS TIME, J. EDGAR HOOVER is looking for Hitler, mostly in Latin America. The Soviets believe they have his body, *but they don't show it to anyone.* They bury and dig up the body again and again and, finally, bury it in Magdeburg in what was then East Germany.

Then panic sets in.

A man with the name Georg Anton Pöch dies in Indonesia on January 16, 1970. A gravestone is prepared, but mysteriously no one seems to know the date of death ... or the date of birth. Someone in Indonesia knows who Pöch really is, so he cannot bring himself to have Pöch's date of birth inscribed. The stone is left blank.

But someone alerts the Soviets. A body has been buried in Surabaya, and eventually someone will come along and say it's Hitler. But Soviet intelligence has records to show that *they* buried Hitler—along with Eva and an entire gaggle of Nazis (and their little dogs, too)—in East Germany. But the records are part of an elaborate hoax that was played on Stalin. The bodies in Magdeburg are not those of Hitler and Braun. Someone in Soviet intelligence knows this. They cannot afford the body in Indonesia to be dug up and revealed to be Hitler. They have to destroy their own "Hitler" and remove any trace of their involvement in his burial. It's called Operation Archive.

And then ... they wait.

The decade of the 1970s comes and goes. Then the 1980s. In 1983, Dr. Sosro Husodo publishes his account of Georg Anton Pöch. There is a brief flurry of interest, which then dies down almost immediately as "experts" ridicule the story. The Soviets breathe a sigh of relief. They can now spin the Hitler story any way they want to.

And they do. In 1992, the Russians make public for the first time that they have skull fragments from Hitler's corpse (a claim that was proven false fifteen years later). They reveal the existence of the order, signed by Yuri Andropov, to destroy the bodies buried in Magdeburg. The operation was carried out on April 4, 1970, seventy-seven days after the death of Pöch in Indonesia. The reason given is they wish to avoid possibility of the burial place becoming a shrine for neo-Nazis.

Neo-Nazis. In East Germany. In 1970.

And who would have revealed that there were bodies buried in the headquarters of the Soviet secret police in Magdeburg? One supposes it would be a logical conclusion, but seriously would anyone want to dig up what might be old execution and torture victims? And what if they *had* found the bodies—after fifteen years in the ground—and opened the wooden boxes in which they had been kept? The bodies had not been embalmed. According to the agents who carried out the secret mission, the state of the corpses was ... well, disgusting. A "gelatinous mass" is how one agent described it. Would anyone really have identified these gelatinous masses as the bodies of Hitler, Eva Braun, and the entire Goebbels family?

This entire account seems doubtful. Another intelligence cover story. And, once again, we have to come back to the single most salient point of all: it has been proven that the bodies the Soviets believed were those of Hitler and Braun were not those of Hitler and Braun.

A Parallel

Perhaps it would be useful at this point to introduce a similar story. A military and ideological leader, a rabid anti-Semite, delusional with dreams of reinstating an ancient Reich, is hunted by the world's democracies. He has committed mass murder, and has urged his followers to continue to do so. He is worshipped, almost like a god. His pronouncements are published everywhere. His photograph is an object of veneration. His enemies are the United States, England, Russia, and the Jews. He warns of a global Jewish-Masonic conspiracy.

One day he is located in a bunker. He is killed. His body is taken away, and his remains dumped into the ocean, so that his grave would not become a shrine. The west breathes a sigh of relief, even as others plot revenge.

We are referring, of course, to Osama bin Laden.

The parallels between the two men could not be stronger. And even as bin Laden was buried at sea—the same way Hitler was presumed to have had his ashes scattered in the Elbe River—American intelligence warned of the existence of "lone wolf" terrorists who would continue to carry out bin Laden's mission even after his death. We remember that American intelligence was concerned about the "Werewolf" operation that was announced by Goebbels: of lone operators who would continue to harass the Allies after the war was over.

This scenario has become iconic. The evil dictator whose body is destroyed and never found. The belief in his continued existence by his faithful followers. The lack of photographic evidence of his death and burial. The control of all of this information by the intelligence agencies. Nursery and Myth, indeed.

Until whoever is buried in Georg Anton Pöch's tomb is dug up and identified, we may never be sure about the truth of this story. It is even possible that no one is buried in Pöch's tomb. Wouldn't that also go a long way towards explaining the lack of dates on his tombstone? Maybe Pöch didn't die at all. Maybe he was snatched—by the Soviets, by the Americans, by the Israelis even—and brought back to an underground cell, a kind of weird exhibit for those with the highest clearance. Who knows? Since we have been lied to so consistently about this since 1945, anything is possible.

If these conclusions and speculations seem wild or paranoid, blame the arrogance of governments and their intelligence agencies that treat the people they are sworn to govern and protect as children who cannot be trusted with the truth, and who are devoted to Hitler's concept of *The Big Lie* as quoted on the very first page of this book. Cynicism is the gap that separates the governed from those who govern; *realpolitik* is the excuse that is made for the worst sins against the soul of nations. And lies—like the lie about the suicide of Hitler in the Berlin bunker on April 30, 1945—become the currency for spies and politicians alike, to be traded like baseball cards until one has a complete set and can call it "the official version of events."

Did Hitler survive?

Look around. Neo-Nazism is on the rise. There is a hard swing to the right in many countries around the world, some of it provoked by fears of a terrorist threat. The instability of the global economies and the widening gap between rich and poor is a familiar precedent for the appearance of populist dictators. Civil liberties are being eroded in the name of national security. Military and political leaders are warming their hands on today's versions of the Reichstag fire. In Latin America and Asia, Hitler is more popular than ever.

What the Allies feared would happen, *did* happen. As the story of Hitler's suicide is shown to be unsupportable by the evidence, the resurgence of belief in this monomaniacal madman and his fanatical ideology of race, purity, and power is guaranteed. Like Barbarossa, he sleeps in a cave—perhaps in a salt mine in Salzburg, or more comfortably in a guest house in Bolzano, in that "monastery in Tibet" or a tropical island in Southeast Asia—waiting for the hurt, the hateful, and the willfully-ignorant to call his name in their hour of need.

SS RANKS AND THEIR AMERICAN EQUIVALENTS

Readers may be bewildered by the use of Nazi rankings in these pages, but there is no easy way around it. The importance of understanding the *Führerprinzip* or Leader Principle is demonstrated by the fact that all of the SS ranks (except the lowliest three who are not leaders but followers) incorporate the word *Führer*. While Hitler was *the* Leader—*der Führer*—he was not the only one. The Leader Principle was designed around a pyramidal structure of allegiances and loyalties. Every person had a leader above him or her, and that leader reported to another leader, and so on to the ultimate leader, Hitler himself. Everyone understood their place in the hierarchy and there was no room for positions outside this carefully-constructed pyramid.

To make it easier to visualize the SS ranks, a table is provided showing them and their American military equivalents. The reader will note the use of the German words *unter*, *ober*, *haupt* and *sturm*. They translate into *under*, *over*, *high* and *storm* or *assault* respectively. This is further clarification of the hierarchical system that begins with *under* and proceeds to *assault*.

SS Rank	American Equivalent
SS-Anwärter ("candidate" or "aspirant")	Recruit
SS-Mann	Private
SS-Sturmmann ("storm man")	PFC
SS-Rottenführer ("foreman")	Corporal
SS-Unterscharführer	Sergeant
SS-Scharführer	Staff Sergeant
SS-Oberscharführer	Technical Sergeant
SS-Hauptscharführer	First Sergeant
SS-Sturmscharführer	Master Sergeant
SS-Untersturmführer	Second Lieutenant
SS-Obersturmführer	First Lieutenant
SS-Hauptsturmführer	Captain
SS-Sturmbannführer	Major
SS-Obersturmbannführer	Lieutenant Colonel
SS-Standartenführer	Colonel
SS-Oberführer	No American equivalent
SS-Brigadeführer	Brigadier General
SS-Gruppenführer	Major General
SS-Obergruppenführer	Lieutenant General
SS-Oberstgruppenführer	General

Reichsführer-SS: This was the title used by Heinrich Himmler, head of the SS

APPENDIX II

RATLINE ORGANIZATION: NAMES, GROUPS, COMPANIES

The structure of the Ratline is vast and complex. For the most part it existed—and continues to exist—underground in a world of lies, deceptions, secret meetings, and covert action. However, the last few years have afforded researchers an enormous amount of new data to understand and organize. The following breakdown is merely an introduction, a basis from which to develop a better idea of the breadth of the organization.

It should be remembered that the Ratline is not a single corporate entity. It is a loose confederacy of fellow-travelers with a similar world-view and identical goals of evading prosecution and continuing their work on the global stage. It began as the war was ending, when the flight of personnel and capital was an urgent requirement. But around those high profile war criminals such as Eichmann and Mengele was an extensive network of safe houses, false documents, slush funds and secret transportation methods that was run by the lower-level SS officer, Catholic priest, and Red Cross bureaucrat as well as various petty criminals such as forgers, smugglers and thieves. In addition, agents of various western governments were also complicit in running the Ratline.

Ironically, the combination of these factors makes the Ratline a very real and very well-documented international conspiracy, far surpassing in its reach any fevered "Jewish-Masonic" conspiracy that the Nazis themselves imagined.

The European Element

The Ratline can be said to have begun in Austria. Salzburg and Vienna were the hotspots, with an emphasis on the CIC (the US Army's Counter-Intelligence Corps) presence in Salzburg whose officers invented the term "Ratline". The CIC utilized the services of Roman Catholic Monsignor Krunoslav Draganovic as well as other Croatian priests.

It is believed by many that Croatian Archbishop Stepinac was also involved in the smuggling of Nazis and Nazi wealth out of the hands of the Communists. Draganovic began the movement of the Ustashe war criminals to Argentina, and then continued with the Nazis in general using the same channels via Rome and Genoa.

In Italy the major centers were in Bolzano (in the Italian Tyrol), Rome, Genoa, and Milan (and to some extent Bari). These were all run by Catholic clergymen with an assist by the International Red Cross. Bishop Alois Hudal was based in Rome at the Collegium Orientalis at Via Tomacelli 132 which served as a safe house for men like Franz Stangl. Archbishop Giuseppe Siri was based in Genoa, which served as the major transit point for war criminals fleeing to Latin America. The address of the Genoese safe house was Via Albaro 38. Archbishop Ildefonso Schuster was based in Milan and provided assistance to war criminals such as Walter Rauff on their way to Genoa.

And the German Archaeological Institute has been revealed in this book to have been another leg in the Ratline from its base at Via Sardegna 79.

Mgr Krunoslav Draganovic, when he was not in Salzburg working for the CIC and, later, the CIA, was in Rome at the Collegium Illiricum running the "Bratovatina Relief Organization" which was a cover for his Ustashe escape routes.

Also in Rome was the headquarters of Caritas, the Catholic relief and welfare agency whose name translates from the Latin as "charity." The element of Caritas that was involved in the Ratline was run by Cardinal Montini who later became Pope Paul VI.

We must also include the International Red Cross and the International Relief Organization as elements of the Ratline. They provided the temporary identification documents that the refugees would need in order to obtain passports and visas.

All of the above was in place as early as 1946, if not earlier.

In Spain, Madrid was the focal point for the Spanish Ratline as it was the capital of the Franco regime. Franco was very sympathetic to the Nazi cause and welcomed the assistance of the Nazi Condor Division in his fight against the Soviet-supported Republicans in the civil war that lasted from 1936–1939. The Nazis were able to use Spanish ports to refuel their U-Boats—the Etappendienst service that was started by future Admiral Karl Dönitz in World War I—and Spanish banks and corporations to launder their funds.

A key figure in the Spanish Ratline was SS officer Carlos Fuldner who began making arrangements to move men and money (particularly gold) through Spain before the end of the war, through such front groups as Sofindus. Later, as the war ended, Hitler's favorite commando—Otto Skorzeny—became intimately involved with the Franco regime and the movement of men and money continued. In addition, Spain's close relationship with Argentina and particularly between the national leaders Franco and Perón meant that Spain would remain an important element of the Ratline long after the end of the war. Franco and Perón were also conservative Catholics and saw the Catholic Church as a bulwark against Communism; for this reason the Fascist-Nazi-Catholic nexus was an important factor in creating and maintaining the Ratline globally, with the Church providing both logistical support as well as moral legitimacy.

Latin America

Pride of place in the Latin American segment of the Ratline must go to Argentina. While there was a noticeable pro-Nazi element in Argentina before the war and a thriving Nazi Party organization there, it was not until the election of Juan Perón in 1946 that the Ratline could make Argentina its destination of choice. Shortly after his election, the number of war criminals fleeing to Argentina increased dramatically.

One of the organizations that served to obtain Argentine visas for the refugees was Vianord which operated offices in Buenos Aires as well as in Spain. It was a tourist agency with no tourists. The European element of the Ratline made extensive use of Vianord among other agencies and individuals with similar capabilities in both Argentina and Spain.

Cardinal Antonio Caggiano was the Roman Catholic prelate most identified with the Argentine Ratline. He personally visited Rome to ask the Pope to let Argentina accept war criminals who were still in hiding in that city in 1946.

The subject of the Argentine Ratline has been covered extensively by Uki Goñi, but in addition to his work the following sites have been uncovered:

Walter and Ida Eichorn of the Eden Hotel, in La Falda, Argentina offered their resort to Hitler personally during a meeting with the Führer in Berlin in 1935. There have been many rumors that Hitler did, indeed, make it to La Falda after the war's end.

In addition, areas of Argentina that were known as both remote and hospitable to fleeing Nazis included Entre Rios, Chaco and Misiones. It was an element of the Ratline that was financed by Karl Dönitz himself, along with Count Lutz Schwerin von Krosigk, Hitler's Finance Minister. Dönitz—from his background with the U-Boat fleet, with the Etappendienst, and as the official successor to Hitler—would have been in the ideal position to know of escape routes and to ensure their success. Companies such as Lahusen of Argentina served as fronts for Nazi organizations in the country and would have lent their aid to any war criminals, in concert perhaps with the operation at the Eden Hotel in La Falda.

But Argentina was not the only country in Latin America to serve as a conduit for the Ratline. Colombia, Venezuela, Brazil, Paraguay, Bolivia and Chile were also important destinations. In Chile we had a large Nazi Party organization during the war. Chilean ambassador to Austria (1964–1970) Miguel Serrano was a devoted Nazi Party member who was friendly with Otto Skorzeny, Hans Ulrich Rudel and Hanna Reitsch, among others, and was thus in a position to assist the Ratline using his credentials as ambassador. He was also intimate with the leaders of Colonia Dignidad in Chile, a notorious safe house on the Ratline route.

In Brazil, the towns of Rio Grande and Casino were populated by immigrant Germans who were pro-Nazi both during and after the war. The Grande Hotel de Casino was mentioned as one of the possible locales of a Hitler sighting in the 1940s.

Bolivia, of course, became the home of Klaus Barbie, the "Butcher of Lyons", before he was deported to France to stand trial in the 1980s.

The Middle East

Syria and Egypt were the most important sites of the Ratline in the Middle East. More than eighty Nazi specialists in torture and interrogation techniques found work with the Nasser regime in Egypt.

Johannes von Leers, a friend of Grand Mufti Al-Husseini, fled first to Argentina and then to Egypt.

Nazis such as Franz Rademacher, Walter Rauff, and Alois Brunner all found sanctuary in Syria, Rauff being assisted directly by Bishop Hudal and Archbishop Schuster.

Paul Leverkühn, the Bilderberger and Nazi, found refuge in Lebanon.

But the most important figure in the Middle Eastern Ratline was, of course, Emir Al-Husseini who raised an SS division to help the Nazis in the Balkans. The Arab resistance to the creation of the State of Israel opened the doors to an acceptance of Nazi influence in the region and some personalities and organizations became pro-Nazi in sentiment as they accepted at face value the stories of a global "Jewish Masonic" conspiracy to rule the world.

Asia

The Asian element of the Ratline is only being revealed in the present time. Although it is known that many Nazi war criminals wound up in Australia—where some are still fighting extradition to this day—Asia has been ignored by historians as a potential Nazi refuge. Yet the relationship between crank German scientists and the Tibetan government before, during and after the war is well-known. The search for Hitler in the Ashinoyu region of Japan has been noted. And, of course, the story of Indonesia and the Nazi Party of Indonesia has been discussed in these pages. Asia was also a destination for Nazi war materiel and engineering designs, via the U-Boat traffic from Europe to Malaya and Indonesia, and possibly also for Nazi gold. It is safe to assume that the men running the Ratline did not dismiss any area of the world as a potential sanctuary, and Asia—due to its remoteness from the European battlefield—would have held some definite attractions.

The United States

There can be no doubt that agencies of the US government (as well as of the British government) actively cooperated in the escape of several Nazi war criminals. Allen Dulles, William Pawley and Frederick D. Hunt are only a few examples of well-placed government agents who were involved in the Ratline. We must also consider Operation Paperclip—which brought numerous Nazi scientists and doctors to the United States—as an element of the Ratline. Klaus Barbie and Krunoslav Draganovic both worked at one time for the CIA with the full knowledge of their Nazi past.

The Roman Catholic Church

As we have demonstrated, the Catholic Church was most intimately involved in the rescue of war criminals from apprehension and prosecution. Every level of priesthood, from cardinals and bishops to priests and monsignors, found themselves involved in protecting men like Eichmann, Rauff, Mengele and so many others. Church participation extended from Austria to Italy and Spain and thence to Latin America among the radically anti-Communist and pro-ecclesiastical regimes in that region.

The Eastern Orthodox Church

The Eastern churches are nationalistic by nature. Each country has its own Orthodox Church (Russia, Bulgaria, Serbia, etc.). The Ukrainian Orthodox Church was involved in pro-Nazi activities during the war as was the Russian Orthodox Church Outside Moscow. An entire division of Ukrainian Waffen-SS was allowed to immigrate to North and South America as well as to Australia after the war. In Serbia, however, the Orthodox were considered the enemy of both the Croatian Catholics and the Bosnian Muslims, adding to the general confusion. Thus, in addition to the Catholic networks aiding Nazis there are also Eastern Orthodox networks which should not be overlooked in any investigation. Valerian Trifa, a member of the Romanian Iron Cross (a Nazi organization responsible for war crimes), became the head of the Romanian Orthodox Church in the United States before he was identified as a war criminal and fled to Spain.

Appendix III:

Hitler's DNA

One of the critical factors in determining Hitler's fate has been the absence of forensic evidence that would prove that a skull, a body, or any part thereof actually belonged to the German leader. The skull that was in the possession of the Russians for more than fifty years after the end of the war has been shown to be that of an unknown woman. The dental work that the Russians have so far not allowed anyone to examine would also prove inconclusive, since—as we have seen—multiples of these dentures were made by Hitler's dentist in Berlin.

Thus, we are left with DNA evidence.

In 1945, there was no such thing as determining a person's identity on the basis of genetic matching. In the past twenty years, however, DNA tests have become an indispensable tool of law enforcement. This new technology has permitted death sentences to be overturned all across the United States as innocent men and women have been released on its basis. It has also permitted many cold cases to be resolved, as the DNA of convicted felons have been added to criminal identification databases, thus linking new prisoners to old crimes.

In the event that the body in Indonesia is ever exhumed, or in the event that other forensic evidence is uncovered elsewhere in the world, the only reliable tool we will have for identifying any given set of remains as Hitler's would rely on the availability of Hitler's genetic material for establishing a match. Unfortunately, even though members of Hitler's family have survived the war, they have resisted providing DNA samples to researchers.

That hasn't stopped some investigators from procuring Hitler family DNA using means that would not survive a legal challenge, however.

In Belgium, Marc Vermeeren and Jean-Paul Mulders have claimed that they had been stalking Hitler family members for years and insist that they have tracked down all living survivors for a total of thirty-six in Europe and three in the United States.

Most of the European descendants live in Austria—Hitler's home country—under names they have changed to disguise their lineage. In the United States, the same strategy was employed. Now living in Patchogue, Long Island—a suburb of New York City—they live quiet, unassuming lives. They did not know they were under surveillance by Vermeeren and Mulders, who took a napkin one of the descendants had used in a fast-food restaurant and matched it with a sample of Hitler's DNA they claim they have stored in a safe.

They also extracted DNA from cigarette butts and from stamps that had been licked by one of the survivors.

The type of DNA extracted is from the great-grandchildren of Alois Hitler, the Führer's father. The admissability of this evidence in a legal proceeding would be moot; it was not obtained during a legal search. However, as a means of testing other evidence in an effort to determine Hitler's fate, it could be worth a great deal. It is entirely possible that Vermeeren and Mulders are the only people in the world at this moment with a quantity of the Hitler family's genetic material, material which could be used to make a definitive judgment as to whether or not the body in Surabaya is that of the twentieth century's most notorious political leader.

ACKNOWLEDGMENTS

It is nearly impossible to acknowledge all the people who have influenced the process of writing a book. Writing an article or even a short story or essay one is struck by how many individuals have had some impact on ideas, information, voice, structure, and point of view. How much more so a book, especially non-fiction: something that marshalls information from various sources and tries to put a face on events that transpired long ago.

If this were an Oscar acceptance speech, I would be getting the five-second warning already. I would have mentioned God for some reason, as well as family, producers, directors, a great cinematographer, a charming co-star ... and extended gratitude to the Academy for making the right decision in the face of so much talented competition. Instead, and since I have unlimited space and no time constraints, I would like to acknowledge the people who in so many ways really helped write this book.

Donald Weiser and Yvonne Paglia deserve pride of place because this is not a book that neatly falls into their list as publishers. An investigative work on the Nazi underground now rubs shoulders with books on spirituality, psychology, Eastern religions, and my own *Tantric Temples*. I may have taken some chances in hunting Nazi networks in Latin America, Europe and Asia, but they took a chance in deciding to publish the results of my work. History will show who made the greater gamble!

Maya Gabrieli, a friend of long acquaintance, lent her support in so many ways to this and other works and while she is reluctant to take credit she deserves at least this mention. It is due to Maya that I was able to make presentations before various groups in South Florida that were interested in the survival of the Nazi underground and the political decisions that enabled the escape of war criminals for decades. This helped me organize my information and formulate my approach. For this, and so much else besides, thank you.

John Loftus was gracious with his time and information. A well-known expert in the field of US government collusion in the cover-up of the Ratline, he was able to guide my investigation into areas I had not considered previously.

Nick Bellantoni, the State Archaeologist of Connecticut, was equally gracious. He had gone to Moscow to examine the putative Hitler skull and who had come back with fragments to be tested, thus proving that the skull in question did not belong to the Führer (the story that is told in these pages). As an archaeologist, Dr Nick gets involved in the strangest cases, including the famous "vampire" graves in eastern Connecticut, but is always a calm and rational voice in the midst of the hysteria. While he believes that Hitler did, indeed, die in the bunker his investigation of the Hitler skull was a critical factor in my decision to take the Indonesia story seriously.

Uki Goñi was kind enough to respond to emails concerning the International Red Cross passports, which was important to my understanding of the documents used by Pöch when he entered Indonesia. Uki is probably the best-known researcher in the field of the Nazi networks in Argentina, working from the Argentine side. His contribution to the knowledge we have of how the ODESSA organizations functioned is invaluable to all of us who work in that area.

Heather Pringle was a great help in the writing of this book as she and her team provided some important documentation concerning the German Archaeological Institute. Her book on the SS-Ahnenerbe is the definitive text in English on this bizarre organization. Her kindness and willingness to help in this endeavor were deeply gratifying.

Clemes Brünenberg of the Deutsches Archäological Institut was helpful in answering email inquiries about the current state of research into the Institute's war time activities.

Marc Frings of the Konrad Adenauer Stiftung in Jakarta, Indonesia was a tremendous help in enabling me to prove that Pöch could not have met Adenauer in Bali as was claimed by his Indonesian widow.

Joseph Farrell toils in the same vineyards. His inexhaustible energy when it comes to writing and thinking about the effect the Nazi underground has had on modern politics and science is astonishing. I am in debt to his published work on Nazi scientific experiments and projects which by now has become an imposing, and heavily-documented, ouevre.

Journalist Tom Beyerlein helped in my research on the background of Ohio murderer Frank Spivak. It is one of the strangest elements of the Indonesian story, and one that has yet to be understood.

Annie Azzaritti was supportive through the entire arc of the project, from the discovery that there were strange Germans in Indonesia who might have been Nazis to the idea that one of them might have been Hitler. We have collaborated on a number of television documentary projects, and she has been gracious enough to introduce me to many of her associates and colleagues in Los Angeles with whom we have been brainstorming concepts on how to treat this story in the best possible way. A good friend and a helpful colleague, Annie has never wavered in her belief that this would make a good documentary some day!

James Wasserman. What can I say? I have known Jim for decades and his aesthetic sense as well as his grasp of historical realities contributed to the completion of the artifact that is now in your hands. The revelation that the US government—as well as the governments of many other nations—actively or passively collaborated in the escape of war criminals and in the establishment of their underground networks is not an easy one to stomach, let alone digest. Throw in the Catholic Church and the Red Cross, and one's belief in the inherent goodness of the human race is sorely tested! But Jim has never lost his moral compass, even in such heavy electromagnetic storms.

It is also necessary at this point to mention my Indonesian partners in this endeavor. Indonesia is not an easy country to move around in, or to understand. It is a complex matrix of cultural relationships and influences that involves language, religion, politics, history, and mysticism. An Indonesian would probably not compartmentalize her life the way I have just done, and this is the strength of the culture.

That said, the one person who helped me the most on this project desires not to be identified. I was fortunate enough to have enjoyed the partnership of various individuals associated with the Universitas Gadjah Mada in Yogyakarta, but they are in no way responsible for the conclusions I have drawn or for the way I have described Indonesian history in these pages.

In addition, all attempts to contact the authors and publishers of the two original Indonesian-language texts on this subject were met with silence. Much of their work had to be independently verified, and this is where my story began as I deconstructed the events described in their books. There were errors in their work, errors of fact mixed with errors of understanding European history and the war, and these I believe I have addressed and answered. In the end, however, the story of Georg Anton Pöch is a remarkable one—whoever he was, and whatever he was up to in Indonesia—and it is to those Indonesian authors that I am grateful for sending me off on this wild ride.

It is customary at some point to include thanks to more intimate members of one's immediate circle: spouse, children, siblings, parents, brothers-in-law, family friends, pets, imaginary playmates, stuffed animals, spirit guides, etc. The nature of this work, however, and the possible reception it may receive in certain quarters, makes me hesitate to unburden myself of familial references for their safety as well as my own. As someone who has received threats in the past, it seems that discretion is the better part of advertisement, and for now that is how I will leave it. However, you know who you are, and you know the contributions you have made, and you know how grateful I have always been.

Thank you!

PETER LEVENDA
2012, The Year of Living Dangerously

BIBLIOGRAPHY

The primary source material supporting the contentions made in this book come from declassified American, British and Soviet files, most of which only came to light in the last ten years. The Soviet files on Hitler's death had only been published in 2005, fully sixty years after the end of the war, and American intelligence files from World War Two are in the process of being declassified. Those that have already been released still, in some cases, contain portions that have been redacted.

Aside from the FBI, OSS, MI6 and CIA files that have been cited in the text, secondary sources include the following. It should be noted that some of the research done on the Nazi underground outside of Europe was published as early as 1939; there was thus an abundance of evidence to support the contention that the Nazis had escape routes in place at the time the war started, using their existing intelligence networks in North America, Latin America and Europe. There was a strong Nazi presence in Mexico, Chile, Argentina, Colombia and elsewhere in Latin America since the 1930s and those files—when they exist—also are being declassified and revealed, albeit in piecemeal fashion.

There are two excellent online sources for declassified government files, and they are Paperless Archives (http://www.paperlessarchives.com) and The Black Vault (http://www.blackvault.com). The interested reader will find many thousands of scanned files on these sites. Paperless Archives is a great source for World War Two-era files, and The Black Vault specializes in Freedom of Information Act (FOIA) declassifications. Both come highly recommended. One can, of course, download some of these files from the FBI website as well as several other US government sites, but the value in Paperless Archives and the Black Vault rests in their organization of the files into specific categories that make the investigator's life easier. Also, in the case of Paperless Archives, one is able to purchase DVD-ROMs with the entire file sets which means less on-line browsing and downloading.

Andrew, Christopher & Mitrokhin, Vasili, *The Mitrokhin Archive: the KGB in Europe and the West*, London: Penguin, 2000

Artucio, Hugo Fernandez, *The Nazi Underground in South America*, New York: Farrar & Rinehart, 1942

Basso, Carlos, *El ultimo secreto de Colonia Dignidad*, Santiago (Chile): Editorial Mare Nostrum, 2002

Bellant, Russ, *Old Nazis, The New Right, and the Republican Party*, Boston: South End Press, 1991

Bird. Lt. Col. Eugene K., *Prisoner #7: Rudolf Hess*, New York: The Viking Press, 1974

Black, Edwin, *IBM and the Holocaust: The Strategic Alliance between Nazi Germany and America's Most Powerful Corporation*, London: Little, Brown 2001

Blum, Howard, *Wanted! The Search for Nazis in America*, New York: Quadrangle, 1977

Bower, Tom, *Blind Eye to Murder: Britain, America and the Purging of Nazi Germany—A Pledge Betrayed*, London: Warner Books, 1995

Bower, Tom,, *The Paperclip Conspiracy: The Battle for the Spoils and Secrets of Nazi Germany*, London: Michael Joseph, 1987

Breitman, Richard, *Official Secrets: What the Nazis Planned, What the British and Americans Knew*, London: Penguin, 1998

Breitman, Richard & Goda, Norman J.W., *Hitler's Shadow: Nazi War Criminals, US Intelligence, and the Cold War*, Washington (DC): National Archives, n.d.

Clay, Catrine & Leapman, Michael, *Master Race: The Lebensborn Experiment in Nazi Germany*, London: Coronet Books, 1995

Coogan, Kevin, *Dreamer of the Day: Francis Parker Yockey and the Postwar Fascist International*, Brooklyn: Autonomedia, 1999

Cornwell, John, *Hitler's Pope: The Secret History of Pius XII*, New York: Viking, 1999

Cornwell, John, *Hitler's Scientists: Science, War, and the Devil's Pact*, New York: Penguin, 2003

Dabringhaus, Erhard, *Klaus Barbie: The Shocking Story of How the US Used This Nazi War Criminal as an Intelligence Agent*, Washington (DC): Acropolis Books, 1984, 2009

Dulles, Allen W., *The Secret Surrender: The Classic Insider's Account of the Secret Plot to Surrender Northern Italy During WW II*, Guilford (CT): The Lyons Press, 1996, 2006

Eberle, Henrik and Uhl, Matthias (eds), *The Hitler Book: The Secret Dossier Prepared for Stalin from the Interrogations of Hitler's Personal Aides*, New York: Public Affairs, 2005

Farago, Ladislas, *Aftermath: Martin Bormann and the Fourth Reich*, New York: Simon and Schuster, 1974

Farías, Victor, *Los nazis en Chile*, Barcelona: Editorial Seix Barral, 2000

Feigin, Judy, *The Office of Special Investigations: Striving for Accountability in the Aftermath of the Holocaust*, Washington (DC): Department of Justice, December 2006

Fest, Joachim C., *Hitler*, New York: Harcourt Brace Jovanovich, 1974

Galvis, Silvia and Donadio, Alberto, *Colombia Nazi 1939–1945*, Medellin (Colombia): Hombre Nuevo Editores, 2002

Goda, Norman J.W., "CIA Files Relating to Heinz Felfe, SS Officer and KGB Spy", Washington (DC): National Archives, n.d.

Goeritno, Ir. KGPH, Soeryo, *Hitler Mati di Indonesia: Rahasia Yang Terkuak*, Indonesia: Titik Media, 2010

Goldhagen, Daniel Jonah, *A Moral Reckoning: The Role of the Catholic Church in the Holocaust and its Unfulfilled Duty of Repair*, New York: Alfred A. Knopf, 2002

Goñi, Uki, *The Real Odessa: How Perón Brought the Nazi War Criminals to Argentina*, London: Granta Books, 2002

Grover, Warren, *Nazis in Newark*, New Brunswick (NJ): Transaction Publishers, 2003

Higham, Charles, *American Swastika*, New York: Doubleday, 1985

Higham, Charles, *Errol Flynn: the Untold Story*, New York: Doubleday, 1980

Hinckle, Warren and Turner, William, *The Fish is Red: the Story of the Secret War against Castro*, New York: Harper & Row, 1981

Howes, Maj. Alfred L., *Dachau: G-2 Section, US Seventh Army*, Bennington (VT): Merriam Press, 2002

Hutton, J. Bernard, *Hess: The Man and His Mission*, New York: Macmillan, 1971

Infield, Glenn B., *Secrets of the SS*, New York: Jove Books, 1990

Infield, Glenn B., *Skorzeny: Hitler's Commando*, New York: St Martin's Press, 1981

Jones, R.V., *Most Secret War: British Scientific Intelligence 1939–1945*, London: Hamish Hamilton, 1978

Kaplan, Jeffrey and Weinberg, Leonard, *The Emergence of a Euro-American Radical Right*, New Brunswick (NJ): Rutgers University Press, 1998

Kirkpatrick, Sidney D., *Hitler's Holy Relics: A True Story of Nazi Plunder and the Race to Recover the Crown Jewels of the Holy Roman Empire*, New York: Simon and Schuster, 2010

Kisatsky, Deborah, *The United States and the European Right, 1945–1955*, Columbus (OH): Ohio State University Press, 2005

Langer, Walter C., *The Mind of Adolf Hitler: the Secret Wartime Report*, New York: Basic Books, 1972

Lee., Martin A., *The Beast Reawakens*, New York: Routledge, 2000

Levy, Jonathan, *The Intermarium: Wilson, Madison, and East Central European Federalism*, Boca Raton (FL): Dissertation.com, 2006

Lifton, Robert Jay, *The Nazi Doctors: Medical Killing and the Psychology of Genocide*, New York: Basic Books, 2000

Linklater, Magnus and Hilton, Isabel and Ascherson, Neal, *The Nazi Legacy: Klaus Barbie and the International Fascist Connection*, New York: Holt, Rinehart, Winston, 1984

Loftus, John, *America's Nazi Secret*, Walterville (OR): Trine Day, 2010

Loftus, John and Aarons, Mark, *The Secret War Against the Jews: How Western Espionage Betrayed the Jewish People*, New York: St Martin's Griffin, 1994

Loftus, John and Aarons, Mark, *Unholy Trinity: The Vatican, the Nazis, and Soviet Intelligence*, New York: St Martin's Press, 1991

Manning, Paul, *Martin Bormann: Nazi in Exile*, Secaucus (NJ): Lyle Stuart, 1981

McGaha, Richard L., "The Politics of Espionage: Nazi Diplomats and Spies in Argentina, 1933–1945", Ohio University, 2009

McGovern, James, *Crossbow and Overcast*, New York: William Morrow, 1964

Melchior, Ib and Brandenburg, Frank, *Quest: Searching for the Truth of Germany's Nazi Past*, Novato (CA): Presidio Press, 1994

Meskil, Paul, *Hitler's Heirs*, New York: Pyramid Books, n.d.

Müller-Hill, Benno, *Murderous Science: Elimination by Scientific Selection of Jews, Gypsies, and Others, Germany 1933–1945*, New York: Oxford University Press, 1988

Phayer, Michael, *The Catholic Church and the Holocaust, 1930–1965*, Bloomington (IN): Indiana University Press, 2000

Posner, Gerald L. and Ware, John, *Mengele: The Complete Story*, New York: Dell, 1986

Pringle, Heather, *The Master Plan: Himmler's Scholars and the Holocaust*, New York: Hyperion, 2006

Roberts, Andrew (editor), *Hitler's Death: Russia's Last Great Secret from the Files of the KGB*, London: Chaucer Press, 2005

Rollins, Richard, *I Find Treason: The Story of an American Anti-Nazi Agent*, New York: William Morrow & Co., 1941

Sandford, Robinson Rojas, *The Murder of Allende and the End of the Chilean Way to Socialism*, New York: Harper & Row, 1976

Serrano, Miguel, *El cordon dorado: Hitlerismo esoterico*, Bogotá (Colombia): Editorial Solar, 1992

Serrano, Miguel, *NOS: Book of the Resurrection*, London: Routledge & Kegan Paul, 1984

Serrano, Miguel, *La resurección del heroe*, Bogotá (Colombia): Editorial Solar, 1987

Serrano, Miguel, *Jung & Hesse: A record of two friendships*, New York: Schocken Books, 1968

Simpson, Christopher, *The Splendid Blond Beast: Money, Law, and Genocide in the Twentieth Century*, New York: Grove Press, 1993

Simpson, Christopher, *Blowback: The first full account of America's recruitment of Nazis, and its disastrous effect on our domestic and foreign policy*, New York: Weidenfeld & Nicolson, 1988

Smith, Richard Harris, *OSS: the secret history of America's first Central Intelligence Agency*, Berkeley: University of California Press, 1981

Spitz, Vivien, *Doctors From Hell: the Horrific Account of Nazi Experiments on Humans*, Boulder (CO): Sentient Publications, 2005

Spivak, John L., *Secret Armies: The new technique of Nazi warfare*, New York: Modern Age Books, 1939

Steinacher, Gerald, *Nazis on the Run: How Hitler's Henchmen Fled Justice*, New York: Oxford University Press, 2011

Stevenson, William, *The Bormann Brotherhood*, New York: Bantam, 1974

Suciu, Eva Mirela, "Signs of Anti-Semitism in Indonesia," Sydney: University of Sydney, Department of Asian Studies, 2008

Thomas, Hugh, *The Murder of Adolf Hitler: the truth about the bodies in the Berlin bunker*, New York: St Martin's Press, 1995

Timmerman, Jacobo, *Chile: Death in the South*, New York: Alfred A. Knopf, 1987

Tim Investigasi Solomongrup, *Melacak Garis Keturunan Hitler di Indonesia*, Yogyakarta: Pustaka Solomon, 2011

Varas, Florencia and Orrego, Claudio, *El caso Letelier*, Santiago (Chile): Editorial Aconcagua, 1990

Wallace, Max, *The American Axis: Henry Ford, Charles Lindbergh, and the rise of the Third Reich*, New York: St Martin's Griffin, 2003

Waller, John H., *The Devil's Doctor: Felix Kersten and the Secret Plot to turn Himmler against Hitler,* New York: John Wiley & Sons, 2002

Walters, Guy, *Hunting Evil: The Nazi War Criminals who Escaped and the Quest to bring them to Justice,* New York: Broadway Books, 2009

Wilson, *Orang dan Partai Nazi di Indonesia: Kaum Pergerakan Menyambut Fasisme,* Jakarta: Komunitas Bambu, 2008

Von Lang, Jochen (editor), *Eichmann Interrogated: transcripts from the archives of the Israeli Police,* New York: Vintage Books, 1983

Zeiger, Henry A. (editor), *The Case Against Adolf Eichmann,* New York: Signet, 1960